Sincerely

Marieke Hardy is a writer, broadcaster, columnist, and television producer. She is a regular panellist on ABC's *First Tuesday Book Club*, an award-winning blogger and the creator of the acclaimed comedy series *Laid*. Her first collection of essays, *You'll Be Sorry When I'm Dead*, was published in 2011.

Michaela McGuire is a writer and columnist. Her first book, *Apply Within: Stories of Career Sabotage*, was published in 2009. She writes a fortnightly column for *QWeekend*, and her second book of non-fiction will be published by Melbourne University Press in 2013.

womenofletters.com.au

Edgar's Mission is a not-for-profit sanctuary for neglected, abused and discarded farmed animals.

Edgar's Mission's Farm Sanctuary, located in the foothills of the Great Dividing Range at Willowmavin, via Kilmore, Victoria, is currently home to over 250 animal residents. As an animal sanctuary, the mission has a policy to 'Rescue, Rehabilitate and Rehome' wherever possible. Edgar's Mission also runs adoption programs for people willing and able to provide permanent homes for rescued animals.

For the sake of the animals that could not be saved, public outreach is also a big part of everyday life at the sanctuary. With farm tours, school visits and appearances at markets and community events around the state, Edgar's Mission aims to inform and educate the public as well as expand their circle of compassion to include all animals. Feeling the warmth of a farmed animal can clear the mind and inspire change in people's attitudes and actions. After all, the ongoing decision to choose kindness is the greatest contribution a person can make to ending animal suffering.

And it all started with a pig. Edgar's Mission was founded by Pam Ahern and named after her first rescued pig, Edgar. Edgar Alan Pig, aka 'the pig who started it all', sadly passed away shortly after his seventh birthday party in April 2010. Edgar, a gentle giant, touched so many people and was an amazing ambassador for pigs and farmed animals everywhere. He is missed beyond words – but his mission will continue.

edgarsmission.org.au

CURATED BY
MARIEKE HARDY AND MICHAELA McGUIRE

Sincerely

Further adventures in the art of correspondence from
Women of Letters

VIKING
an imprint of
PENGUIN BOOKS

VIKING

Published by the Penguin Group
Penguin Group (Australia)
707 Collins Street, Melbourne, Victoria 3008, Australia
(a division of Pearson Australia Group Pty Ltd)
Penguin Group (USA) Inc.
375 Hudson Street, New York, New York 10014, USA
Penguin Group (Canada)
90 Eglinton Avenue East, Suite 700, Toronto, Canada ON M4P 2Y3
(a division of Pearson Penguin Canada Inc.)
Penguin Books Ltd
80 Strand, London WC2R 0RL, England
Penguin Ireland
25 St Stephen's Green, Dublin 2, Ireland
(a division of Penguin Books Ltd)
Penguin Books India Pvt Ltd
11 Community Centre, Panchsheel Park, New Delhi – 110 017, India
Penguin Group (NZ)
67 Apollo Drive, Rosedale, North Shore 0632, New Zealand
(a division of Pearson New Zealand Ltd)
Penguin Books (South Africa) (Pty) Ltd
24 Sturdee Avenue, Rosebank, Johannesburg 2196, South Africa

Penguin Books Ltd, Registered Offices: 80 Strand, London WC2R 0RL, England

First published by Penguin Group (Australia), 2012

1 3 5 7 9 10 8 6 4 2

Cover design by Alex Ross © Penguin Group (Australia)
Based on an original concept © Tara Nielsen
Text design by Allison Colpoys © Penguin Group (Australia)
Typeset in Tribute by Laura Thomas
Printed and bound in Australia by McPherson's Printing Group, Maryborough, Victoria

National Library of Australia
Cataloguing-in-Publication data:

Sincerely / Marieke Hardy, Michaela McGuire.
9780670076710 (pbk.)
Australian letters. Australian literature.
826.408

penguin.com.au

*To Liam Pieper, David McCarthy
and the lady in the hat, Pam Ahearn*

CONTENTS

INTRODUCTION

It's fair to say we had absolutely no idea Women of Letters would grow to be what it now is. When we first started throwing ideas around in January 2010 for a modest literary salon 'of sorts', little did we expect the sold-out shows, warm and wonderful crowds, and oddly potent combination of barnyard animals and diverse women writers to weave their magic in such a fashion.

Since its inception in March 2010, we have taken our strange and beautiful little Melbourne-based roadshow to Perth, Darwin, Brisbane, Byron Bay, Sydney, Woodford and Canberra, raising over $100 000 for animal rescue shelter Edgar's Mission. We have held events in perfectly dilapidated ballrooms, velvet-curtained co-ops, cathedrals, music festival forum tents and one particularly memorable outdoor 'enchanted amphitheatre', where we experienced Perth's only hour of teeming rain in months. 'That's odd, we've had perfect weather every other day,' locals told us, peering at the sky with confused expressions as we ran indoors and set up a temporary stage.

And how exactly does a Women of Letters event run, if you've never been to one? Well, most afternoons consist of five readers who have written a letter to a topic we have foisted upon them – 'A letter to the best decision I ever made', for example, or 'A letter to the person I misjudged'. In a candlelit room filled with about 350 people, these are read aloud. There is wine. The audience is given the opportunity to write postcards and aerogrammes of their own. Pam, head honcho of Edgar's, brings an ambassador sheep or pig along to see what all the fuss is about. Marieke sits up the back and has a bit of a weep. Michaela holds things together onstage with customary aplomb. It is exactly as you might expect, although with a little more cake.

You may notice a lot more contributions here from our gentlemen friends than there were in Volume 1. This is due to the fact that we decided to extend our Men of Letters shows to our friends in Sydney and Brisbane, too – meaning thirty blokes onstage in three days! This may make this book appear more testosterone-heavy than the events actually are. Our once-yearly MoL shows are very dear to us, though our show remains a strong, female-driven enterprise and will stay that way for as long as it is operational.

We are so immensely proud of Women of Letters and the sense of community it has created. We hope that through reading you will be able to share a sense of its overwhelming specialness.

Warmest,
Michaela and Marieke

A complaint letter

TRACEE HUTCHISON

I'd like to start by complaining about the topic.

I told Marieke that my head really wasn't in the complaint space any more. That I'd grown weary of the need to shout about quaint notions of social justice and the nonsense of grown men consuming fossil fuels at 350 kilometres an hour under the auspices of sport. Shouting just makes you unpopular and unemployable and is bad for your health.

I'm living gently these days, I said, trying to tread lightly on the planet because it's got more than enough problems. And I'd reasoned that the only thing I had control over was my own little footprint. No point complaining about things you can't change.

So I'd decided to make jam instead of word-war. Plum jam, from the fruit of my own trees. And tomato relish from my own tomatoes.

Marieke, of course, saw opportunity in my protestation, and insisted I start with:

Dear Complaint Letter,

I've been looking everywhere for you . . .

It's true we used to be such great friends. In fact, some of my finest moments were spent in your company. There've been times when I've felt like my whole life was a slavish homage to your intoxicating appeal.

3

We started young, you and I. Back in those heady twenty-something days of the early 1980s when the world was ripe for changing. Those halcyon years of unshaved armpits, feminist mantras, the Socialist Left and singing from the Oils handbook.

Gosh, we really showed them.

1983. Remember that 'Stop the Drop' banner we painted? The one that stretched right above the stage at the Sidney Myer Music Bowl? The Oils, Goanna, Redgum and INXS. What a night.

We were there – you and I – in the inner circle, taking our first fledgling steps as card-carrying members of the protest movement. Anything was possible with Pastor Pete leading the way.

So much to complain about – so little time.

And we followed our protesting heart to the Jays – when working there was a political statement. We had a workplace agreement to up the ante and say 'fuck' on air without a language warning. To really *care* about vinyl and the significance of *not* playing Kylie. To 'Fuck tha Police' . . .

Ah, Niggaz With Attitude. That first great test of our conviction. We played you. Oh yes. A high-rotation favourite in the summer of 1989/90. And we defied the wrath of the expanding national network that baulked at our freedom to cuss with such abandon. We even went on strike in your name. Proudly flipping the bird with Heaven 17's '(We Don't Need This) Fascist Groove Thang' playing on a loop as we left.

Gee, we really showed 'em, didn't we?

Right up to the moment they sacked the lot of us and installed a group of more malleable presenters who were happy to ditch Ice Cube for Kylie – no questions asked.

Oh, yes, those were the days. What a grand protest it was. And just look where it got us. All that youthful idealism smashed in one fell swoop.

But we had our dignity and the courage of our conviction to keep us company in our unemployment. And that had to count for something, didn't it?

And wasn't it exciting when we finally got the chance to interview Ice for that cool TV show on SBS called *nomad* in the early 1990s? There I was – a small white girl with a right-on attitude – all ready with my 'Fuck Tha Police' versus Triple J story to regale him with in the preamble.

And in walked Ice with twenty-five men from the Nation of Islam who stared me down with such folded-arm hatred I was rendered mute.

There was no getting around it. I was white. Middle class. And a woman. What would I know?

Their disdain was as palpable as my despair. I felt tiny. And ridiculous.

'I've played No Fixed Address and the Warumpi Band and Yothu Yindi on the radio – before the 'Treaty' remix.' It was all in my head, jumbled up with land rights marches and nights in my swag in Arnhem Land. But I couldn't form a sentence. It seemed pointless.

That once-defiant complaint we shouted so loudly and proudly about seemed hopelessly misplaced. Like old Ice had stomped on my moral compass with such ferocity that large chunks of it had lodged in my eyeballs.

But you stuck by me, dear Complaint Letter, and reassured me it was the process – not the outcome – that mattered. And we intellectualised and rationalised with astounding success for our cause.

To complain was part of our democratic right. The foundation of our freedom. Our raison d'être. Remember? And so we proudly maintained the rage, but choosing our moments and our targets a little more wisely as the years rolled on. And we did it publically, which was quite a privilege.

On community radio, where you can't get sacked (especially when you're the Program Director), and in print, where, incredibly, we got paid. We railed and railed and railed on the op-ed page of the *Saturday Age* for four glorious years . . .

Flat-earthers, bigots and general village idiocy were particular favourites.

Refugee policies, Closing the Gap, the drowning island states of Tuvalu and Kiribati.

Iraq. Afghanistan. The state-sanctioned logging of old-growth forests.

Remember? The hate-filled politics of the 'we will decide who comes to this country' years that scratched open a still-weeping sore of fear and loathing. Lest we forget . . .

We were useful then. I really do believe that. If only to send a literary lifeline to our kindred spirits huddled around the teapot every Saturday morning.

They were testing times. But we stuck it out. You and I. Loading up week after week in the vain hope of sanity – and humanity – prevailing. And you were great company.

Until I became surplus to complaint requirements at *The Age*.

I think that's when I started reassessing my relationship with you.

A new political broom had swept through and our mate Pete was Environment Minister – what use would I possibly have for you? Flat-earthers and bigots would be banished. Pine Gap and uranium mining be damned. The day of reckoning had come . . .

Of course, it didn't quite pan out that way. But we squeezed in a few parting shots. About the Bay and Pine Gap and the unbridled resilience of general village idiocy.

Occasionally we'd branch out to give the Spring Street mob a whack. Remember Bracksy? The unlikely premier who looked like Hymie from *Get Smart*? It's always the ones you suspect the least that you have to keep the closest eye on.

Remember how he stepped down as premier just after the dead fish started washing up in his electorate, on Williamstown beach?

The ones we wrote would wash up once the Port of Melbourne started dredging the mouth of the Yarra so that big ships from China could bring in more trinkets? And it stirred up all that arsenic and heavy metal that no one wanted to talk about?

Except you and me. We talked about it. A lot.

My beloved Bay churned up and its entrance blown apart in the most indecent fashion. We really did bang on about it, didn't we?

Until we worked out that the trinkets were more likely steel sheeting made from Australian iron ore that was being turned into warships at Williamstown in a deal stitched up by Victorian Labor, the Feds and the ADF. Checkmate.

We didn't have much swinging room after that. And I felt quite small and broken when that dredger arrived. Our grassroots community campaign – and everyone who'd been part of it – smashed by the money and might of an all-powerful triumvirate.

Our idealistic little offerings to the broadsheet just seemed hopelessly naive.

We had our annual crack at the Grand Prix. We even joked that one day, if the planet was still spinning in a hundred years, people would look back on the obscene waste of a finite resource and exclaim, 'They still had fossil fuel then? And they did *what*?'

But the Grand Prix keeps on keeping on and the weather gets madder and madder, just like the Orwellian madness of the flawed rationale that keeps propping it up.

Integrity. Honesty. Conviction. What is it good for, really? And putting a face on shame never makes you popular.

Which is why I've just found life a lot simpler and gentler and easier – and infinitely more wonderful – not to bother with it anymore.

So much to complain about. So little time to actually *live*.

So I make jam. For me and my neighbours. My plums. Their apricots. With lime, for a jaunty twist. And there's something tangibly good about the olde-worlde charm of handmade labels and a real fruity taste.

It just feels like a much better way to engage with our battling blue planet than shouting about how wretched everything is.

None of it has gone away, of course. But I guess it finally dawned on me that if that's all you look for, then that's all you'll find.

Which is why, dear Complaint Letter, I haven't been in touch much lately.

I'm living quite differently now – in ways that don't drain the life force out of me.

I can love and laugh and dance and sing. Freely. I have my health and I have a job. And I appreciate these are hard-earned victories for many people.

But not us. Not here. Life is good. Really good. Of all the places in the world to be – we really are blessed.

And it just seems a little churlish to complain.

So, to you, dear Complaint Letter – my trusted, fiery friend – thank you for the good times. I shall cherish them when I'm old and grey and will always admire your courage and conviction.

But I really think it's best for both of us that we go our separate ways.

Au revoir, ma chérie, au revoir.
(Ou peut-être, peut-être, à bientôt . . .)

SOFIJA STEFANOVIĆ

Dear Doctor Ted DiGeorgio,

I came to see you six months ago with writer's block and I'm not happy with our progress. Below is a list of six issues I have compiled during our time together.

Issue One: *My expectations, regarding you as a therapist, were not met*

To be honest, I thought you'd be more like the character Paul in the television show *In Treatment*. He's a hot psychotherapist, played by Gabriel Byrne, who's not much at first glance, but he becomes sexier as you get drawn in by his tender eyes and the remnants of his Irish accent. Watching his good work in that series gave me the push to see you.

But it turns out you aren't like Gabriel Byrne, are you, Ted? Gabriel is your age but – more fortunate build and bluer eyes aside – he takes care of himself. I'm not trying to tell you how to do your job; I'm just saying that your patients might be less disappointed if you scrubbed up.

And while Gabriel is passionate and supportive towards his patients, I can only assume you follow a different school of psychiatry. Which must be why you fell asleep just as I was saying I worry about not being interesting enough. Closing your eyes for a full twenty seconds and then cartoonishly jolting to attention was your way of confronting me with my fear.

Issue Two: Despite this, I have become obsessed with you

Don't flatter yourself that this is erotic transference, because it's not. As we've established, I already did that with Gabriel Byrne.

Though, if we're being honest, I should mention that I had a sexual crisis a few months ago. I'd arrived at your rooms and realised that I was wearing lipstick. But I wasn't going anywhere else afterwards, so I must have put on lipstick *especially* to see you.

I wondered if you would notice this and take it as a sign that I was coming on to you (which I wasn't) and I also wondered if I had subconsciously put it on because I *was* attracted to you but didn't realise it.

Infuriatingly, this made me think about sex with you, which I hadn't done before, and then the whole session was ruined because I was trying not to do things that my mind was irresistibly forcing me to do, like crossing and uncrossing my legs and undoing my top button. I glanced at your watch to see if our time was finally up, and I'm sure you thought I was looking at your penis, so I blushed, making it seem like I had been.

Issue Three: I have ulterior motives

You suggested that it might help with my writing problem if I put aside some time each week to do 'private writing'.

Somehow I've convinced myself that this writing time can be dedicated to researching psychotherapy on the internet. And I've developed a little fantasy.

Now, I know there's a lot of competition among the world's best case studies. Anna O, Wolf Man, Little Hans and, of course, Rat Man. They are the superheroes of the mentally unstable world – Anna O, paralysed with anxiety and phantom pregnancies; Wolf Man, nightmares of six white wolves haunting his every move; Little Hans, whose fear of horses turned out to be castration anxiety; and Rat Man, who couldn't stop fantasising about a pot of rats attached to his fiancée's buttocks gnawing her anus.

Well, my secret desire is to join their ranks. I've been trying to work out what my own sex-related glitch could be. There are many to choose from, like when I kept dreaming about going into an elevator with groups of men I work with, and I told my mum about it and then we found out that the elevator was the most common dream symbol for sexual intercourse. Or when I dreamt that one of my dogs became a human and she and I became lesbians.

I imagine you holding a seminar using a pseudonym to present my circumstances to a fascinated audience of students.

That way, I would feel that my insane moments were for a good cause. And you could end your seminar with a brilliant resolution, which sees me, Dog Lesbian, resolving my issues and becoming the acclaimed writer I always wanted to be.

Issue Four: I am dishonest in the sessions

My favourite parts of the sessions are those golden moments when I get you interested in an anecdote. Or when you are impressed by my insights.

I know this is counter-productive – but I sometimes make things up to entertain you. I imagine you in your spare time, comparing me to your other clients. I want you to decide that I am definitely your favourite.

Do you remember when I told you that my grandmother married my grandfather because in her village everyone had to marry someone the same height as them? And so my grandma stood on a box, to make sure she got my tall, handsome grandfather instead of a midget?

In my defence, I *did* initially believe this had happened to my grandmother, and then as I was saying it I realised it had happened in *The Golden Girls*. But I couldn't tell you because I didn't want you to think I was experiencing false memory syndrome, or, worse, that I was delusional and thought I *was* a character in *The Golden Girls*.

Issue Five: We aren't perfect

Ted, don't you wish we could just start again?

Imagine that: instead of this endless sitting, you in your chair and I in mine, stabbing in the dark, clearly unimpressed with each other, we could just be deleted out of our listlessness. You, grey haired, cross-legged, weary. Me with my incessant monotone.

Both gone. An unimpressive first draft.

If I was able to just sit and actually write for five minutes, I'd write us from scratch. We could become each other's dreams – you more like Gabriel Byrne, I more like Freud's Anna O. Rich with meaning, answering questions, untangling threads.

You could be whatever you dream of when you doze off. And I could use an eraser to smooth out the knots in my psyche so I could be the woman I wish I was and know I can become.

Issue Six: You insist on talking about the real world

Despite my best efforts to distract you, you keep going, on your dull, drawn-out mission. Each week we find ourselves talking about writer's block again.

'What made you so upset when the boy in *Toy Story 3* grew up and left his toys behind?'

'I wasn't that upset! I told you, the children I was babysitting overreacted!'

'You said they called their parents because you were crying.'

'They would have been crying too, if they weren't sociopaths! The boy gave away Woody and Buzz! He gave up the fantasy world! It was tragic!'

'Is reality really that bad?' you ask.

'What do you mean?'

'I mean, let's talk about reality: sitting down and writing. If your work doesn't live up to your fantasy – is that really so terrible? Is that a reason to never write anything?'

'What, you think I'd rather play with my toys, watch films and fantasise about *you* instead of actually sitting down at the computer? Because I'm scared of not being the best writer in the world?'

'Is that what *you* think?' you ask.

'Is that what *you* think?' I ask.

'Maybe it's just something to be aware of,' you reply.

And, unlike Gabriel Byrne, you sit in silence, letting me squirm, and I can't turn the television off, and you just continue to stare at me, like a real person looking at a real person.

I glance at your penis, and it's time to go home.

See you next week,
Sofija Stefanovic

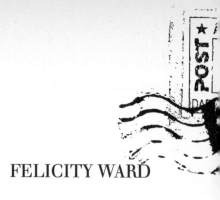

FELICITY WARD

Dear Reputable Music Magazine Editor,

There's a serious, unaddressed problem within the music industry. I'm talking about music that makes me want to have sex. There are some songs and some bands that make me want to grab a man by the collar, push him and his pelvis up against a wall, and plant one on him. Then say nothing, drop my business card at his feet and mouth the words 'you weren't special' as I walk away.

Here are some problems with that particular scenario:

1. I don't have a business card.
2. That is sexual assault.
3. I don't even know this guy; what if he has lip herpes?
4. How do I know there's a wall there if it's a hypothetical situation?

And the list goes on. There is music that exists that deludes me into thinking with all the sexual confidence of a porn star or a dog. Think about it: dogs are pretty sexually confident. They go up to a stranger's arse, give it a sniff, decide whether it's something they want, jump on and hump on. I'm not into it, I just respect it. Anyway, that's beside the point.

Here's what I mean. On one occasion, I remember getting ready for work. Now if I'd had no music playing at the time, I may have left the house fully dressed. *But* because I had the Pixies' 'Tame' blaring in my ears, I left the house wearing nothing but heels, thick stockings and a 'long-enough' business shirt, à la Carrie Bradshaw. It wasn't until I was halfway through my gig, when I had to say the words, 'You're right, sir, I'm *not* wearing any pants', that I understood this wasn't the time, nor the place, for a high-stage, low-set audience and no protective measure between us.

And this doesn't stop in my head. Songs by the Cold War Kids have made choices for me in the bedroom that I still regret. I won't go into details but let's just say there are a few things that you don't do on a first date, and I learned the hard way.

Bands need to tone it down. When I listen to The Black Keys, I'm not sure I'm not pregnant afterwards; that's how sexy it is. Once I thought my imaginary baby was kicking – turns out it was doing the Hustle. Even *it* couldn't fight the funk.

And this is very different to music that makes you feel in love. *This* is music that takes a little friend called Sexual Insecurity and gives it a line of cocaine, a push-up bra and a finger in the arse.

And it is doing damage to thousands of mediocre people who could otherwise be setting their sexual bar at a realistic level. There is a statistic, which I have made up, that shows the music of Sharon Jones & The Dap-Kings increases sexual hubris and proportionate amounts of disappointment by 67 per cent. That is devastating (mostly because of its scientific inaccuracy).

This is a pandemic that needs an antibiotic and Dr Ward is prescribing three days of Joni Mitchell and a turtleneck.

We say no to cock rock, and we say no to 'Best Bonk Songs of All Time' compilation albums.

Yours sincerely,
Felicity Ward

Felicity Ward

HELEN MARCOU

A complaint letter: an angry topic, a topic that was apparently made for me, something I've spent the last year doing. Well, I personally don't like whingers, haters or complainers. If I'm just complaining, I get so riled up I want to explode. I can't sit still – my whinging drives me nuts and I have to do something about it. Whether it's the quality of the school sausage sizzle or the state of live music – if I take control and get off my arse, I feel better.

Every complaint letter I've written this year also came with a big dose of responsibility. After getting 20 000 people out onto the streets for the SLAM rally, we then had to sit at the negotiating table with the government – we had no experience, but we had to fight for what we wanted.

For this event, I could have chosen one of the many letters I've written to politicians or councillors, or even Sue Maclellan, the old director of liquor licensing. However, I can't help but be moved by the state of the world at the moment and by thinking about the future. So this letter is from my yet-to-be-born granddaughter. My youngest child, Lola, is now seven, so she's not expecting yet! If she's anything like me, she'll probably wait another thirty years to have a child.

Dear Grandma Helen,

I always love visiting you in what you call 'the nursing home for old punk rockers'. Is it true this place was once the National Gallery? Wow – the nation really bought art?

I love your cuddles, warmth and hugs, and the ancient bottles of gin from the minibar and the vials of biomorphine from the medicine cabinet that you've nicked and have hidden in your thick black pantihose. Did people really wear black tights in your day? I can't imagine it with all this heat – what a peculiar image.

Grandma, as your dementia gets worse and Mum and I work around the clock to pay all your bills and feed you, clothe you and love you, I look at the thousands of old people in this big, run-down space and want to ask you: 'What were you and your generation doing while the world melted around you?'

Your people, your friends, lived in McMansions with fewer than twenty people in one house, and drove big trucks in the city (four-wheel *whats*?), and bought furniture that would break and then they'd chuck it on the nature strip three months later. And your people habitually bought things called 'homewares' – what the hell were homewares? Luckily the Swedish banned anything as crazy as that years ago.

Grandma, I'd also like to complain about the size of your wardrobe. You went through so many clothes over the years, by old dead designers I've seen on history sites, who are now known as the 'decadent old masters of fashion'. You could've bought my mum and uncle a house each with the amount you spent on handmade shoes. And what about the sweatshops – didn't you ever feel guilty? You'd max out that David Jones card every week, without ever stopping to think about what you were buying. Did you really think people respected you more because of what you wore? Grandma, let me tell you, the only thing that is 'this season' any more is edible, not wearable.

I'd like to complain about the years you spent pampering yourself on the then Greek islands, which no longer exist (the only Greek island left is Athens). You were a free, promiscuous, drug-addled bum in your youth – you never considered the future, and you damaged your brain and body while living off your parents. And you frivolously dropped out of uni, a uni that was paid for by the government. What privilege! My mum is still paying off her HECS debt and she's fifty!

I don't have the dole or free education or air travel or the Greek islands. I'll never have a pension; I can't lie in the sun without second-degree burns; the air is stale and thick with pollution; the only travel I'll ever get to do is on the few remaining trains left in the city, to go and see you to clean your dribble and wipe your arse. I'll never get to taste French champagne or real truffles or Ligurian honey, or see a King Island crab, or bask in the golden Aegean. I can't even eat lettuce or drink fresh milk for fear of contamination. Did you ever stop to think that I'll never experience these things? I still can't understand the greed and gluttony of your 'what about me' generation. Your generation lived better than any king in years gone by, or the CEOs that run the world now. Was it ever enough? Did you think you could fill that void in your soul by consuming more?

I looked up on TweetFace politicians from your time. A guy called Tony Abbott went to a fourth term with a parliament of talk-show shock jocks. The war cabinet was led by Alan Jones and Andrew Bolt, and then they were all assassinated by the Maori warlords after invading New Zealand. Now we have Prime Minister Alannah Hill, who was apparently the only really famous person to put her hand up for the job. She has been so successful with her renewable energy program that we have power between 6 p.m. and 7.30 at night.

My Grandma Helen, I do appreciate all the work you did for the music community; it really helped for a few years. However, with gentrification and rising property prices, the only solar-amplified gigs left nowadays are out in Dandenong. But at least I can get a ferry out there since the new beach came in.

I still love you and will never forget the way you and Yiayia Maria spoiled us with organic home cooking and beautiful handmade things, and how you and Mum would take us to gigs and you would make us dance with you in the mosh and blow our heads off in the speakers . . . I can almost forgive you for the constant ringing in my ears (our whole family has tinnitus). Wasn't it you who said, 'Wearing earplugs at a gig is like sex with a condom – never as good'?

Well, Grandma, to you and all your hedonist mates of the past: I love you, I respect many things about you, and I feel sorry to be complaining. So I'm rolling up my sleeves and I'm gonna make a big difference, you'll see. I'll give my children the things I didn't have, just as your parents gave you the things they didn't. One day I'll make my granddaughter very proud!

With lots of kisses,
Your loving granddaughter,
Adidas Jägermeister Vegemite McLean xxxx

Helen Marcou
X

To my most treasured possession

LIBBI GORR

My dear iPhone,

Firstly, I need you to understand: I don't hold it against you that you are powered by Telstra. You can't help your parents. You didn't choose us for yourself. But we've got a plan for you. You are in our little bundle of joy, along with the internet and the home phone.

The home phone asked me the other day what my favourite form of communication is. I told the home phone that mummies don't have favourites. That I love all forms of communication equally. But it was clear from that response – the home phone wasn't it.

Secondly, iPhone, you need to get that I am fully aware I haven't owned you for very long. But I believe that elevating you to the status of my most treasured possession – above even my beloved Snoopy doll which I've had since I was seven, with his cracked left eye and his chargrilled feet from a Sunday night spent far too close to the heater – is a pragmatic and sensible decision. I don't have time to bask in the glow of sentiment and nostalgia nowadays, given my constant need for more time in the present. And if I was to allow myself the pleasure of just concentrating on one thing at a time, I would also have cited my brain, which I treasure beyond all my body parts, including my vagina, because my brain is where my most pleasurable explosions occur. Even those explosions that originate in my vagina culminate in my brain.

But my most treasured brain explosions revolve around my

imagination. And indeed, my most consistent and trusted relationship in this lifetime has been with my subconscious. It's given me
friendships – some real, some imaginary, some that I thought were
real but which turned out to be imaginary (that's what came from
working in television), and some I'd always dreamed of, which then
actually turned out to be real (that's the beauty of radio). Indeed,
it's my brain, that most delicious part of myself, that has led me to
cite you, dear iPhone, as the winner of the award – most treasured
possession – today.

Treasure implies sentiment, and its not sentiment I feel for you
per se – I'd replace you in a second if my daughter dropped you in
the toilet just for fun – so let's not get narcissistic about this. It's
what you hold for me, what you embrace, what you keep close to my
heart, that means in this busy world I cannot even come close to doing without you. That is your value to me. Me, me, me, it's all about
me. All of the bits of you that are me.

You connect me, constantly, with all the things in my life, while
I'm busy concentrating on only one of the many parts of it. In earlier
times, this would've necessitated abandoning the rest.

You are made for me, a girl of what I call the Cinderella/Greer
Generation – Cinderella because we were brought up to think we
would be rescued, and Greer because, despite that, we were feminists.
At school we were told to burn our bras and run hard against the boys
– and many of us burned our bras and ran hard, bra-less, against the
boys and then came home with two black eyes. We still expected to
be rescued. But by whom? Men? That's far too great a responsibility
to heap upon another sex. I love men, as you know, iPhone – I have
one at home. I found him in a catalogue. But be rescued? No – not by
another human. I rescued myself, iPhone, when I bought you.

Intelligent Phone, I should call you, really – iPhone is a generic
nickname, like J.Lo or TomKat – but I feel like if I addressed you by
your full moniker, you'd think you were in trouble. And you're not.

Not at this moment. You would be if you'd slipped yourself onto silent and slid down under the passenger seat while I was driving, or behind a couch at someone else's place, and let your battery run down so I couldn't find myself in an abstract sense. In that case, I'd call you every damn name under the fucking sun. I need you in my reach and fully charged, ready to go whenever I want you. Ours is the only relationship I have in my life that's allowed to be completely on my terms. And it doesn't bring the repercussions of divorce or DoCS knocking on my door. No, that's silly – DoCS being proactive and knocking on a door? There's my imagination again.

But, dear iPhone, back to the point. When you are lost, I don't use the phrase 'can't find myself' without understanding the significance of such a phrase.

Because you are me, in a sense. You don't have my soul, my vibrancy, my thighs, but you do operate as an annex to my brain that makes my life manageable. You are compartmentalised and easy to access. The ambivalence with which I hold you – with all your capabilities, your functions, your memory, your slimness – is exactly the ambivalence with which I observe my whole life, how it's structured, what I can achieve with the time I have to achieve it. What you are capable of makes me more capable. Your functions allow me access to sentiments and memories, wherever I may be, at whatever time. My children, my partner, my work, my imagination, my shopping, my music – I can be close to every aspect of my life when you are close to me, despite being pulled in a million different directions at any given moment of the day, and despite the ambivalence I may feel about such a lifestyle.

Ultimately, it is this ambivalence I treasure. Because if I didn't have it, I wouldn't have everything. And I do believe I have everything. Back in the '80s, the American comic Steven Wright once said, 'You can't have everything. Where would you put it?' Well, I put it in my iPhone. That's thirty years for you.

As long as I am close to you, you make me close to me, and connect me to those who are close.

[Here I break into a rendition of 'Close to You' by The Carpenters, switching between live vocals from myself and prerecorded audio and vision from my family at home. I then video the audience's vocal response, all on the iPhone.]

How to now sign off from an epistle to an inanimate object with so many capabilities, innumerable functions and, most importantly, no feelings to hurt if I use and abuse you?

'I'm powering down now' seems a little fey.

'Warmest' sounds like a battery malfunction.

'Thank you for having and holding my life, so I may have it close by me as I globally roam' sounds like we are getting married, and I just don't subscribe to that social abnorm. I'm happy being in a committed relationship.

But now I know how I must end this note, in a way that reflects us both at our best and most resourceful:

Dear iPhone, I must go, because our time is capped.

Sincerely charged,
Libbi

LOENE CARMEN

To My Grandmother's Silver Lamé Showgirl Bikini,

There you are, tucked into a corner of my bottom drawer, alongside other rarely worn and strange items – dazzling silver lamé, hand-made but beautifully stitched, full of secrets and housewife dreams and defiance and devilry. And you fit me like a glove.

You came into my possession when I was a young girl, a gift from my grandmother, who I did not really know. She had been an unwed teenage mother and was sent to the nunnery like all girls in her 'un-fortunate position', then forced to give up her baby for adoption to a respectable family. Mother Superior must have had a soft spot for her, though, as shortly after my father's illegitimate birth, she sent my grandmother to fetch something from her desk, where she had left the address of my father's new parents in an obvious place. This allowed my grandmother to surreptitiously keep track of my father through his childhood, and later, too, as he married and my brother and I were born. She was finally brave enough to make contact with my father when I was a kid and began a hesitant relationship with us, in a time when family secrets such as this were not spoken of.

I think she quickly cottoned on to the fact that she and I had similar interests, and, in a bid to make up for lost time, I was lucky enough to be the recipient of many of *her* most treasured posses-sions – which quickly became mine – such as a double-tailed fox fur replete with one grinning head; a green lurex and real-gold-thread embossed swimsuit; see-through vintage nighties; 1950s pink and purple shimmering ball gowns; pointy-toed silver stilettos; and, for some reason, enough boxed cakes of flower-stickered soap to wash a whole posse of Tivoli showgirls clean. I was also the beneficiary of hundreds of tubes of Avon's Make Mine Roses lipstick and bottles of Imprevu perfume over the years.

Our family left Adelaide for the bright lights of Sydney. Parcels began to arrive stuffed with old tutus and *TV Week*s with items of interest circled, as well as Chinese dressing gowns, Japanese fans, theatre programs, silk scarves, gold-plated cake servers and floral letter-writing sets. But nothing was quite as splendid as you, oh silver showgirl bikini. Yes, you really took the cake. You spoke to me. You came in a package alongside a racy set of unworn nylon knickers hailing from the 1970s bearing embroidered slogans such as 'Ooooh' and 'Call me!' This finery was also accompanied by a fabulously long and florid letter assuring me that, should I find myself pregnant, my grandmother would be happy to take the baby and raise it. I think I was twelve or maybe thirteen by then, and at the time I found it hilarious. Looking back, it seems terribly poignant, sweet and courageous for her to even mention such things.

Long-distance phone calls were a hurried and rare event in those days, but I did manage to slip into a quick conversation a question about where she wore you, this wonderfully glamorous item. There was a very long pause before she quietly answered, 'Oh, just around the house, darling.'

———

I now see you as symbolic of so much. Of the undeniable tenacity of bloodlines – despite the fact my grandmother and I barely knew one another, we shared a frighteningly similar fascination for tinsel, for showbiz, for silver and gold, pink and purple, roses and lipstick and Spanish lace. And of the indestructibility of the feminine spirit, and of the power of visualisation. Because, despite being in a desperately unhappy marriage to some dull, angry, alcoholic bastard who squandered away everything they had, my grandmother retained a playful fondness for dressing up to entertain herself and a dedication to losing herself in beautiful imagined worlds and passionate love affairs. She was a willful agoraphobic, a true domestic goddess who existed on Chantilly Cream, coffee and sweet biscuits, whose inner life was far more real and more important to her than her reality. I recently discovered she wrote copious amounts – magical Harry Potter-style children's stories and potboiler romances, all lost now, as well as the pages and pages of extravagantly curly, purple, cursive-filled letters she wrote to me and my family every week or so, more often than not enclosed within her parcels of treasures. Laugh if you will, but I still maintain a bulging suitcase full of 'dress-ups' myself – although my daughter has charmingly re-named them 'heritage items'.

You're a spectacular enigma, a whimsical whodunnit masquerading as an innocuous showgirl bikini. Getting one's hands on something exotic like you in the mid-1960s can't have been an easy feat, especially in a small, ultra-conservative town like Adelaide. So did she make a concerted effort to find you? Did she have a secret job dancing lunchtimes at La Belle – where coincidentally one of my father's first professional piano playing jobs was providing bump-and-grind tunes for the strippers as a teenager? Did she carefully cut out a glamour-wear ad from the back of *Australian Post* and send away for you? Were you a gift from her husband, or maybe a lover? I have a hunch that simply the subversive act of owning you was enough to give her a secret thrill. I suspect you gave my grandmother an escape route, something to slip into on a cold, dreary afternoon and dance a little in the warm, golden glow of her mirror, to transport her to a place where she was adored and admired. Although it's also entirely possible this was no mere act of imagination, as there are whispered

29

rumours that her six children were all fathered by different men. But that's another mystery for another time.

I regard her legacy now as something akin to having a grandfather who was a war hero. I'm proud to be descended from her, to have her wild blood running through my veins, and to carry her torch. In her own quiet and ladylike way, she was unafraid, unrepentant, and she ran her own race. As an adult I have come to know her other granddaughters a little, her progeny from the 'other' side of the family, and I'm pleased to report they are equally feisty and intelligent, and similarly inclined to follow their hearts and their instincts and indulge their lovely and bohemian tastes. They also have their own little bizarre and cherished stashes inherited from our generous and wayward granny.

It requires a healthy degree of delusion, a talent for illusion and an undying faith in one's own self – tempered, of course, with complete denial of hard cold reality – to be a musician, or indeed to follow any kind of creative pathway in this country. And, somehow, I see you as embodying all of these elements. A mesmerising silver force to be reckoned with on the outside, and, inside, plain white cotton and hand stitched, frayed, exposed elastic. Let's dance, you seem to say, with an artfully raised, pencil-thin eyebrow. You're the call to arms. The flagship of the family business. The invitation to the blues. A ticket to another dimension. You expose the secret showgirl, the unashamed, the bold, the brave, the dangerous, the existential entertainer that lurked and malingered in the veins of my grandmother to finally find expression through an unknown son, grandchildren and great grandchildren – musicians, songwriters, entertainers, philosophers, authors, feminists, lovers, fighters, imagineers.

I'd love to take you out one day, to show you off and give you your due. However, despite an immense admiration and respect for showgirls, I have no personal interest in getting down to my smalls publicly and so far I've only ever worn you around the house. In the mirror. In my mind. But please, rest assured, you may be hidden away out of sight but your reputation still glows and grows.

You represent to me now an indomitable female spirit, a flagrant *fuck you* to moral rectitude, an empowering totem of a willingness to be an outsider, a weirdo, a bohemian temptress in a suburban waste-land, a cultural revolutionary. You are a glittering ode to mystery. Rebellion. A signpost spruiking 'Trouble This Way'. Hunger and demons. Forbidden afternoons and a bite of the apple. Pulp fiction. Waking dreams. A strange bird. A lioness's roar. A strutting peacock. Edward Munch's *Scream* and a sailor's delight. A pounding heart at the dark end of the street. An unread book. A triumph of the will. A declaration of independence. A refusal to conform. You're stoic. You're desire. You're behind the curtains and under the skin. You're proof of life. A shining victory for untamed imagination. An ever-sparkling testament to bad-girl spirit. You're tantalising evidence of a grandmother I wish I'd taken the time to get to know. You're the right to bear arms and you're a stolen moment. A brazen beacon and a candle in the window. A lonely stretch of highway. Gin and tonic on the sly. A smokin' hot tamale. You're wham, bam, thank you ma'am, and hello Mrs Robinson. You're the ginchiest. You're the question on everyone's lips. You're strangers in the night. You're the twilight zone, a voice from the grave, you're not alone. You're why, why, why, Delilah. You're slipping into something more comfort-able. You're the reason why and the *raison d'être*. You're the *pièce de résistance*.

You're thank you and goodnight.

Loene Carmen

COCO (AS TOLD TO MANDY SAYER)

Dear Mr Bowl, my favourite possession,

This is the story of how I won you at the Kings Cross Dog Show; of how hard I worked to have you in my life, morning and night, filled with beef treats, kibble and smelly bones.

The sun was shining, the band was playing, and about forty dogs were milling around the stage, pulling on leashes and sniffing each other's bums. Boston terriers and bulldogs, poodles and Pomeranians; there was even a pair of Mexican hairlesses, who looked like they'd had thirty rounds of chemotherapy. Fortunately, as I scoured the competition, I noticed there was only one chihuahua – me.

I began to relax a little when I realised who the judges would be for the dog show: Rhonda, who was a friend; Warren Fahey, an acquaintance; and Rubella the singing drag queen, who works in a local pharmacy (sometimes in costume) and who always fawns over me when I enter the store. The fourth judge was the jazz singer Edwin Duff, who'd been a friend of my owner Mandy's family since the 1940s; he'd performed in bands with her jazz drummer father for decades. I already knew I had a pretty good chance of winning, but, with the panel stacked as well as it was, I now sensed victory was in the palm of my paw.

All right, the lookalike section didn't go so well. Yes, I was certainly clean and well-groomed, but Mandy was suffering from a red-wine hangover and lack of sleep, having hosted a dinner party the night before for guests who didn't leave until three o'clock in the morning. In winter, I usually wear a red and black jacket to keep me warm, and I had planned to wear it during the lookalike section, while Mandy was supposed to wear a matching black dress with a vintage red velvet coat. Unfortunately, in the rush to get ready that morning, she couldn't find the coat anywhere, and had to race out the door in a different ensemble – some black '40s number that was too small for her and made her arse look fat.

Of course, I was annoyed when a very organised owner, wearing a blue and red football jumper, paraded her fox terrier, who was wearing an identical jumper with the same number stitched on the back. And then there was the man with salt-and-pepper hair and beard, who proudly displayed his two bearded salt-and-pepper Airedales before the grinning judges.

When it was our turn, Mandy and I bravely trotted across the stage, but even then I sensed we'd already been outshone. And things went from bad to worse when the drag queen MC, dressed in a pink and white '50s dress, asked Mandy why she thought she and I looked alike. Brain-dead Mandy took the microphone and, in an effort to win over the judges, attempted some coarse humour: 'Well, it's not so much that we look alike, it's that we act alike – when we hear our names called we both immediately come.'

I could already feel that trophy slipping out of my paws.

Next was the category of 'Best Dog Trick'. My other owner, Louis, confidently took to the stage with me and, I must say, I wiped the floor with those other mutts. I begged obediently, I high-fived, I pirouetted perfectly on my hind legs before the judges. The crowd went wild with applause and whistles, and scores of cameras clicked as I danced. Convinced I'd receive a perfect score, I sat back down and anticipated my accolades. Rhonda held up her score: 10; then Warren: 10; Rubella: 10. Then Edwin riffled through his cards and held up his score: 1. The crowd booed and I found myself wondering if Mandy's eighty-year-old friend was blind, or senile, or both. Still, dear doggy bowl, in spite of Edwin's low enthusiasm, I won 'Best Trick of Kings Cross' and was gifted with you, engraved with my name and my winning category.

But, Mr Bowl, I left my best trick until last. After the show finished, Mandy let me off my leash and allowed me to roam around the park. Five minutes later, I looked up to see Edwin Duff himself talking to the then Leader of the Opposition, Malcolm Turnbull. I saw my chance for revenge and promptly took it – while Edwin bragged loudly about once having known Frank Sinatra, I lifted my leg and pissed all over his sequinned cowboy boots.

Lots of love and licking,
Coco

To the moment I knew it was time to go home

KK JUGGY

Dear (oh dear) rock 'n' roll disappointment,

Lights flashed, strobes blinked, glitter bombed, smoke engulfed, audience cheered, drums pounded, sloppy bassline thundered and a big hook at the back of the stage swung unemployed as Gene Simmons stood there, tongue hanging out, looking up at the platform above him. I could only assume the swinging hook was meant to have hoisted him up to the platform during the extreme pantomime dramatics. Ladies and gentlemen, it is with great pleasure and some amusement, I introduce you to Kiss.

It was May 2004 and Machine Gun Fellatio were opening for Kiss's third 'last ever' tour of Australia. An offer we just couldn't refuse – the chance to tour with the closest thing to Spinal Tap since, well, Spinal Tap. As a kid I wasn't a Kiss fan, but many of my friends were, so I inevitably heard their music at birthday parties. I do have distant memories of playing Pin the Tail on the Donkey to 'Detroit Rock City' at a friend's eighth birthday party and, funnily enough, that is the one Kiss song I do actually like.

During this tour I had a certain prop/costume I'd made for a character I'd invented called Fanny Warhol. She is a New York feminist performance artist who has multimedia 'happenings'. Her most celebrated performance was and still is the 'Mono Vag' (inspired by the comparatively dull *Vagina Monologues*). However, instead of reciting monologues she shouts and hollers names and phrases for the vagina. 'Glistening Slit! Beef Curtains! Growler! Fur Burger! Beaver! Coochie! Snatch! Nookie! Muff! Cunt! Putang! Velvet Mouse Trap! Love Tunnel! Poonani!' I think you get the drift. She also interpret-dances orgasms and makes paintings with her vagina such as 'Gash Slash' and 'Portrait of Young Vagina as an Artist'.

She can queef (that's a fanny fart in case you didn't know) musical compositions and her performances often end with a sublime version of Celine Dion's 'My Fart Will Go On'.

Throughout her performances she wears a billowing pink and red kaftan and a cardboard cut-out vagina with her face cheekily peeking through the slit. It was the cardboard cut-out vagina I took on tour with Kiss, as I hoped to photograph Gene Simmons and/or Paul Stanley wearing it, joining the ranks of the Darkness, Duran Duran, the Dandy Warhols, Peaches, the Black Eyed Peas and Sir Les Patterson, just to namedrop a few who have cheerfully posed wearing the vagina on their heads. I thought some Kiss shots would be hunky-dory. I was wrong.

As the tour progressed, it became apparent that Gene Simmons lacks a sense of humour, which is a pity considering he looks like Krusty the Klown made up for a Halloween special. After a while of trying to coax him backstage to wear the vagina, it became clear that he wasn't going to wear it and we rather disliked one another.

He has bedded many, many women and boasts of his lovemaking skills. This modern-day Casanova is in fact so extraordinary that, according to one of his songs, women call him 'Dr Love'. This does seem a little far-fetched, especially if you've ever seen the video of him on YouTube having remarkably uninspired sex with a beer model, with his tube socks on and trousers around his ankles. For someone who loves women so much, it did seem odd he was so shy of a vagina.

Paul Stanley, on the other hand, was quite a different kettle of fish. While Gene plays ooga-booga woman master, Paul plays campy, flamboyant, fruity theatrical type, if you know what I mean. Gene stomps 'n' groans 'n' sticks his tongue out. Paul skips 'n' pouts 'n' wiggles his bottom. His introduction to a song called 'Lick it Up' was the highlight of their show. He yowled to the audience, 'Wooooo! Thith one ith for all the laaadieth out there! You know how it ith, yeah? Jutht lying back and taking it and really enjoying it? All right! LICK IT UP! LICK IT UP!'

The flock of fans known as the 'Kiss Army', a very dedicated lot, screamed and cheered. As I looked around at the Kiss Army, who turn up to Kiss concerts dressed and made up as the band members (it feels like being at a convention for mime artists – really noisy and not very good mime artists), I noticed that, as a rule, Dad turns up as Gene and Mum turns up as Paul and their kids are the other two (the original band members were sacked long ago so I couldn't even guess who the other two band members really are now).

It then dawned on me as I watched the flock sway and stomp to 'Lick it Up' that later that night, when the Kiss Army got home, all frisky and fuzzy with post show glow and looking all hot and sexy in their mime/Kiss makeup . . . Dad (Dr Love) probably gives one to Mum (Paul) 'lying back and taking it and enjoying it and licking it up. Woooooo!' Urgh. I still shudder at the thought of it. Funnily enough, Paul happily posed with the cut-out vagina on his crotch. Snap!

The last night of the tour we were in Brisbane. I was feeling festive and in the mood for mischief. That night, backstage, I met some of the members of Melbourne's Philharmonic Orchestra who were performing with Kiss. One guy, a French horn player, was an MGF fan and loved the Fanny headdress. He asked if he could wear it on stage during their performance. Well, of course he could! I certainly wasn't going to let him down. Also backstage that night were a couple of girls Gene had organised to party with him after the show. They were from the Gold Coast, they were attractive and they were young. They were friends of friends of Gene's.

Fascinated by groupie mentality at the time, I approached the girls. 'So, do you think you'll sleep with him?' I asked

'Don't know,' they responded, 'we haven't even met him yet.'

They had been picked up by a stretch limo, driven to Brisbane, put up in a hotel and given the obligatory backstage passes. This set-up is probably quite normal for some rock bands but it was all pretty foreign to me.

As Kiss finished their final show that night and invited the Melbourne Philharmonic Orchestra to stand and take a bow, the French horn player took the cardboard vagina off his head and handed it to Gene. Gene was furious. He grabbed the vagina and ripped it before throwing it across the stage and stomping on it. Dr Love! Now that is no way to treat a lady.

Later that night I was carrying on at a nightclub when Dr Love's lady friends called. Dr Love was being Dr Yawn and they were bored. Did I want to come up to the penthouse and drink champagne with them?

Knowing who was footing the bill, I just couldn't resist.

Bubbles were drunk, giggles were giggled and then the phone rang. It was Dr Love and he requested his patients visit him for a check-up in his hotel room downstairs. The girls suggested I join them. I explained I wasn't feeling sick enough to see a doctor and had no need for a check-up. I then downed a glass of champagne and said, 'Bugger it! He tore Fanny's vagina, I need a word with him. Let's go!'

We went downstairs and knocked on his door. Gene answered and was not impressed to see me swaying between his lady friends. An arm over each girl and grasping a bottle of Bollinger, I felt like one of the Keiths – Richards or Moon – and believe me, I felt a lot more rock than Gene looked that night. He asked what I was doing there and the girls complained that he had been no fun and was ignoring them whereas I had been entertaining and partied with them.

I then chipped in and let him know what a disappointment he had been to meet. Admittedly I hadn't really been expecting much but I had no idea he'd be such a dullard.

Dr Love, who stands quite tall even without his space booties, looked down and flared his nostrils and said, 'You're just saying that because you're d-d-d-d-d-d-d-d-d-d-d-d-d-d-d-d-drunk!' Wow, this doctor really knows his shit. I *was* drunk.

I laughed and replied, 'No, I said it because it's true, and guess what? You're not getting l-l-l-l-l-l-l-l-l-l-l-l-l-l-laid tonight! C'mon, girls!' I spun around and, bless 'em, they followed me back down the hall as I strutted my 'hahaha, I just stole your pussy line-up' walk whilst crooning 'Lick it Up'! We went back to their room, ordered more champagne and took turns performing 'Lick it Up'.

Now, ain't that just the sweetest thing? Just when I thought rock 'n' roll was an old man's game, it turned around and embraced me. Not so disappointing after all.

Yours forever,
KK Juggy xxx

KK. Juggy

PIP LINCOLNE

There were so many things I could have chosen to write about here.

Sitting in a bogan car at the drive-in, in a tiny town in the far north-west of Australia, with a boy I did not like.

Finding my fifteen-year-old self dressed a lot like Madonna at the Street Machine Summernats.

Standing triumphantly in the front row at that 1986 festival only to be told by the girl next to me that the boys in the band were looking down my top.

But I decided to go for something with fewer boobs, less hair and no cars. My letter is about my brother and me.

———

Dear Moment,

It has been quite some time since we were together. You came with a Famous Five mindset, long crisp days and the promise of cheese on toast and a cosy couch once you'd passed. So great. Not that life isn't full of those things now. My couch is cosy, my toast is cheesy and my days are often crispy. But I am slightly more grown up, I guess.

Here is the lead up to where you came in, back then, when I was ten.

We sat in the lounge room, my brother and I, on well-worn club chairs. We looked at the fire, crackling cosily. We looked at the grey floral carpet dotted with little burns and singe marks. We looked at the cricket flickering, green and soundless, on the telly. We looked at the dead flies, legs crossed, on the window sill. We looked out the window at the quiet, still day, at the glassy water and at the boats sliding slowly back and forth in our little bay below. We looked at the stack of faded comics at our feet. We looked at each other.

Do you want to go fishing? I asked. Sure, he said.

We pulled our jumpers over bed hair and wriggled our feet into our sneakers. We walked to the room at the back of the shack and rummaged in the cupboard for a bucket. I grabbed two rods from outside the bathroom door as he stuffed a packet of biscuits and a bottle of ginger beer into his backpack. He fished around in the old chest freezer for bait while I looked for Minties and scribbled a note to the adults. They seemed to be missing. Maybe they had done the big drive into town to get bread and milk.

I yanked open the back door and fly strips slapped our faces. We squinted as we pushed our way out into the bright white daylight, slamming the door behind us. We strode across the back patio of our blue shack, past the little piles of shells, sea urchins and pieces of driftwood. Past the clothes line, with flapping beach towels and someone's bathers. Past the old barbecue where the shack key was hidden beneath a secret brick.

We walked past the woodpile, shortcutting across the grass and crawling under the house for some extra hooks and sinkers. It was dark down there. It smelled like metal and petrol. I pulled my jumper up over my mouth and tried to breathe shallowly as we sorted through old jars full of lures and weights and hooks. The rust-coated bits and pieces made me shiver. I couldn't wait to get out of there.

Outside again, we breathed the sea air deeply. We walked across the crunchy grass and through the front gate. We were on the unsealed road now, still crunching along beneath the huge cliff-top gums. Below were the rocks and then the beach further along. It seemed a long way down.

We walked along the road, which had a single row of houses on each side bordered by paddocks to the left and the cliffs and the sea to the right. There were only about fifteen little houses, their gardens dotted with the same hardy red hot pokers, agapanthus and geraniums. Some shacks were deserted, their front yards sporting long grass and littered with shards of bark or broken branches from the overhanging trees. Others were neat as a pin with elderly residents tucked quietly inside, tidy cars in the driveways and smoke trailing from their chimneys.

At the end of the road, past all the shacks, neat and not, was an old wooden fence. We hoisted ourselves over it and walked along the grass towards the cliff edge. It felt scary and exciting. It felt *high*. The best climbing spot was marked by a towering gum that jutted from the cliff top. The ground was bare there, exposed to the elements and our constant clambering.

I went first. I kneeled in the dirt and scuttled backwards away from the big tree, clinging to its roots as I shimmied carefully towards the rocks and blue sea below. I had my arm looped through the bucket handle and it bumped noisily as I climbed, pretending to be fearless and feeling like a Charlie's Angel (with a bucket).

A minute or two of bumping and bravery and I landed safely on the rocks. He reached the same spot at the bottom of the cliff about a minute after I did and we unloaded our things onto the ground. We were right by the water's edge. It was calm, and sunny, but not hot. The breeze was slight, a sea sigh, I suppose.

He baited our hooks, first slicing the bait bag open with his pocket knife, then skewering the half-frozen nuggets of yuck with difficulty. I held my nose as I put the rest of the bait in the sun to defrost. We washed our hands in the rock pools and chose our fishing spots. We were going to catch a fish, maybe even a few fish, enough for all the kids to have fish and chips for dinner. That was the plan.

So there we sat. By the sea. Waiting. I think we sat for 256 hours.

Well . . . Actually we probably sat for a good four minutes without a bite. I reeled my line in and looked at the bait. Surely there was something wrong with it. I cast my line again. I waited. For 143 hours. Or three minutes. Still no dice. He had no bites either. We waited. We watched. We listened to the seagulls. We saw boats putt by. We yawned. Nothing. I can't tell you how boring it was. This was not part of the plan.

I wedged my rod into a hole in the rocks, the line still trailing in the water, and wandered about a bit. I picked up some shells, and looked at starfish and sea urchins. Ate a biscuit. Stubbed my toe. Sobbed. Ate a Mintie. Pretended to be a mermaid. Glugged some ginger beer. Wandered some more. Looked at my sore toe. Talked to myself a little bit. Pretended to be Marie from *The Swiss Family Robinson*. Checked my line. Nothing. He pulled his line in too and perched himself on a rock eating mildly fishy biscuits. It was not fun. I wished we were back with the comics and the singed carpet watching *Welcome Back, Kotter*.

We decided to freshen up the hooks with new bait. Um . . . There was no bait. The seagulls had stolen it, staging unnoticed air raids while we were eating biscuits. Bugger it. We had not caught a single fish. Our bucket was empty, our biscuits were all gone, and we only had five Minties and the soupy bit of the ginger beer left. Things were dire. We were desperate and baitless.

I was mad now, Moment. I would not be beaten by seagulls. Hungry cousins were relying on me. If we didn't catch any fish it would be spaghetti bolognese for the third night running. I took the empty bucket and began pulling periwinkles off the rocks. (I know it's brutal, but these were tough times and we were running out of rations with nothing to show for it.) I scooped the inside of a periwinkle out with the pocket knife. It was rubbery and weird. I pushed my hook through it, wincing and gagging a bit (as you do with things that are rubbery and weird). I don't know how I knew to do this, but I did.

I carried my rod to the water's edge and sat with my legs tucked under me. I plonked my line in so the hook floated a little way under the surface. All was quiet. The water was so still and shallow, I could clearly see the baited hook moving with the current and the seaweed swirling beneath it. Then I saw a fish. There was a flash of silver as a flathead swam up and bit the hook. I got such a shock I yanked the rod over my ten-year-old shoulder and the now-hooked fish flew up onto the rocks with a thud. I stood with my mouth open. He shrieked with laughter and, wide-eyed, grabbed the fish. I turned away as he gave it a quick whack and put it in the bucket, clattering the periwinkles onto the rocks to make room. We stared at each other, and then at the fish. We were awe-struck.

We tried again, lowering our periwinkled hooks, waiting until we saw a fish swim up just seconds later and then yanking our short lines out of the water without even having to reel them in. The fish were flying onto the rocks with stunned regularity.

We caught eight fish, enough to feed two shack-fuls. We puffed our chests up proudly. We were Periwinkle Pirates, swaggering in soggy rolled-up jeans, *Goodies* songs our sea shanties, chewing Minties like tobacco. He was so swashbuckly he drank the last soupy bit of the ginger beer. Yuck. I screwed up my nose and dug in my pocket for another lolly. I dug deep, retrieving three empty wrappers and a hair clip. I dug in my other pocket then, and, even more hopefully, in each back pocket. Nothing. No dice.

I looked at my stubbed toe. I looked at my soggy rolled-up jeans. I looked at my mermaid legs and at the sea before me. I looked at the empty periwinkle shells and at the bucket full of shiny fish. We looked at each other.

Sean, the Minties are all gone, I said. He shrugged. That was the moment I knew it was time to go home.

Pip Lincolne

COURTENEY HOCKING

Hey you,

Sometimes when my parents go away on holidays, I like to borrow their car and take it for a drive back to where I grew up – Nunawading, which is an Aboriginal word for 'home of crime and boredom'. Though Nunawading hasn't been my home for over fifteen years, it's still the place I've always returned to by instinct, to remind me where I came from and where I belong.

When I was little, there weren't any factory outlets in Nunawading, aside from the Chinese grocery where my mum would buy huge bags of rice to make her special 'Chicken Chinese' dish – which involved chicken, definitely, and rice, which perhaps was meant to account for the Chinese element. Less distinguishable in their relevance, though, were the celery and pineapple.

As you can imagine, it was an incredibly multicultural suburb, where I was honoured to be the only tall, awkward white girl included in the traditional Cambodian dancing demonstration on Australia Day. I can still speak a little bit of Mandarin and Vietnamese – yi, er, san, si, wu, liu, qi, ba, which is Mandarin for one, two, three, four, five, six, seven, eight; and doh mah, which is Vietnamese for motherfucker.

In my mind, Nunawading was the kind of working-class, egalitarian suburb that Bruce Springsteen would have written about, if Bruce Springsteen had grown up in Forrest Hill. The most exciting excursion we had at primary school was when we were all herded out onto the school oval while a gunman held some people hostage in the nearby commission flats.

We lived in Nuna until I was about fifteen years old, when we moved further in to be close to the girls' school I'd been admitted to. I never felt like I fit in after we moved – among all those kids with money and entitlement and that disturbing combination of all the opportunities in the world and all the indifference as well. I gave raging yet shaky orations about female genital mutilation in the third world to groups of teenage girls who thought feminism was some sort of fungal infection that their mothers had warned them about. I wrote furious treaties about Pauline Hanson and the benefits of multiculturalism for girls who came from old Australian money, families with long lines of relatives from England, Ireland, Scotland, Europe – all the colours of the white rainbow. I also wrote a lot of bad poetry about Paul McDermott, but that was just the teenage pants-love talking.

At that school I always felt like an outsider – someone who knew what it was to go without, and who longed for my old home where no one cared whether I had the right PE shorts, or whether I was on the rowing team, or which of the boys at the local boys' school talked to me on ICQ. I hated my parents for sending me there. I felt like the underdog in a room full of bitches.

My empathy for people who are unlucky or disadvantaged is still a huge part of my character. But who am I kidding? I've always had an incredibly lucky and privileged life. I'm a white, middle-class girl with a voice and a brain and arms and legs that aren't painted on. But I still identify with the underdog. The teenage years are all about struggling to find out who you are, how to exist and what clothes you can wear to look attractive next to your best friend who has a huge rack while you have a chest flat enough to paint art on. But once you finish all those years and think you've finally survived and thrived – where are you then? Where does that leave you?

Back in Nuna, I walked to the shops, where my brother used to piggyback me around until it was time to go home and watch *Magnum, P. I.*, and past a restaurant where I could see three generations of the same family sitting and having ('having' is the word – they were certainly not 'enjoying') a meal. They all had the same facial features, the same disinterested look on those features, and they all sat in a row, pulling the same face into the very same face reflected before them. It looked like a really shitty Saturday night out. A bit further up the street, I picked up a newspaper that was littering the road and put it into a bin. A woman walking past said, 'Tut, tut, that's not a recycling bin, is it?' And I said, 'Sorry,' though I immediately wished I'd said, 'Fuck off,' – finding the honest yet civil point between those two phrases is ever the bane of my existence.

I walked along the main road, where there used to be a tyre shop and a petrol station, and now there's a giant Harvey Norman and a Bunnings and the McDonald's, where the drive-through had been expanded onto the block where the boys who set fire to the dental van used to live. I went into the local fish and chip shop and in the doorway I knew just what it was like for those cowboys in the movies when they step into a western saloon and the music stops. Literally everyone – the cook, the lady at the counter, the bored guy reading the local paper and the woman with her kid (and the kid) – all stopped to stare at me. Perhaps I was being hypersensitive, but I felt so out of place. Not as though all my years away had changed me so much that I obviously no longer belonged, not that, but something more

I could finally see why my mother had been so desperate to get me out of there. She very kindly describes me as 'a bit eccentric', and perhaps becoming a bolshie, smart-arse political comedian isn't necessarily what she always dreamed of for me. But my mum fought to give me the opportunities she never had, and the importance of a good education can't be underplayed in that. She was never allowed to read any books other than the Bible when she was a girl, and yet she somehow raised a daughter who, sometimes, when the going is good, is able to write for a living.

Driving home again, I wondered if this is what becoming an adult was about – some kind of final 'the grass is not greener' realisation? An end of that need to shine a torch down all those paths not taken, or even the final moment of clarity when you realise that your hometown is not so much Bruce Springsteen as it is Bryan Adams? But I think it was more than that. I came away from that last trip out to Nunawading strangely free from all that old nostalgia. What I truly miss and had been searching for were not just memories or an actual place where I belong, but the sense of belonging that I felt back then. Of feeling at home without ever having to question why – even as a tall, gawky white girl dancing amongst half a dozen delicate, beautiful Cambodians. And I'm still looking for that. I feel as though I'm on that strange part of the road that's both too far between my origin and my destination to feel anywhere but very far away. I think Bob Dylan is an incredible artist and also an unbearable wanker, and I think he explains it best. He said once, 'I was born very far from where I'm supposed to be, and so, I'm on my way home, you know?' Yeah, Bob, I do. Guess I'll see you out there.

Love,
Courteney x

A love letter

KRISTINA OLSSON

To the alphabet,

I knew you before I knew myself. Prenatal, a thumb of flesh beneath my mother's heart: even then, swimming in darkness, I heard you. Pa boom, pa boom, pa boom. The blood's percussion – my first alphabet.

Sound is our first sense, learnt in the womb, but my young mother knew nothing of that. She had no Brahms or Beethoven to hold to her belly, to calm the anxious blood she pumped to me. But music came to me anyway, long before my birth: it was in the cadences and rhythms of my father's Swedish vowels, his song-like sentences. The way his words curved and twisted around that darkness I swam in.

In contrast, my mother's words were straight, clean lines. Her vowels plain and broad, without decor, as ordinary as the streets of the city I was born into, and as honest. That's what they loved first, my mother and father, the elegance and decency of the other's words. When you've suffered enough, when you have felt, at times, less than human, these two things – elegance and decency – are what you long for. More than anything.

Moving blind inside my mother's skin, I knew nothing of suffering. I heard the sounds of my parents' tongues and even then knew language as comfort but also as shapeshifter, as disguise, as multiple: the alphabet of possibilities. I have been in love with your possibilities ever since.

I've been in love, I think, not just with letters and not just with words, but with the look of them, the music of them. The way they slide together to make language, the way their rhythms make meaning. The way their shapes make a map to live by. Sometimes I think the books I've written, the stories, the postcards and poems, have just been love letters to language. The alphabet of desire.

My granddaughter is learning to read. Her fingers trace over the letters in her reading book, on the porridge packet; her quick eyes find them on road signs, in grocery aisles, on t-shirts and envelopes, the notes I leave for her around the house. Everywhere. She is learning that the world is letter-shaped: round and comforting like a C; sharp and prickly like a capital A; as devious as an S or as wondrous as O; full of rules like the marching capital K.

I've watched this slow accumulation of letters for a while. But last week, something special happened. Propped next to me on the bed with an old Dr Seuss, she ran her finger along the letters and joined them in the casual way we peruse our mail, or our daily paper, or a billboard. She'd done that before but stumblingly, searchingly, one word at a time. This was different: it was comprehension. The letters ran together into words and the words tipped over into sentences and became story. She understood that, I could hear it: the words were no longer random but part of something bigger, something with meaning and shape. Somewhere, deep down, she began to understand that she was too: she was part of something bigger than she was, and it might have meaning and shape. It might have magic.

In the meantime, her finger kept moving along the lines, as if it was creating the story. I thought of Michelangelo's famous mural, the finger of God touching the world into being. The power of it, the majesty. My granddaughter doesn't know it yet, but this was also a moment of power and majesty. She got to the end of the page and looked up at me, smiling her angel's smile. The alphabet of magic.

But it wasn't all smooth sailing. She sat puzzling over 'might' and 'light'. Got stuck on the G and the H. Mig? she said. Lig? Frowning the frown she was born with. These guys don't make a sound here, I told her, and placed one finger over the middle of might. Another over the middle of light. They're silent. That frown again. She's six, after all, and not much acquainted with silence. She shrugged and flipped the page. Dad, she read, her fingers tender on the 'D'. Dad is sad. Dad had a bad day.

I managed not to weep. I managed not to frighten her with my joy, my own ecstatic memory of this: the suddenness of meaning, of the world making sense. At six. Beneath my finger probing D-A-D. The bulge of possibility and, yes, of love, in that D with its chest puffed out, in the golden stretch of play and wonder she now knows as D-A-Y. That she now owns, because it is no longer simply a collection of images and sensations before her every morning. She has made meaning of it, not just by naming but by seeing, by owning it. It has a name, and she alone – or so it must seem – has named it. As if it has emerged from her, or her from it.

As much as any rite of passage, learning to read is about finding power. When you are six, and the world still frightens you, and when you feel in all your cells that you have no authority, no volition, this is important. It isn't just being able to give a name to things, though this truly is a source of power. It is the ability you now have to transcend yourself, to be more than yourself. To fly with Peter Pan, meet the White Rabbit, to ride a tiger's back or live in a castaway's treehouse. To be as cheeky as Huckleberry Finn or as brave as Bunyip Bluegum, or as free as Pippi Longstocking. To be Pippi Longstocking.

To have your own alphabet of wonder.

I looked at my granddaughter tucked beside me, a colourful fairy against white pillows and a white doona, and saw the moment for what it was: a glimpse of the real future. I wanted to celebrate it, to mark it in some way, perhaps as the medieval Jews did, by transforming words into food. First the new reader – usually a boy – repeated the words written by his teacher on a slate: 'May the Torah be your occupation'. When he finally got it right, the slate was covered with honey for the child to lick, so that he bodily ingested the words. Or they would be written on hard-boiled eggs or on honey cakes for the child to eat. I love this idea of words becoming us, that they are literally part of us, inside us. We become our own ingredients, our own alphabet soup.

But, alas, we have no such traditions, and besides, that particular night, we'd just cleaned our teeth. We celebrated instead by singing our favourite words, nonsensical, fantastical, out loud and all around the room. I think I allowed myself a few tears after she'd gone to sleep.

The tears, though, weren't just for joy, and weren't just for her. I can't tell her yet but one day I want her to know that you, my alphabet, you who are music and desire and wonder and nourishment and power – and as such should belong to us all – don't really belong to everyone. Because you are about power, you are often used by the powerful to keep the powerless in their place. How better to dispossess a people than to remove or forbid their language? To obliterate their alphabet of survival and strength? How better to maintain our own place in the world than by ensuring that many have none? That some children have and some children do not have an alphabet of optimism?

In the end, to celebrate my granddaughter's Age of Reading, I told her about the Butterfly Alphabet. About the Norwegian photographer who discovered that, if you look carefully, you will see the entire alphabet spelled out on the collective wings of the world's butterflies. It was night so we couldn't go looking, but we lay there and imagined letters fluttering about us as we walked and played and swam. Inscribing the sky with words. We thought that, as we slept, they too would settle for the night, making beautiful sentences in darkened trees and grasses, whole stories beneath the folded wings of flowers.

I let her believe for now, my alphabet, that you are as free with your favours, as subversive, as butterflies that, not knowing one garden from another, one person from another, brush their indiscriminate wings against us all. My alphabet of elegance and decency.

Kristina Olsson

KATE MILLER-HEIDKE

Dear twelve-year-old Kate,

Kate, I'm writing this out of love for you, but it's also a kind of love letter to myself, now, aged twenty-nine. I've been feeling a bit lost lately. So I'm going to give you some warnings and advice, and tell you some stories, but I'm mainly telling them to myself, as a reminder.

I don't write many letters these days. Just the occasional verbose email to old friends. The mechanism might be a little rusty – bear with me. Here we go.

- Kate, remember your first kiss, a few weeks ago? He's going to turn out to be gay. You should consider the possibility that 80 per cent of your boyfriends over the next decade will turn out to be gay. They will like you because you can belt out a campy rendition of 'On My Own' from *Les Mis*, and because you have a general surliness they are drawn to. Some of them will use you to test the murky waters of heterosexuality. One of them will make you sit through a twenty-minute silence, by candlelight, in memory of Princess Diana. Don't despair, though, because eventually you'll end up with one of the most finely tuned gaydars in Brisbane.
- If you decide to recount personal events in your diary, particularly those that involve smoking pot or being fingered, it's best to wrap tape around the diary and hide it. Otherwise your mother might casually wander into your room and read everything in

your desk while you're out. If this happens, don't overreact. She is acting out of love, no matter how it seems at the time.

- Be prepared to lose your virginity in a pretty undignified way. It's not as uncommon as you might think. Your boyfriend's 'best friend' *may* be in the next room, playing 'Like a Virgin' by Madonna over and over, and whooping sporadically. It *could* be quite distracting. The next day, your boyfriend *might* come out of the closet. Try not to take it too personally.

- When you go to France for a year to stay with family friends, resist the temptation to masturbate on their couch if there's even a slight chance one of them is home. Believe me, it's not worth it.

- When you start doing gigs, you might want to give some thought to a stage name. Otherwise you risk being known as Kate Miller-Whatsherface forever. Radio DJs will routinely call you Katie Millie Hi-Dickey. Just give it some thought now, before it's too late.

- If my memory is correct, a short while ago you saw Wendy Matthews on TV, singing 'The Day You Went Away' at the 1993 ARIA Music Awards. I know you pictured yourself up there on the stage, singing 'On My Own' to an enraptured audience that included a misty-eyed John Farnham. You will get to go to these awards several times when you're older, but don't be too disappointed if they've turned to shit by then.

- There is a pharmaceutical drug in America called Adderall, prescribed for children with ADHD. Do not take two Adderalls before you walk down the red carpet at your first ARIAs. The only thing it will do is make your armpits as sweaty as Bob Hawke's. Also, you might want to rethink your outfit. One popular fashion website called Go Fug Yourself printed a step-by-step guide of how to achieve my ARIAs 'look', which suggested downing a few shots of tequila, spinning around in a swivel chair for five full minutes, and then grabbing random accessories donated by (among others) Kelly Osbourne, Cyndi Lauper and Sarah

Ferguson. Then they posted a photo of me in all my resplend-
ent armpit glory. Again, I recount these things out of love. What
I'm trying to tell you is that your choice of profession will result
in you being insulted in a variety of ways – some entertaining,
some hurtful – but I think you've already developed a kind of
steeliness that will see you through. Most of the time.

- When signing your first management contract, read it carefully.
  Pay particular attention to page four.

- Keep an eye on the artwork on your album covers. It is possible
  that when they come off the press the pictures of you will have
  acquired an inexplicable orange Hollywood tan that definitely
  wasn't there when you initially approved the artwork. Pay attention. Do not approve anything under duress.

- Don't worry too much about the bitches at your school. Later in
  your life many of them will start coming to your shows and asking you to sign their CDs. But it won't feel like vindication, it will
  just feel bizarre – so enjoy knowing that now while you're still
  young and naive enough to hate with pure focus.

- When getting a bikini wax, use a different name for the booking.
  When they ask what you do for a living, just say you're a teacher,
  unless you're prepared to talk about your new video clip, which
  features mainly fish, with a woman who is completely focused
  on your crotch.

- Don't use the word 'cuntie' in your first ever tweet. It's not
  worth it.

- Please, please don't google yourself. Under no circumstances go
  to the *Time Off* or *Mess+Noise* forums. This is the biggest gift
  of love I can give you. I know you have no idea what all this
  means, because it's 1993 and you've never been on the internet,
  but someday these things will acquire a deep significance.

- When you're invited to speak at Women of Letters, don't spend
  three days writing a fictional letter from shock jock Alan Jones to

his young male lover. It might seem like a good idea at the time, but ultimately it will just come out weird.

Twelve-year-old Kate, I miss you. I miss your deep curiosity and potential. I love it when I sense your ghost breathing in my lungs. When I'm writing a song, if it's a good song, you are guiding me. Your echo, your shadow, your playfulness. When I'm taking a walk, and that ultra-ultra-rare feeling of joy and lightness descends, I can feel you smiling within me.

I know I have let you down in all sorts of ways, and I'm so sorry about that. And I know this letter is of no use to you. I can't stop you falling in love with gay men, signing bad contracts, or spraying the word cuntie all over the internet. I can't take away your sadness.

They say that nightmares are a way for your brain to prepare itself for the worst-case scenario. If that's the case, you and I have been very well prepared for a long time. Don't worry. You'll be fine.

I nearly forgot to mention that you will eventually meet a man who is your ideal – articulate, well-read, funny, smart, hot, sensitive and fluent in French. Okay, he doesn't speak great French, but he plays guitar like a motherfucker. You and he will be kindred spirits, just like Anne of Green Gables and Gilbert Blythe, who I recall you're quite fond of at the moment. You and your soulmate will travel the world together writing, recording and playing music, and almost every element of your life will be transformed by this miraculous partnership.

Don't feel the need to reply to this missive. I just got a reply to the letter I sent my ninety-year-old self and it's largely incomprehensible. She talks about cheese a lot.

Sincerely, with love and empathy,
Kate aged twenty-nine

MORAG KOBEZ-HALVORSON

Dear H,

Looking back, I know I took you for granted. I see now how naive it was, but I thought we'd be together forever.

You walked out of my life so suddenly, my dear health.

It felt like the bottom fell out of my world with that one phone call from the gynaecologist. Let's call her Doctor Glass-Half-Full. The one who performed minor surgery to remove that pesky polyp from my uterus. A procedure she performed almost every day, she'd told me – simple day surgery, painless, and certainly nothing to worry about. 'But we always take a pathology sample just in case.'

The call came later that week. 'Hello, Morag, it's Jodie from Doctor Glass-Half-Full's rooms. She'd like to see you as soon as possible.'

Then the visit.

Dear Doctor Glass-Half-Full,

I am writing to tell you that when you say to somebody, 'These abnormal pathology results don't necessarily mean it's cancer; try not to worry too much' – that will probably make the person quite worried.

Doctor Glass-Half-Full, can we please cut the crap? You have just told me I need to see an oncologist, *as soon as possible*. A doctor whose

62

core business is mortal tumours. I think we can all guess where this is headed.

———

Dear Doctor Tumour,

I am writing because I would like to address a number of issues.

Unlike you, I do not count my hitherto-unknown ability to grow rare and unusual womb-tumours as an achievement of any note.

The fact that a tiny collection of my cells travelled halfway around the world from a laboratory in Brisbane, to Sydney, and then on to the womb-tumour guru at Harvard Medical School does not excite me in quite the same way it does you.

'Ninety-five per cent of uterine malignancies occur in the endometrium, so it's quite rare to find a malignancy like this in the uterine wall. And most of that rare five per cent of malignancies are carcinosarcomas. But you've gone one rarer than that with adenosarcoma. It's very rare!'

Might I suggest that this was a conversation best had with your tumour-doctor buddies over a few beers at the pub, rather than me, the patient?

And another thing, Doctor Tumour – when you tell somebody in no uncertain terms that the definitive treatment for their exquisitely rare womb-tumour is to remove the offending womb, there's a good chance they're going to think that sounds like pretty sound advice.

That wretched womb gave me a lot of trouble over the years, and I wasn't all that sad at the thought of seeing the back of it.

If you'd bothered to enquire, Doctor Tumour, you'd have discovered that using that womb for its God-given purpose was not very high on my to-do list. I understood from your attitude, and from the pictures on your desk of your four lovely children, that you felt differently to me – that reproducing was very important to you.

The fact that you then suggested we leave the defective womb where it was and 'watch the situation closely', until such time as I had a chance to bear a child, was a teensy bit presumptuous now, wasn't it?

Finally, a little disappointedly, you agreed to take it out, even though that had been your idea in the first place!

I have had the dubious pleasure of visiting you regularly over the last few years, so that you could have a good look up my twat. You are, at least, not afraid of long-term commitment, Doctor Tumour.

I have become accustomed to our enchanted encounters, the little tete-a-tetes that always begin with, 'Any lumps, bumps or bleeding "down there"?' You are nothing if not methodical.

But I don't think I'll ever get over the fact that you resemble a burly rugby player. Each and every time you stick what feels like your entire burly arm up my front bottom for a feel for 'anything untoward', as you always say, I am ready for the words that alarmed me the first or second time I heard you say them: 'Sorry this might be a bit ouchy-ouchy! Sorry to be yuck!' If I had my way with you, Doctor Tumour, the way you always have your way with me, the words 'ouchy' and 'yuck' would be erased from your vocabulary.

For a long time after the surgery I felt like a marked woman. But, over time, the feeling faded.

Dear Health,

I began to harbour hopes that you'd come back to me, so I could stop seeing all these other people. I stopped drinking Diet Coke and began buying organic vegetables in an attempt to lure you back to me. I was making an effort to exercise more. I even started going to yoga classes.

But there was this niggling twinge in my right hip.

It wasn't painful in the beginning, just a bit wonky. So I ignored it and hoped it would go away.

I remained in denial until people around me began to comment on my limp.

'How did you hurt your leg?' someone would ask every few days.

'You are starting to resemble an injured animal, the way you drag your leg along behind you,' my partner eloquently pointed out.

So I started seeing someone else – Doctor Yanky.

Dear Doctor Yanky,

I admire your commitment, truly I do. You yanked my right leg with a little more gusto each time I came to see you. But no amount of yanking seemed to help. And to your credit, Doctor Yanky, you eventually conceded that all the yanking in the world didn't seem to be improving matters. In fact, the hip was getting worse. It was starting to hurt, quite a lot, even when you weren't yanking on it.

Time for some x-rays, you decided, and a referral to an orthopaedic specialist. You let me down gently, even introduced me to somebody else. Let's call him Doctor Blunt.

Dear Doctor Blunt,

Nobody could ever accuse you of bamboozling your patients with complicated medical jargon, or beating around the bush in making a diagnosis. No whispering sweet nothings in my ear.

You sat me down, looked at my hip x-ray for roughly two seconds, then turned to me and delivered your three-word prognosis: 'That hip's shot.'

'What do you mean by "shot"?' I asked.

'Well, no wonder it hurts, it's almost worn out. Arthritis. Have you played a lot of sport – professional tennis, perhaps?'

'Doctor Blunt, do I look like a professional athlete?'

I've always avoided sport, Doctor Blunt. I had a note from my mother to get out of PE more weeks than not.

A couple of weeks later, you did an arthroscopy, making a small incision in my hip, poking a teeny-tiny camera in and taking a look inside the joint, just to make sure it really was shot.

'Yep, it's definitely shot. The arthritis pain is only going to get worse. Stick it out as long as you can, but there's nothing else for it. You'll need to get a hip replacement.'

Dear Health,

It was a harsh blow. More than ever I had been considering your needs, putting you first, and this is the thanks I got?

No more organic vegetables for you, H.

Instead, a steady diet of painkillers. Stronger and stronger painkillers in ever-increasing quantities in an attempt to combat the feeling of being stabbed with a hot knife in the hip joint with each and every step.

My regular GP went on maternity leave and when next I needed the prescription filled, I saw another doctor at the same clinic.

Let's call her Doctor Corset.

She became rather animated when I told her how many anti-inflammatories I was taking. Said it was a wonder I didn't have a stomach ulcer.

I'd seen two orthopaedic surgeons by this time, and had had numerous x-rays in addition to the arthroscopy. I had a disabled parking permit. Everyone agreed the hip replacement was a done deal; it was just a matter of when.

But Doctor Corset was determined to make her own diagnosis.

'Where is this pain?' she demanded.

'In my right hip.'

'Bend over,' she barked.

She poked and prodded extensively before arriving at her final diagnosis.

'What you need is a good corset,' she said.

'I beg your pardon?' I said.

'A corset. David Jones has a good range. It will brace your pelvis and keep your hips in place.'

———

Dear Doctor Corset,

Please leave the underwear advice to my mother and the good ladies of David Jones' intimate apparel in future, and stick to sharing the medical knowledge you allegedly possess.

———

I booked in for the hip replacement not long after with Doctor Cocksure.

He was very sure about everything. Sure of the procedure and its success rates —one of the most common and successful procedures, apparently. Very sure of his own ability. What he didn't seem too sure about was how many years this new hip might last.

'A very long time,' was the vague answer to that one. 'One thing's for sure – it won't be my problem. I'll be retired by then.'

I had read a lot about the process. More than I should have. It involved a very large incision, cutting through the muscle and tendon to reach the hip joint, then dislocating the hip by pulling the leg into an extreme position on the operating table.

Doctor Cocksure would take a bone saw and lop off the top of the femur bone, to remove the diseased cartilage from the joint. A new metal socket would be installed, secured with a large screw driven into the pelvic bone, followed by a new lining. Doctor Cocksure would then take a chisel to carve out a cavity in the femur, and a new stem would be driven into that cavity. He'd seat the components of the new hip joint and check to make sure both legs were the same length, before closing up the layers of muscle and fat with a scar to make Frankenstein proud.

Doctor Cocksure mentioned a lot of blood, but said he would try to avoid a transfusion if possible.

I remember sitting on the operating table as the theatre staff administered an epidural, and glancing down at their feet. No little cloth booties covering their shoes –they wore shiny, white, knee-high gumboots. Galoshes! Would there be that much blood?

The next week in the orthopaedic ward of the hospital passed in a haze of morphine. The morphine dulled the pain, but not the vexation of the never-ending chorus of, 'Oh, you're a bit young to be in here, aren't you?' Nobody could pass up the opportunity to comment on my age: every new nurse who came on duty, physiotherapists, the tea-trolley lady and all my geriatric neighbours.

On the second day, I was issued with a lovely bottle-green and maroon Zimmer frame, dubbed 'Bertha' by a friend. Given permission, and with supervision, I was allowed to stand with Bertha's assistance.

On the third day, I was encouraged to shuffle, under supervision, the ten or so steps to the toilet, where one of those lovely raised toilet-seat frames awaited me.

On day four, I made it out of my room on the Zimmer. I joined the procession of elderly folk, all of us in our gowns and white knee-length compression stockings doing slow, shuffling Zimmer laps around the ward, as directed by our physiotherapists. I was pretty chuffed to be leaving my room, even if it was only for a walk with a Zimmer frame called Bertha.

I thought I was making good progress, until dear Doctor Cocksure shattered those allusions.

'Your gait is shithouse. Have you been doing your exercises?'

Slowly but surely my gait improved, and I left Doctor Cocksure and his harsh words behind.

Once again I allowed hope to creep in, dear H, that now, finally, I had paid the price for treating you the way I did. That you might come back into my life.

But you weren't satisfied that I had learned my lesson. Oh, no. You had a few more surprises up your sleeve, didn't you?

Three more hospital visits in six months, in fact, including a particularly dramatic New Year's Day surprise, in the form of a trip to the emergency room. An excruciating pain in my side that had me begging for more morphine, writhing and moaning like a mad woman.

Enter Doctor Panic Merchant, who turned up like a knight in shining armour to my bedside.

CT scans and ultrasounds were ordered. The writhing and moaning and begging for more morphine continued.

Doctor Panic Merchant got the results of the CT scan and told me he could see a 5-centimetre mass near my right ovary. He wanted to talk to Doctor Tumour, but Doctor Tumour was on holiday at the beach and couldn't be reached.

He talked about immediate surgery to remove the last remaining accursed piece of my reproductive system, my ovaries, along with that 5-centimetre mass, and I was admitted to the ward, still writhing and moaning.

Then Doctor Panic Merchant rode off on his white horse and Doctor Knickers arrived in his board shorts and thongs. I was officially dating down now, it seemed.

Dear Doctor Knickers,

Regardless of whether it is New Year's Day, or any other holiday, board shorts and thongs are not appropriate attire if you are attending a hospital room for a consultation that involves donning rubber gloves, lubing up and performing an internal examination of somebody's ovaries. Especially if you intend to charge in the vicinity of $400 for the pleasure.

Furthermore, call me old-fashioned, but it is my heartfelt belief that the phrase 'slip off your knickers' should really not be part of a gynaecologist's repertoire.

Still, compared to Doctor Panic Merchant, you were the bearer of good news. He was perhaps a bit mistaken.

You thought that 5-centimetre mass near my right ovary was my right ovary, somewhat enlarged due to a now-ruptured cyst. That would explain the pain. But we'd have to wait a couple of weeks until Doctor Tumour returned from the beach to find out for sure.

———

Dear Doctor Panic Merchant,

Next time you go diagnosing a tumour near an ovary and scaring the bejesus out of somebody, perhaps you could locate said ovary first as a handy point of reference.

———

Please, H, no more tumours. No more doctors. I don't want to see anybody else.

It's been exactly four years and 351 days since you left me, H, but not a day goes by that I don't think about you.

Can we put the past behind us now? We had so many good years together.

I promise that if you come back to me, things will be different. I'll treasure you, and never again take you for granted.

JACQUI PAYNE

Dear Babies,

I loved it when you were babies. I loved being pregnant and I loved it when you were little babies.

To each of my babies: Joseph, Sebastian, Greer, Georgia, Mia and Zoe.

To Joseph,

You are the 'baby from another mother'. I was a solicitor at the Aboriginal Legal Service. I was young, had never been a mother, and I was in love with a handsome young doctor. My life was free and easy.

Your parents were clients of mine in the Children's Court. Their circumstances overwhelmed them, and, totally unplanned, you came to live with me from the age of five days old.

I had not planned this in any way. It really was that one day I didn't have a baby and then the next day I did. No planning, no preparation. If I was asked why it was you came to live with me, I would respond that it was because, at the time, your needs were greater then mine.

My money then was for clothes and going out and travelling, so I hadn't wasted any of it on a washing machine. Now I had a baby. It was the time of cloth nappies – I had to handwash all of your nappies and clothes. OMG – do you know what that takes? I hung a small line across my lawn and had to hose the pooey ones. My life was controlled by those nappies. You do not know how liberating a big pile of clean nappies could be.

Of course you were bottle-fed. If microwaves were around then, I didn't have one. I would make a few bottles for during the night and when you'd wake I'd have to boil water to heat them. In the dark it seemed to take so long. I remember I thought it was a good night if I could add up all the sleep I got to four hours. A total of four hours sleep a night became the benchmark.

You came to work with me every day. When I went to court the secretaries looked after you. Then, when you were about eight months old and crawling, you were creating havoc and ripping up files, so you were packed off to day care. I remember filling out the form and they asked me how I would describe you. I just wrote 'happy'. You were such a happy baby.

I know I must have done some of it so badly, since I'd never been a mother before. But I also know I did some of it right, because when your own baby was born you named her Jacqueline after me. She is so wild and robust and playful. I still smile when I think about the other night, when I tucked her into bed and she said, 'Goodnight, Nana.'

———

To Sebastian,

I fell pregnant with you at the end of a five-year relationship with that handsome young doctor – in fact, it was really after it had finished. You were my biggest surprise. I went to a friend's house and they were cooking sausages and the smell of them made me nauseous. Why? I love sausages. But I couldn't eat them and I felt weird. I went to the doctor and said, 'I think I'm pregnant.' He asked me why I thought that and I told him, 'I suddenly can't stand the smell of sausages.'

I loved being pregnant with you. I loved everything about having another person growing inside of me. I even loved *looking* pregnant. I maintained my commitment to high heels and would have maternity dresses made for work. I remember being about five months pregnant and walking to court in my red maternity dress, with my lipstick, pearls and heels. A truck with some men drove past and whistled at me. I remember feeling fake indignation that they would whistle at a pregnant women. (Men would be too scared to whistle at anyone these days.)

The other great thing about being pregnant was that I allowed myself to eat whatever I wanted. I had such terrible morning sickness with you for the first three months – I was so nauseous, I would eat to try and stop it. Then I just kept on eating. I put on 22 kilos. I was so big.

The Simpsons was new to television then. One evening, I was in the kitchen standing and watching it when I got a Braxton Hicks contraction. I was laughing at the show and the unexpected contraction hit me and I fell to my knees from the pain, but I was still laughing. Only a pregnancy could cause such a surreal moment.

When I went into labour with you, I didn't know at first if it was real. I just felt different. But eventually I had no doubt. In fact, the labour lasted for twenty-seven hours, of which nine hours was really, really hard labour. In the end you were an emergency caesar. You still owe me for that smiley face just below my belly – the one that gets more prominent as I age.

You were such a beautiful baby. When I would walk down the street with you, strangers would stop and comment on how beautiful you were.

I loved it when you were a baby, but I was single and had to work to support you, Joseph and me. You went into childcare from the age of three weeks. I worried about leaving you but the love and care you were given by those women in the childcare centre was extraordinary. You were rarely left by them in the nursery, and I remember coming to get you to find you curled up like a possum on the lap of one of the women as she worked in the office. You would have a little heat rash on your face from being nursed all day.

When you were first in childcare and still being fully breastfed, I had to express milk – has anyone ever found that easy? Those bags of mother's milk were the most precious things I have ever owned. My breasts were full of milk as I went about my work, and I couldn't always express because I was in offices, courts, prisons. I used copious amounts of breast pads but at times my breasts were hot and full and painful. I was in court one day, on my feet, cross-examining a witness. I felt my milk come in, which it often did, but this time it wouldn't stop flowing. I looked down and saw big wet circles appearing on my pink linen suit. I picked up a plastic folder and held it against my chest. When I sat down I leaned forward to try to stop the milk from making my suit even wetter. But by then the folder had rubbed against my suit and left dirty marks. If anyone noticed, which they must have, no one said a word.

In the evenings, Sebastian, I would race to the day care and rush to feed you. One night I was the last parent to arrive, and you, Joseph and I didn't even make it to the car – we just sat in the gutter of the car park. I fed you, and Joseph laid his head on my lap.

———

To Greer,

My first girl baby. When your father and I got engaged, I was three months pregnant. But I miscarried a couple of days before our wedding. I had a curette and the doctor told me that, for medical reasons – including, I suppose, a scrubbed uterus – I should not have sex for some weeks. But I was madly in love with your dad and, against medical advice, I fell pregnant with you on my wedding night. There is the evidence you were conceived in love.

I didn't think it was likely I would fall pregnant so soon, so I was very surprised but also very happy. I think we paid a bit of a price for me falling pregnant when I did, though. When I was about four months pregnant, I was out walking in West End with Sebastian in a pram and Joseph and our big German shepherd, Texas, when I started to bleed. It was not like a brief but noticeable trickle – it was a tap. I started to walk home, the blood running down my legs. By the time I got home, the inside of my shoes were squishy with blood. I sat down on the edge of a chair with a towel on the ground below. In that moment, I learnt that blood and guts is too much for your dad. He looked worse than me.

At the hospital, our doctor told us that if the pregnancy continued and you were born, I should call you Lucky as it would mean you were born under a lucky star. Greer, how amazing that you are lucky and perfect in every way. Whatever that secret ingredient is that is needed for a person's life to turn out well, you have it.

When you were born, I learnt about things that happen in labour that pregnant women are never told about in advance. This is despite billions of babies having already been born before you. I had you naturally – not through a caesarean as our doctor wanted – so I found out that when you are pushing the baby out you can push poo out as well, and some poor nurse has to wipe your bottom. And I learnt that the most painful part is not the delivery of the head but the shoulders. But the greatest injustice of all is that after you deliver the baby and you think the pain is all over, you have to deliver the placenta. WTF – why didn't anyone mention that!

Greer, you were such a fat baby. In the baby height/weight charts you were in the top percentile – in fact, you were nearly off the chart! It was my fault, as I'd pop my titty in your mouth after any noise you'd make. Sometimes after I fed you I couldn't lay you down, as you were so full the milk would trickle out of your mouth. I had to prop you up so gravity would keep it in.

One day when you were little, I found you with your shirt pulled up and a doll against one breast and an inverted medicine cup against the other. When I asked you what you were doing, you said you were feeding your baby and expressing milk.

I was so happy to have a girl baby and I had so much fun dressing you. Today you are the best-dressed person I know. You have the gift of being very groovy and cool in how you dress, and I hope I contributed to that.

To Georgia,

I was pregnant with you when your dad was involved in the Ivan Milat trial. He was so daring and it was often a David and Goliath battle. The day I went into labour, he was in Sydney. He was to appear in the Supreme Court against Keith Mason QC, who was then the NSW Solicitor General and later became the President of the NSW Court of Appeal. I rang your dad and told him I thought I was in labour and asked if he could come home. He had so much on his plate, and so he asked me if I was sure, and if I could wait. But, Georgia, you didn't wait. That night, your dad called to tell Keith Mason that I was in labour and to see whether they could adjourn the application so your dad could come home to Brisbane. Your dad got Keith Mason's wife on the phone, as Keith wasn't home. He told her I was in labour and she told him not to worry, to go home and that she would tell her husband. Even Keith Mason answers to a higher power.

Georgia, you arrived before your dad made it back to Brisbane, and you know one of our favourite stories about you is about how after you were born, when they brought you in to me in the crib,

I couldn't see a baby – it was as if there were only two big brown eyes.

You were a beautiful, delightful baby, just as you are now as a young woman. We have always called you Gorgeous Georgia; you even had a jumper once with 'Gorgeous' on it. But underneath that wonderful nature, you have a steely and determined will, and you can show your displeasure. You showed this side from three months of age. I remember you crying and wailing to be fed, and, although I hurried to finish what I was doing, you had a short wait. I started to feed you and you drank, but then you would stop, set your jaw and growl at me from deep in your throat. You would drink and then growl some more. Even to this day you do that growly thing when you are displeased, and you still set your jaw first.

As you grew, you became even more gorgeous. You loved books and you were such a good girl. You would come to me and ask, 'Mummy, can I go to bed now but may I read a book first?' I could hardly believe my ears; with all of my other children I'd had to battle to get them to bed, but you would go off on your own and look at books before you fell asleep. I would look at you with pleasure and disbelief – I hope I didn't look at you like you were an alien. I could hardly speak, I was so gobsmacked.

When your sister Mia was born, you were still a baby yourself – not even two. I would lay and feed her on one side, and you would lie in the crook of my arm on the other. When I had to put her on the other breast, you would roll across me and lay on the other side. How lucky was I to be cuddling two babies at once!

Georgia, you are still as precious and loving today as you were as a baby.

To Mia,

My dear Mia. You are so adventurous, maybe because we went on so many adventures together when you were a baby. I was running my own criminal law firm at the time, and I went into labour at work. I was in my office speaking to a client when my water broke. You are the only baby with whom my water broke early. I did not say anything to the client and just kept talking. I could feel the warmth in my seat. I finished my conversation with him and said goodbye. I couldn't walk him out because my clothes were wet, so I just stayed seated. As soon as he left, I got up, drove myself to the hospital and, Mia, you were born. Two days later, I was back working full time. You were often cared for by my staff. When you were first born, I had a clerk who was young and single. You often slept in his arms as he worked at his desk.

You always came with me to court, so I had to bring one of my secretaries with me to care for you. We'd take off for the day – briefcase, nappy bag, secretary and baby. I would feed you in court adjournments. Once we went out to Petrie Courthouse and forgot the nappy bag. I was in a trial and the magistrate would adjourn when you were crying outside – I never asked for this but was just shown such goodwill. You pooed your nappy and we had no clean nappies. The contents of your nappy went all over my skirt. I had to go into the women's toilets and wash my skirt under the tap, and then go back into court in a wet skirt.

I also took you into all of the prisons on legal visits. I got special permission from the general managers of the prisons to take you in with me. The prisoners loved it when you came in.

But I knew it was time for you to leave the office for good when one day you ate a paperclip. That was a drama, getting that thing out of your mouth.

Today, Mia, you are bold and fun and great with people – maybe it was that early start to life that gave you those skills.

———

To Zoe,

You were baby number six. I was too scared to tell your dad I was pregnant. When I was about twelve weeks along, he told me I was putting on weight. I didn't reply and he probably thought he should leave the subject alone. A couple of weeks later he said to me, 'You're not pregnant, are you?' I told him that if I was, he was the last person in the world I would tell. Which was true – he was. But he took that as a no. Maybe it's like asking your teenage daughter if she's pregnant – you just don't want to believe it is true.

I was twenty weeks pregnant before I let him know. We were walking down to the West End Street Festival and I decided I had to tell him; it was inevitable he would find out and I couldn't keep it a secret any longer. I was really showing and I'd been wearing baggy clothes. That night I wore a Burmese sarong called a *longee*, which wraps tight across the belly. He looked at me with so many emotions flashing across his face that I couldn't describe a single one. He said we had to tell the kids. They all knew already, but I'd sworn them to secrecy. After I told him the children knew, he told them they were traitors. I don't think he could put a sentence together for two weeks.

He said to me that he thought I was responsible for contraception. I told him the most amazing thing about that comment was that he was soon to be a father of six, and that he was the first person in the history of the world ever to use my name and the words 'responsible' and 'contraception' in a sentence.

Zoe, I was a magistrate when you were born and I was the first Queensland magistrate to have a baby in office. Like all my babies before you, you came to work with me, but because I was no longer self-employed, a nanny had to come to work with us as well.

You were my last baby and you were breastfed until you were two years and seven months old. I knew it was time to wean you when one day you finished drinking on one breast and tapped me on my other breast and said to me, in your lispy baby voice, 'Udder side.' The use of the word 'udder' instead of 'other', combined with the fact you could now discern and articulate when one breast was empty, convinced me it was time to change.

———

To my babies,

I loved being pregnant with you – I never felt more beautiful and vital. And I loved it when you were babies. You all came to work with me and we raced around the courts, offices, conferences and prisons. We hung on to each other during thick and thin. And I learnt, from all the other people in our lives who cared for you and cared for me, that it is true that it 'takes a village to raise a child'.

mum
X

PATIENCE HODGSON

I find writing love letters hard. I can only recall ever writing one before. I was in grade nine and he was beautiful. He went on to be a male model – I like to brag about that. Immediately after graduating, he commenced relations with the film and TV teacher, and they now reside in Paris. She is a full-time clairvoyant. She contacted me telepathically last night to tell me she knew I'd be talking about them today, and to let me know that neither of them mind.

> *The letter I wrote:*

Dear Dan, you are like a Clydesdale and I am like a wild vine. From, Patience.

I handed it to him before school and at morning tea he told me how right I was, and that we should break up. How could I argue? They were my words. I was a wild vine that needed to be free, and he was very much like a Clydesdale with his massive feet. If only I'd understood what that meant then . . . Our love was over before it started.

> *He got super hot a couple of years later and we tried again, but by that stage I was selfish and sixteen. He was just way too nice. He suggested we doorknock for cancer and I was like, Ew, ohmahgawd, what a huge massive dork, as if! But I went along with him anyway and had a brilliant time, and then dumped him shortly afterwards because he was frigid.*

But it's not just love letters I have trouble with – it's love songs as well. Though I try to pour my heart out, I'm always more inspired by break-ups, pain and loss. All the good stuff in between has trouble sticking around. Or so I thought, until I moved to New York. There I timidly step out of my comfort zone on a daily basis, and, finally, I think I've learnt to love, in letters.

To my precious, darling New York City,

Oh, how I miss thee. I miss every beat, every honk and every street argument. Not one minute goes by when I am not distracted by thoughts of your wide sidewalks, cheap beer or fresh tamales. How you – a city so vibrant, so intelligent, so regarded and courted by all – let a simple island peasant such as myself, into your dazzling world, I could never understand.

New York, I am tortured by thoughts of your delicate spring awakening. I can see the first tips of green breaking through frosted dirt, the early whispers of tulips emerging from hibernation. The darling buds smiling from elegant branches in tree-lined streets. Energy swelling with the flood of one's natural anticipation – it seeps from the pores of every hot-blooded soul in the city. Strangers becoming friends in an orgy of excitement about the coming warmth.

Majo, my upstairs neighbour – wasn't she something else? Her beauty was a reflection of your beauty, her long Spanish locks hanging in cascades much like the morning glory growing from Brooklyn balconies. Her generosity was a reflection of your generosity, and she was very giving. Eighteen months of free internet; she never asked for a penny. Tools whenever I needed them, blenders, jackets, bed wear, doonas (or comforters, as your people like to call them, a term I never used because I think it's kind of slimy), baking trays, chorizo, and a smiling face. I'll always cherish her smiling face. The face

I would see whenever we crossed paths riding our bikes along 6th or met in the stairwell. Living below Majo was like having a big sister and the world's best flatmate rolled into one. We never argued over washing and had all the personal space you could need. Majo's sweetness could not be faulted, New York, and nor can yours.

New York City, I remember the first time I ever went to your food vendors at Red Hook. I could never figure out if that neighbourhood had a bad reputation or a good one. I came to understand that neighbourhoods were split into blocks and that one block could differ drastically from another. The corner of 22nd Street and 6th Avenue is adorable, while the corner of 22nd Street and 7th Avenue sends chills up one's spine. Such is the complex nature of you, my darling. My first trip to the good/bad Red Hook was in perfect weather: cool enough for a cardigan, warm enough for a shirt. I rode my bike along 6th before turning left at 9th, a route I took every day on my way to the band room. The difference today was that I would not stop at the hot dog stand and cross the road to the lone door on the huge red brick building that housed forty bands and forty artists. This time I continued forward, riding under the formidable Brooklyn-Queens Expressway, turning left, turning right, turning left again, then arriving at a sports field where children of all colours were diligently practising baseball. Then I saw the food vans, massive hunks of metal balanced on big black tyres. I locked my bike with my industrial-strength chain, took a deep breath and surveyed the vans for the truck with the longest line, which was where I would be heading. The best food always has the biggest line in New York. The poupousas were divine and I returned many times, before winter took hold and the vans stopped coming.

My Park Slope South neighbourhood seems like a fairytale when I think of it now. It is on the last corner of 6th Avenue before the grand Green-Wood Cemetery with its monumental Gothic entrance and aristocratic headstones. I lived in a brand-new three-storey building that sported a luxuriously rare wide, level staircase, with plenty of sunshine and room to hang an upside-down tomato plant in my apartment. Majo was above me and below was sexual Christina. Oh boy, New York City, you turned her on. I was a jealous mess. Just how much seemingly amazing sex can one girl have? All of her screams and panting at 4 a.m. on a Sunday morning – it was enough to turn me green. Screwing for two hours in the magical first light of a new week, a minimum performance of three orgasms, five or more screams of 'Jesus', plus a lot of wall pounding – and I never saw the guy. But I did have fun pressing my ear against the wall to hear the subtleties of their love making, and I also enjoyed cruelly stomping around to disturb them.

I guess one part of you I miss most, New York, is my kindred spirit, the Park Slope Food Co-op. Thirty years ago, it was no more than a stall frequented by a handful of progressive lesbians, who over the years were integral in transforming it into the micro-metropolis it is today. But still it's so understated you'd most likely walk past it if it wasn't for the members bustling in and out like bees in a hive. When I became a Co-op member, I had no idea how deep I would sink into its rugged, no-frills, communal nature. Each of us served the store as unpaid workers for three hours per month in return for membership and low-priced, ethical produce and products. Seduced by the smell of garam masala in the air and the blush of organic apples at $1.16/lb, which is roughly $2.25/kg ... I felt blessed and rewarded for my work. The pushing and shoving of trolleys in small aisles had no effect on me, for I was under the spell of wholegrain French couscous and enchanted by ethically raised, hormone-free chickens selling for $5 each. You could see me close to tears standing in front of big bunches of emerald lacinato kale, around $2.18 each, or amazed at every kind of milk you could imagine: happy cows' milk, almond milk, hemp milk, rice milk, oat milk, hazelnut milk, and soy milk in original, sweetened, chocolate or unsweetened chocolate.

Oh, and I haven't even got to the vitamins aisle, or the beauty products aisle, the cereal aisle, the baking aisle, or the bulk aisle where you could buy vanilla beans at three for sixty cents ... The Co-op was the size of an IGA, had 14 000 members and sold almost everything you could think of that wasn't a tool or an electrical item. It was packed floor to ceiling, stuffed full like your great aunt's house, and the aisles were small, with trolleys passing each other only having millimetres between them. These days I'm pathetic, dragging my heavy heart around like a ball and chain, straining in Australian supermarkets at the limited selection and the price of celery.

Everybody adores you, New York City, but they're shallow and they're predictable vermin. They talk of your art galleries, which are impressive and inspiring; they praise your restaurants, many of which I frequented and I can say I've had almost every one of my best meals in your town (not including Mum's lasagne, bolognese, rum balls or trifle). Others celebrate your many nationalities and the intercultural exchanging of ideas. Some regard your architecture, while some discover nature in Central Park, or pay tribute to your fallen at Ground Zero. But I love you more, New York, and my love for you is as real as the gentle breeze that blows hats off pretty ladies posing for photos on the Brooklyn Bridge. My love is authentic in its need for a quiet, family-friendly Brooklyn street where kids skateboard in summer and battle snow wars in winter; a three-storey building, humble in size and character, with Liberty views from the rooftop when you stand on a bucket; a nightmarish, grey-carpeted band room with a beer vending machine; a bagel shop whose speciality is Mexican tamales; a blue vintage Schwinn bike with a large basket covered in tacky plastic flowers that often delight children; the opportunity to observe, from the discreet vantage point of my window, a cult of gay men known as 'Radical Fairies' who grow woolly beards and wear kilts; a tiny balcony only big enough to comfortably fit two; a fridge next to my bed whose loud operation noises

I become accustomed to; and a Food Co-op whose membership card becomes proof I am a New York local and a reason to sing proudly in the streets, to ride my bike through red lights, to exclaim of the simplest of things loudly, a reason to enjoy being out of my comfort zone, my passport to trying new things.

New York, I love you because you accepted a third-rate tin-pot such as myself and challenged me to be more. With the heat of a jalapeno, I crave to ride my bike once more through Prospect Park. To roll on your grass is to be given a second life. I feel you in my veins, my love. Forever I am your unworthy servant.

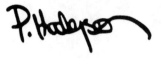

To the woman who changed my life

GEORGE NEGUS

Dear JB,

This is it!

It's time, after all these miserable years of avoiding the issue – in fact, close to three dreadful decades – to come clean.

Our secret history has to be written. And now, thanks to the sensitive souls who conjured up this idea of Men of Letters, it's possible for me put it on the public record, once and for all. If you like – and if you'll tolerate my almost criminally unforgivable wordplay among such illustrious literary company – I am not coming out of the proverbial closet. I'm going down into the basement!

JB, I can't go on any longer without you knowing what I am about to recount. This note is not driven by nagging guilt, but rather by unrivalled gratitude, boundless appreciation and constant, daily, even hourly recollection of how your very existence has changed and continues to change my life. In fact, I drop off to sleep nightly and wake every morning worshipping the ground you sprang from into my life forever!

What am I trying to tell you? I had no idea the sad old lady of the media – television – would bring us together with such an impact. How could I? But then again, fate and coincidence are, after all, the explanation and religion of the sceptical non-believer – which you know me to be.

But, that aside, those early years of professional camaraderie between us – common interests, mutual friendships, social compat-ibility – led to you, JB, becoming the most important woman of all those I'd met and liked and even maybe loved (and there were a few in my totally illegitimate, unattached period of public recognition as a pumped-up-rubber inflatable sex symbol – 'the thinking woman's crumpet', according to that august literary mag, *TV Week*). You were the game changer of my life, the woman who set me on a journey of love, on which I am still travelling twenty-seven years later.

How can I thank you, other than by doing what I am doing right now – blurting it out to a roomful of hopefully understanding folk, probably 95 per cent of whom are total strangers? I am sorry that un-til this day, this moment, I've never had it in me to come out and tell you of my real feelings. You single-handedly brought meaning to my flim-flam, jetsetting, irresponsible, frivolity-filled, Kerry Packer-funded life. There! I've said it. I can't go on without your knowing it, although I suspect you always have known. Without you, my life would have remained superficial, self-styled, globetrotting, ratings-driven, specious nonsense!

How can I ever thank you for saving me from myself? I was happy but anchor-less, probably staring down the barrel at a love-less, lonely life as a national household name, with not much to show for my glamorous, continent-flitting, testosterone-assisted lifestyle but millions of frequent flyer points, one too many crates of Piper-Heidsieck and an encyclopedic knowledge of international cuisines. I bounced from five-star hotels like the George Cinq in Paris to pay-ing a prostitute in a brothel beside an open sewer in Belize – not, I add, to sleep with me, but to just let me hire her camp stretcher for the night!

JB, I am stumbling about trying to find words – embarrassingly, in such literati company. Well, here I go!

Thank you, thank you, thank you, JB, for standing me up that Friday night in Melbourne. How could I forget the details? You charged off to Tasmania for the weekend with Whatshisname – Mr Whoeverhewas – instead. But before you unceremoniously dumped me, you introduced me to your good friend Kirsty, who became pretty much immediately my live-in lover, and not long after that the mother of our marvellous sons. They would also like me to thank you for that – and for allowing them the chance to get not just my genes but their mother's as well, which they both regard as a gigantic plus. They are both handsome, intelligent, sensitive and politically aware. Ta for that, JB.

You'll recall that we were at the Logies on that fateful night. Who would have thought that the bloody Logies could be that romantic?

So thanks again, JB, for changing my life by bringing me together with the woman who is still changing it. Twenty-seven years later, she quite rightly regards me as a work in progress. But, she told me to tell you, I'm coming along okay.

JB, I will probably go to my grave remembering the day Kirst and I turned up with a bottle to tell you that we were an item. As you opened the door to us, you gasped and said, 'Holy shit! What have I done?'

Oh, and by the way, say g'day to Andrew and Connor from Kirst and the boys. See you guys for a lazy lunch soon, huh?

Rottsa ruv!
GN

MICHAEL ROBOTHAM

Dear Anne Marie,

I don't know if you remember me, but you took my virginity at a Young Catholic Students camp at Woodlawn College near Lismore in December 1975. I was the kid from Coffs Harbour who had curly black hair and freckles and so little idea of female anatomy that I thought girls didn't have pubic hair. I assumed you were all balder than Barbie dolls because I used to share a bath with my sister and she was bald and had lots of Barbie dolls. Apart from that, the only naked women I'd ever seen were in those old pre-1970 *Playboy*s, where genitals were obscured behind draped towels or houseplants.

I must confess that I felt a little used that first time, Anne Marie. I didn't want to lose my virginity. It was too soon. And afterwards I was sure that everybody at the camp could see my shame. I had 'fornicater' tattooed on my forehead – misspelled, unfortunately, because I was crap at spelling.

On the train home to Coffs Harbour, you ignored me. By then you'd hooked up with Eric Bielleiter and you were pashing for Jesus.

———

Dear Pam,

You called me Mike because it was short for Michael. I called you Loose – because you were.

I asked you to the school social because I'd heard you were the sort of girl who let a boy run straight to third base, skipping bases one and two. I didn't get to any of the bases with you, though, because Dennis Crossley gave you his flask of Bundy and Coke and you spent the night throwing up in the toilets.

———

Dear Leonie,

I never told you this, but you were my first love. I even wrote you a song, called 'Save Our Love, Leonie'.

Thirty-five years on, my brothers can remember every word of the chorus and sing it to me when they want to take the piss.

———

Dear Madonna,

We were best friends. We walked home from school together every day. On weekends I would watch you play netball in the winter and sail Hobie Cats in the summer.

Even when you didn't know it, I was watching you. I built a tree house in our jacaranda and I could see your house from the branches. That's why whenever you walked into town I always seemed to meet you on the way.

You told me about the boys you liked and asked my advice on how to make them yours. You cried on my shoulder when these relationships ended, asking me why nobody loved you. I loved you. All the time I was thinking, Pick me, pick me, but you never did. And I could never tell you the truth because I was too frightened of rejection.

I wrote you an entire album of love songs. I drew you a picture of a rose, which I traced and copied from a book, but I told you I'd done it freehand.

I saw you again two years ago at Dad's funeral. We had nothing in common except those memories. They weren't enough to last through the entree before I was chewing the tablecloth with boredom.

I didn't tell you that I once loved you. Perhaps you always knew.

———

Dear Linda,

Your family were friends with my family, so when we got together they had visions of our two great families becoming a mediocre dynasty.

I was a journalist on *The Sun*. You were studying journalism at Bathurst.

You said you loved me. I said I loved you too, but I was lying because I didn't want to hurt you. I moved to Melbourne to get away.

'It's not you,' I said, 'it's me. I just need more space.'

Guys say things like that all the time. You're probably wondering what it means to want 'more space'. It means that I wanted a space exactly the same height and weight and width as you.

You tried to follow me to Melbourne, applying for a cadetship on *The Age*. I didn't want you to get it. I didn't want you in the same city, or the same state. I didn't want you living with me.

I said all this in a letter – but it wasn't written to you. It was meant for a friend of mine. But you found the letter and you read the truth and you filled the Yarra with your tears. I'm so sorry for that.

Then we had the best sex of our relationship, and said goodbye.

———

Dear Rebecca,

You showed me the beauty of so many things I had never seen before, such as a single teardrop hovering on the lower lashes of a child, waving goodbye to her mother on her first day of school. But then it was as if you shot that child, cut out her heart and stomped on it with your three-inch stilettos. You destroyed something beautiful and innocent.

When I stopped hurting, I began hating. I hated you so much it gave me energy.

I used to have a fantasy about you. It wasn't one of those hero dreams where you're captured by terrorists, or held hostage in a bank siege, and I rescue you and win your undying love and we live happily ever after.

No. In my fantasy, you're living in a caravan park in Cootamundra with four barefoot kids by four different husbands, snot running out their noses and nits in their hair.

Your latest partner is a 500-pound abattoir worker with tattoos on his back beneath an old-growth forest of hair. He doesn't wash, he chews his food with his mouth open, and his idea of foreplay is a grunt and a raised eyebrow.

One night, he's romancing you in the caravan and 300 kilos of sweating fat are slick between your thighs. Staring over his shoulder, you spy the TV screen above the bed, which is showing *Wife Swap*. At that moment, your left breast flops onto the remote control and the channel changes. You see an image of me on *First Tuesday Book Club*. I'm saying something incredibly intelligent and erudite, while next to me Marieke Hardy is wearing one of her cute Betty Boop dresses and a flower in her hair, and she's hanging on my every word.

That was my fantasy.

To all of my ex-girlfriends,

You showed me how not to behave, you knocked off my rough edges, you got rid of my flares and my brightly coloured body shirts, you taught me how to cook and fold socks and make love. If it wasn't for you, I wouldn't be the man I am today.

More importantly, if you hadn't thrown me back, I wouldn't have been swimming in the sea when the right girl caught me. She wouldn't be my wife and we wouldn't have three beautiful and talented daughters.

So thank you, Anne Marie, Pam, Leonie, Madonna, Linda, and, yes, even Rebecca.

You were my stepping stones, my false starts, my near misses; you were the Rex Hunts of the romance world – because you kissed me and let me go.

For that I will be forever grateful.

Yours sincerely,
Michael Robotham

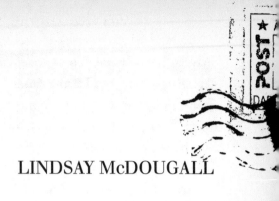

LINDSAY McDOUGALL

Dear woman who changed my life,

It's Lindsay. Lindsay McDougall. Yes, I know, it is a surprise getting a letter out of the blue like this. Especially one addressed to 'the woman who changed my life'. Trust me, if I received a letter addressed to me as 'the woman who changed my life', I'd be surprised too, though more for understandable gender-based reasons.

But make no mistake: you are indeed the woman who changed my life. I suppose you must be thinking, Why me? If you're going to write a letter to read out to a large crowd at a fancy inner-city venue (how did you know that's where I'd be reading this out?), aren't there more important women in your life? Women who have done more? Changed you more?

Well, sure . . .

I suppose I could, of course, write a letter to my mother. A woman who, when I was four years old, put her life on hold so she could make mine safe. Who not only took me to allergy clinics and dealt with my mood swings when I accidentally ate the same fruit two days in a row, but who also taught herself holistic medicine and bought a bloody health food shop. Not just some health food, a whole shop, which to this day provides me with the gluten- and nut-free snacks I desire, and the supplements, tonics and balms that I require to live the life of a fancyman.

I could also write this letter to my sisters, from my dad's first marriage, who I only found out about when I was twelve! Three sisters, named Peta, Andre and Susan. Yes: Peta, Andre. Dad wasn't to know. In fact, he only named his youngest daughter Peta because he was a Peter, and so was his dad, and he figured she'd be his last kid and he wanted to keep the tradition going, gender be damned! My sisters, a few years older than me, taught me about the world outside suburban Engadine, from the moment Peta arrived on our doorstep, on crutches, and acid, asking for money, after she'd finally broken through her mother's wall of silence and tracked Dad down.

Or I could write to ex-girlfriends – the ones who taught me how to kiss, or blow smoke rings, or scull OP rum, or do it heaps good. But most of them have changed their addresses and have me blocked on Facebook.

And yes, I could write to Marieke. In fact, I was going to, but I think George Negus is and I don't want to harsh his buzz.

But who else changes your life, alters the path of your youth as you storm the gates of adulthood, lines the path of your teenage years with the words that blossom into flowers of really stupid and pointless metaphors? Who changed my life?

Well, you did. Because you were my teacher. And not just any teacher. Not Sister Pam, who busted me changing my lunch order from salad sandwich to hot dog with the unforgettable line 'Lindsay McDougall, I have a bone to pick with you.' Or Ms McLintock, who, apart from smoking in the art staffroom with Ms Richmond and giving my brothers cigarettes, taught me that the name of Juliet's family in Shakespeare's play is not pronounced 'the Montages'.

You were my music teacher. But not like Mrs Kelly at St Pat's, who tried to get me back together with Rebecca Smith who I'd broken up with at lunchtime. Trust me, if Mrs Kelly had known what we'd been up to in year eleven, she wouldn't have wanted us back together. Fifteen is a ridiculous age to try S&M. And not like Ms Nicholls, who most likely hooked up with Sam Bennet, or Ms Bishop, who probably hooked up with Steven Mace, and who definitely left the music room open over the Christmas holidays – my brother may or may not have the trombone to prove it.

You were my music teacher in year eight. When I was fourteen. A predominantly uneventful year. I probably got bullied. I probably said some awkward things around girls, although it wasn't until year nine that I finally wrote that love letter to Felicity Morris, who, as I watched through the woodwork room window, walked down the field laughing as she read it out loud to her friend.

A predominantly uneventful year – except that it was the year you taught me how to play guitar.

I'd been learning keyboard. I'd had three separate teachers, all of whom coincidentally left town or left the music school before I'd really mastered it. But I could really impress on those ivories. 'Chopsticks', 'Heart and Soul', all the classics. So when you, Mrs Reddy, told the class we were going to learn guitar that term, I was freaking out. But I'm a keyboard player! I'd even drawn a stage set-up in art class for Ms Richmond. Anonymous nobodies flanking me on guitar, bass and drums, and me, centre-stage, with a three-tiered triangular synth set up! *And a moustache*, goddamnit! Guitar? That wasn't the plan!

Of course, this was year eight, so I just shut up, nodded and picked up the strange conglomeration of funny-smelling wood and nylon.

I won't bore you with the details. Needless to say, I was shit hot. 'Skip to My Lou'? Nailed it. 'She'll be Coming 'Round the Mountain'? She'll be boring 'round the mountain, more like. 'Baa, Baa, Black Sheep'? Don't make me laugh! Soon I was busting out real songs, like 'Patience' by Guns n' Roses; 'Paradise City' by Guns n' Roses; and 'You Could Be Mine', also by Guns n' Roses. Which, incidentally, sounds great played on a crappy, nylon-string guitar.

But still I wasn't sold. Guitar was merely a plaything, a juvenile distraction, something for kids' parties – not like the keyboard.

That's where my future lay. Sure, the moustache was a few years off, but if they'd let me back on those black and white bits of plastic I'd get back on the path.

But then something happened. We reached the end of the term. We'd been marked on our guitar work. I'd probably got an A-plus or double-plus or something, I can't remember.

Mrs Reddy, you were letting us year eight kids decide what we wanted to focus on for the rest of the year. You went around the class asking us: 'Michael Honeysett? Keyboard, nice. Daniel Sydes? Guitar. Good. Meaghan Ryan? Keyboard. Good choice. Felicity Morris? Keyboard and breaking the hearts of innocent young boys in two? Well said . . .'

But when you got to me, Mrs Reddy, you barely looked up. 'Lindsay McDougall,' you said. 'Back to piano, of course.' And moved on, probably to Damian Hardiman or Margaret Ryan, Meaghan's twin sister, who was probably better looking but not as nice to talk to.

Something inside me stirred. And it wasn't because of Felicity. I hadn't been given a choice! Sure, that'd happened in the past, but I'd never cared. I'd never felt like this before. A rush of emotion. Pubescent bile rising in my teenage throat. How dare you make this decision for me! Decide my future (well, six months of it) without giving me a voice! I felt caged, chained, like all those abused animals that I knew nothing about and cared about even less at that innocent age.

It would not stand.

'Actually, Mrs Reddy,' I stuttered, surprising myself with the sound of my own voice, 'I think I'll stick with guitar.'

What was I saying? Guitar? But *why*? What about the stage – the three-tiered synth racks – the *moustache*, goddamnit? Was I really throwing all that away simply to make a stand against (in my fourteen-year-old mind) tyrannical oppression?

It wasn't your fault, Mrs Reddy. You had no idea. I had no idea. But in that split second, I seemed to gain a voice, to learn the self-righteous indignation, to get that leg up onto the soapbox that anyone who knows me knows I've been dragging around with me ever since.

But also at that very moment I decided, purely because I didn't like someone else making the decision for me, that I would properly learn to play the guitar.

It wasn't because I thought I'd be successful at it, or because I thought it'd allow me to drop out of uni after three months to join a punk band and then to spend the next fifteen years drunk. Or even because of the chicks. My success with chicks had, at that point, been entirely limited to awkward 'Heart and Soul' recitals with Meaghan or Margaret Ryan – I got them mixed up.

Thinking back, Mrs Reddy, somehow I doubt that if I'd stuck to keyboard back in year eight, I'd be writing this letter to you now, or speaking it aloud, through a Madonna mic – I forgot to mention the Madonna mic – with six keyboards jutting out in front of me.

I was a little prick to you when you innocently thought I would head back to the keyboard. I insisted on being contrary, essentially just for the sake of it, a trait which hangs around me like a glorious odour to this very day. Because of that, you, Mrs Reddy, are the woman who changed my life. Along with every other chick I've mentioned today. Except Rebecca Smith – she was just weird.

Lindsay Flench

EDDIE SHARP

I was quite nervous in the week leading up to the Men of Letters event. I procrastinated so much that I actually ended up research-ing my astrological natal chart. For those interested, my sun sign is Scorpio but I also have Chiron in my twelfth house, which equals fear of success, which probably explains why I had so much trou-ble writing this in the first place. Apparently us Chiron-in-twelfth guys have a real tendency to shoot ourselves in the foot. We're famous for it.

Writing a letter to a woman who changed my life is a tough one. I don't have a wife or children. I have had female dogs who I loved like children, but that's not the same.

I could dedicate a letter to my mother. She is an incredible woman and I adore her. But as an unmarried, childless man who works in the theatre and loves doggies, it is a daily struggle to maintain a flimsy veneer of heterosexuality as it is, and 'A Letter to Mother' might just be the tipping point.

I recently read my fifteen-year-old diary in front of a large group of people and afterwards a lot of female friends came up to me to tell me that they knew someone like me in high school, and not in a nice way either. It was said quietly, with a certain degree of sadness and with haunted eyes: 'Yeah, I knew someone like you in high school.'

I had thought I was an incredibly witty, precocious teenager, but, after re-reading that diary, it turns out I was simply a sociopath.

I should also mention that I had an eyebrow ring, bleached blond hair and a mean pair of light-green corduroy pants. Which means I ended up hurting a lot of young women's feelings. It was nobody's fault – that was a powerful look in 1998.

When I thought back to the women I knew aged fifteen to seventeen, what occurred to me was the ways I'd changed their lives – for the worse. So this is my letter of apology to all the women who were unfortunate enough to know me at that time. As much as I am sure I influenced their lives in less than savoury ways, all of them have changed mine. Significantly and for the better.

To my good friend Charlotte,

I'm sorry I was never any good at taking drugs, and that on weekends, when we were supposed to be having 'fun' on ecstasy, I was always that guy who is single-minded, obsessed, *fixated* on everyone having enough water.

'Hey, have you had some water? Let me know if you want any water, because I have a whole backpack full of bottled water. But, you know, don't, don't also have too much water, because you don't want to end up like that girl in the *Daily Telegraph* who drank so much water she drowned her brain because she didn't know when to stop. She just filled herself up, all the way to her brain, like a human vase. Listen, guys, seriously, because this is important – do you feel full of water or very, very thirsty? Because there's no in between. Everyone! Stop enjoying your youth and listen to me: you all have to have exactly the right amount of water or you'll die.'

I'm sorry that I wasn't a little more chilled out and laid-back about stuff.

To Sophie Lang, the first girl I ever slept with,

Thank you for sleeping with me. It was a really great and kind thing for you to do. A life-changing event in and of itself. And I'm sorry. Not just for the brief, substandard sex, but also for the state of my room at the time. The terrible smell, the cheap incense I lit to cover the terrible smell, and my choice of Ben Harper's 'Burn One Down' as the soundtrack. I know it was your first time, too, and I just wish for both our sakes I could have made it a little less creepy. But I was young and brash. Full of that misplaced confidence that only comes with having your whole stupid life ahead of you and just the right amount of water inside of you.

I'm also sorry to Amelia Savvides, who was my girlfriend at the time. Like I said, I was a sociopath.

———

To my stepsister Ella,

I'm sorry for the years of subtle but constant psychological torture. Hiding my drug paraphernalia under your bed for our parents to find. Spelling out horrible attacks against you on the kitchen table with foodstuff – a 'fuck you, bitch' carefully arranged in pretzels and then swept away once you started screaming and a parent came into the room. I can see now that I was painting you as a paranoid, delusional Cassandra-figure, who saw grave insults in food that weren't there, caused by drugs that she claimed to have never even seen. They were mean tricks and I'm sorry. You are and always were an excellent sister and a loyal ally.

———

To Emma Stein, who was my girlfriend from 1999 to 2001 – marriage in high school terms,

I'm sorry that we haven't spoken for ten years now. I know it was the last thing you ever wanted to happen. I'm not sorry that we met, but that we met each other too young and stayed together for too long. I loved you so much. You meant as much to me as anyone I've ever met.

I always felt as if you were too good for me. When I sensed you growing up just a little bit faster than I was, I resented you for it and did everything I could to make you feel like you were a bad person. Disloyal. Selfish. So that when you finally did leave, I got the chance to turn around and say, I told you so. I told you that you are a bad person, selfish, disloyal.

And I returned all your things. Not just your things, but my things as well. Letters from you. Photos of you. Presents you gave me. And I said that I would never speak to you again. And I didn't.

We spent every moment together for three years. Our parents were friends. And then I screened your calls, deleted your emails. Walked right past you on the street. It was the coldest, shittiest thing I've ever done to anyone, and I'm truly sorry. It was a calculated move.

Recently I've developed something called 'empathy', which I think comes in later for men. I can see now how much this would have hurt you. Or maybe it's because my Saturn is returning and a lot of past-lives stuff is coming up. Anyway, I'm sorry. You were never a bad person.

I wish we were able to have a pleasant conversation. Or that I had at least one picture with the two of us in it. But I've left it too long. I hope that you are happy.

E S Sharp

DAVID WILLIAMSON

Mothers are the most likely people to have changed one's life. I've imagined four short letters to different mothers, dealing with more or less the same issues, but whose tone is sharply different according to the particular personality disorder suffered by the writer.

1. Daughter with a narcissistic personality disorder

Dear Mother,

I have just had an incredible setback. Despite being clearly the most qualified and intelligent candidate, I have been told that a pallid little suck-up called Phoebe Stromlow has been given the promotion that was all but promised to me.

The whole department is of course outraged on my behalf. My PA, Rachel, assures me that my work colleagues are almost universal in acknowledging that I am the most valued, creative, far-sighted and efficient person in the department. Given the respect and admiration I sense in all who deal with me, I can't help but conclude she's right.

In fact, Mother, this setback is a blessing in disguise, as it's made clear to me that my full talent will never be able to flower in this department, where the truly gifted are seen as threats by an ageing and talentless male hierarchy.

I would have little trouble, given my articulate persuasiveness and charisma, in obtaining parliamentary preselection for the Liberal party, whose belief in the supremacy of the talented individual echoes my own values.

I am sorry to hear of your terminal illness, but I'm assured chemotherapy is more efficient and targeted these days.

You'll understand it's a little difficult for me to fly across to Perth, but I'll make every effort when it becomes necessary.

When you are gone, I will never forget how you mortgaged your house to pay for my studies, and the generous gift of your car. Nor the way you refused to complain when you fell off the bus going shopping and broke your leg.

At least you can die happy knowing that your faith in me has been repaid a thousandfold.

Your loving daughter,
Mirabella

2. Son with paranoid disorder

Dear Mother,

My rage when I read your letter was acute. Those fucking corporate arseholes who pour their noxious polymer wastes into the atmosphere, causing a cancer epidemic, ought to be strangled slowly with piano wire.

Do these pathetic arseholes of the twittering generation I work with ever think, when they buy their dinky iPhones, iPads and iWhatevers, about the carcinogens released during manufacture?

As you would expect, I didn't get the promotion, but I found it almost unbelievable that Phoebe Stromlow got it. She stuffs up everything she touches and is the laughing stock of the office. But then again, she is a lesbian and that lot stick together.

Mum, I'll drive across to Perth as soon as I can. I'm boycotting those corporate thugs Qantas, led by that execrable Irish prick.

I am still angry that you had to mortgage your house to get me the kind of education snot-nosed middle-class private-school little wankers take for granted. And I'm glad that when I pranged your car at least I took out a Mercedes. It's criminal that they forced you to pay the costs.

Your loving son,
Dougal

3. *Daughter who is an anxiety neurotic*

Dear Mother,

That is horrible, terrible, awful news about your terminal illness. I am devastated. And I feel even worse because I couldn't stop wondering whether this particular type of cancer has a hereditary component. Can you possibly forgive me?

I didn't get the promotion I applied for, but frankly I'm relieved as I wasn't sure I could have coped with the job. And Phoebe Stromlow, who got it, is so much more impressive than I am in just about every way.

I have circulated an email through the office apologising for thinking I had any right to expect a promotion, and now I feel so much better.

I cry a lot when I think of you and I am full of remorse for all the horrible things I have done to you over the years, such as that unforgiveable tantrum at my twelfth birthday party because I felt the magician you hired was not appropriate to my level of sophistication.

I have booked a flight to Perth this weekend to get across to see you. I know by rights I should quit my job to look after you full time, but it would be hard, given my undistinguished performance here, to get another one.

I'm still full of guilt that you mortgaged your house to pay for my studies and gave me your car. I am so sorry I panicked at the intersection and wrote it off.

Your loving daughter,
Zoe

—

4. A depressive son

Mum,

Cancer. What an absolute bummer. The only person in the world I can count on to lie to me that I'm of any worth whatsoever, about to be taken from me. Why the fuck did you ever bring me into this vale of tears?

During a brief moment of Zoloft-inspired optimism, I applied for a promotion. If I'd given it a second's thought, I would have asked the obvious question: why would anyone in their right mind promote me? I didn't even get an interview.

I still get depressed when I think about you mortgaging your house to get me through law school. Why did you bother? And giving me your car. Only a moron would have left it unlocked with the keys in it in Darlinghurst.

I painted my flat yellow because I read somewhere it lifts your spirits. It didn't.

Samantha has left me for a guy who smiles a lot and has a big dick.

My irritable bowel syndrome has got worse.
The world is a shit of a place.

Love,
Martin

David Williamson

PINKY BEECROFT

Before I start: This is entirely fictional. Any resemblance to any persons living or dead is an accident.

———

Dear Stepmother,

This is just a short note to say hi and to let you know that you're in my thoughts today. I hope you're in good health.

Actually, that's bollocks. I hope your health is lousy. I mean, I don't spend my days praying for you to get some kind of horrendous arse cancer – but . . . if you did, I would be okay with it.

And this will most likely not be a short note. There are things that need to be said, before one of us really does get arse cancer and expires.

Thinking about it, I'm not sure which one of us is more likely to do that. Yes, you're a lot older than me, but, you know, it's a genetic lottery, isn't it, and someone told me Gollum lived until he was 589. And I've long suspected you two are related.

Meanwhile, I've got appalling genes. I should be dead already. I almost am, some days. My father, as you know, had every medical condition known to mankind, with the possible exception of syphilis. Come to think of it, he probably escaped most of the sexual diseases, but I guess you'd know more about that than me.

Every time I go to a doctor's they say, Right, okay, tell me about your family history. Did your father have any problems? I say, Yeah, he had heart disease, fluid in the lung, vascular issues, five or six hernias, two aneurysms, shitty eyesight and he scratched himself to death. And that's just the tip of the iceberg. He had the record number of full cardiac bypasses in the world. He was pronounced dead at least four times, by qualified medical specialists. On top of which, he loved to booze. He liked red wine, white wine, whiskey, beer, champagne, and all things in between. So long as it was wet, and vaguely alcoholic.

His number-one fantasy was, quote, sitting in the Brisbane Travelodge with a Gin Rickey, unquote. Which, in hindsight, is itself indicative of mental disorders that are too complex to go into right now.

Mostly when the doctors ask me about my father's health, I just say, Look, give me that big book there, yeah, that one, the Encyclopedia of Illness. I'll just cross off the ones he didn't have.

And then I tear out the chapter on STDs.

My mother was strong. She was strong like a tigress, like a wild mother-tiger who's been given a strange unpredictable chemical, and all the handlers have fled the scene, or been eaten, and she's busted out of the jungle with her cubs and gone on a wild rampage across the savanna, along the way somehow discovering Catholicism, and not a gentle God-loving pat-the-kiddies-on-the-arse Catholicism but a hard-edged Irish fundamentalist fever, and that combined with the strange unpredictable chemical has made her nuts, so batshit crazy no-one can get near her – except my dad, who brought her down to Sydney and settled her in the suburbs with four kids under five. All of which is just a long-winded way of saying yeah, my mother was strong.

But she got the cancer. It wasn't, strictly speaking, arse cancer, but it was pretty close. I remember when they operated – I spent the longest day at the hospital with the old man and eventually they wheeled Mum out of theatre, alive, unconscious, except suddenly she looked up and said to me, 'If you're going to cook a roast dinner, then for God's sake do it properly.' I didn't argue, and she just slipped back into whatever transcendental kitchen she was floating in.

Dad and I sat bedside, and on the TV above Mum's bed the movie *Cliffhanger* came on, with Sylvester Stallone, and we both got hooked into it and then just at the climax, with Stallone's character Gabe Walker hanging one-handed from a precarious razor-thin icy mountain ledge – Mum woke up. We turned off the TV. Almost immediately.

And then for the next few years Mum battled the cancer thing; she fought like Stallone and beat it, she beat it like a red-headed stepchild. And we celebrated. And then suddenly she had a stroke and died.

Which is where you came into the picture. Not long afterwards.

My father sank into a black hole of grief, for months he sat in the laundry and read and re-read the visitor's book from Mum's funeral, hunkered down there between the tubs and the drinks fridge. (Every fridge we owned was a drinks fridge.)

It's not even a very nice laundry, as you well know, now that you inhabit it and own it along with every other thing that once belonged to my family. But let's not go into that, I don't want to seem bitter.

And it's true, you did drag my father out of his misery. I remember the day he pulled up at my house in a new car, with a sunroof and a blonde woman. It was like I'd taken acid and wandered into a Mitsubishi commercial. And that year being what it was, that sort of thing was possible. Maybe it's all been a bad trip. I wish.

And thus began your Reign of Terror. I don't know how else to describe it. You got rid of his carpet first, which, okay, fair enough, it was shitty carpet, but then all the furniture got chucked, and then his friends. And his music. My dad was a music nut – Al Jolson, Al Hibbler, Al Bowlly – he was nuts for singers named Al. But you trashed his tapes and CDs, and the house got sad and silent, except for the gleaming floorboards. And *Deal or No Deal*.

And every time I went to visit the old man, you had quail for lunch, quail or spatchcock. *Every day?* All those small dead grey birds on your dinner plate; it was like *True Blood* with pigeons, and I tried to look away, I tried not to think about this endless procession of broiled budgies. I took to calling you The Bird Murderer. We all did. The name stuck, like a fork through a squab.

And then came the cruising thing. It turned out you have a mania for cruise ships, and suddenly my father was on a slow boat to China – every other week. How the fuck? This was a man who wouldn't walk to his own letterbox, but suddenly it was all about docking in Sapporo or Vladivostok or anywhere, really, where Dad could have a stroke, get carted off the ship and be pronounced dead by a team of qualified medical specialists.

Only to rise again, get flown home, spend a month in intensive care pleading quietly, 'No more cruises.' Before going home to sit scratching in front of *Deal or No Deal* while you drooled over Sea Princess brochures and banged on about the wonders of the East.

Look, Bird Murderer . . . I can forgive you for the cruise thing. For most things, really. A lot of time has passed and you were clearly nuts or on acid or both. And I get both those things. And maybe that's what this letter is about: forgiveness.

Except . . . except you poured poison in my old man's ear. You really did. You alienated him from his kids, one by one. You fought and schemed and straight-out lied until every one of us was on the outer. It was no small achievement.

You banned *me* from the house – the house I grew up in.

And so I rarely got to see him in that last year, the year he was pronounced dead for the final time. (They had to get it right eventually.) You'd engineered a situation, and I was exiled.

I guess what I want to tell you is this: a week or two before he died, I waited outside the hospital, waited until visiting hours were just about over, and you came out. I watched you leave. Then I snuck in and found the old man. He was asleep. *Home and Away* was on the telly – he'd taken to watching it, daily, which, well . . . see the above bit about mental disorders.

Anyway, I stood there for a while, and he woke up. And he looked at me, and he said, 'You and me – we're okay. Aren't we?'

At first I thought he was just quoting dialogue from *Home and Away*, but he wasn't. He was serious. And I said, 'Yeah. Of course. We're okay.' And he gripped my hand and went back to sleep and we stayed that way until the bell went for the end of visiting hours. And then I said goodbye for the last time and I left.

And that was that.

I don't know why I'm telling you all this. You're certainly a woman who changed my life. But you didn't win. You didn't get the lot. And part of me wants to tell you that.

And part of me wants to say, 'Hey, I still have keys to your house and every second Thursday when I know you're out, I let myself in and I turn the pictures in the hallway upside down. Just to drive you mental.'

But that second bit's not really true.

Mostly, I just wanted to write it all down, so I can forget about it. I can feel that process has already begun, and it's nice. There's something to be said for this letter-writing thing.

I will leave you to your brochures, and your birds.

Regards,
Me

Pinky Beecroft

RHYS MULDOON

It was a blonde. A blonde to make a bishop crack a massive fat. And she was walking towards me. To compare her breasts with – well, I couldn't compare them. They were perfection. And they rose and fell, or, rather, pressed forward with the glory of all that is good and right in this world, against her black cashmere dress. Beneath her breasts beat the heart of a wild animal. Her lips were full and wet and dark red, and made me want nothing more than to drop to my knees and thank God I was a man. Her hips matched the insolence of her lips, and swayed with a rhythm that screamed, '*Jungle!*'

Her eyes were like tropical seas in a thunderstorm and were looking deep into mine.

'I've heard talk,' she whispered, her warm breath reaching down inside me and doing whatever the hell it liked.

'What have you heard?' I asked.

'I've heard about you and your inevitable cock. And I want it inside me every which way but Friday.'

'What's wrong with Friday?'

'Okay, you've talked me into it.'

She held herself against me, her nipples filling with blood and pressing into my chest like thumbs. I thought her dress might split open.

'Wait,' I said. 'Who do you barrack for?'

She licked her top lip. 'I barrack for the greatest football team God ever shovelled guts into – the St Kilda Football Club.'

I felt a South Sea pearl erupt from the eye of my manhood. She smiled. She knew. She spoke.

'Now, take me to the MCG, take me to my private box, press my face against the glass, and push that beautiful cock of yours into me each time the Saints score a goal.'

She ran her finger along the length of me, the veins straining like the steel cables of Centrepoint Tower in a high wind. She slowly lifted the back of her dress, revealing nothing but perfect flesh, and pushed two fingers inside herself.

'Taste me,' she said.

And I did, reader, I did. The top note, middle note and bass note of this scorching oil of truth had the beauty, strength and fragility of a handful of daisies thrown into a cyclone. A cyclone in a country where danger and beer and motorcycles make life cheaper and better and more worth living.

'My turn,' I said, and pushed my fingers inside her. At least I think I did, as the heat and strength that met me caused me to reflect on the Kelvin scale and why Kelvin didn't talk enough about what's *hot*.

A shoe was dangling from one of her feet. It had the elegance and slight breath of Sacher-Masoch and de Sade, which all good shoes have, and I noticed it dangle, then fall. As it should have. She was coming like an Arab revolution in the springtime, but with nicer sounds.

I pushed a third finger into her and the revolution went worldwide.

As this shuddering temple to magnificence and wonder and beauty and mortality found rest, we looked down at our hands, wet, white-knuckled and bound together. We raised our dizzy heads and our eyes fell into each other. In hers, the tropical storm was easing and there were small native children splashing in the waters we had created. My eyes were only the colour of love and awe. Much like a young Solomon who has been allowed to approach the tabernacle.

The Holy of Holies. Much like the eyes of a young Russian train driver as the sublime Anna Karenina's eyes meet his for one blissful, yet fearful, second. Like the mental eye of the scientist who suddenly sees the Theory of Everything. I breathed in.

'MCG?' she asked, letting that breath of hers fall into my soul and then my toes.

'Yes,' I replied, quietly. She reached down and took my Elgin Marbles in her hand like an English plunderer. I knew I was never getting them back, no matter how Greek things got.

We got in the cab.

'I'll give you $300 for your rear-view mirror,' I told the driver.

'What?' he asked, as I tore it from the windscreen and threw him the cash.

'MCG. Members entrance,' she said. And he instantly forgave and drove.

My cock ached like it had its own heart, as she reached down and ran a nail along all the bits that hurt most.

I looked at the crimson ottomans that were her lips. As they headed to a land that was aching for an explosive and velvet revolution, she paused, and delicate, wise words fell from those lips:

'You will never, in your life, see, or know, or experience, or feel anything as beautiful as a beautiful woman.'

Reader, she was right.

TOBY SCHMITZ

I'm writing to a younger you because I don't want to reminisce. We never do that, you'll find, when we meet. We fill each other in.

The open coffin is a fiasco. Your daughters wail, and all the grim men brace themselves at the back of the funeral home viewing vestry for their moment with a corpse. And the smell, man. Hamlets are always so cool handling Yorick's skull – Hamlet should be dry-retching.

And all these toddlers wailing, on laps, on plastic chairs, slumped on the tiles. See, your eldest daughter has heaps of kids and in turn they have heaps of kids. You'll meet them all, don't worry. And there are inevitably more to come, but they'll be of the same genre.

I give your carcass a perfunctory once-over and it appals me – all that propping up of something so intent on pooling – spare me. Spare everyone.

I'm not telling you so you'll actually spare us by attempting to change fate, insisting on a closed-coffin clause in your will wouldn't work, this letter would be erased as I was writing it, or something of the sort. That's not the gist of the line I'm dropping you. I'm letting you know what's going to happen because I happen to know you *want* to know, and that you won't – can't – change a thing.

Just saying – open coffin: no wonder everyone's wailing.

Terrific exit. You've got cats over for a sundowner, and, rising to make gin and tonics, you have a turn. Last words: 'There's more champagne in the fridge.' Whatever your turn involves, it gets you from gin and tonic to champagne. The anecdote continues to impress both hedonists and hostesses. And off you trot dreamily in the ambulance. We are such stuff as dreams are made on, and our little life is rounded with a sleep.

No one can desire to know exactly *when* they die; let's say you're well into the good-innings bracket. Top of the ninth. Ish.

I'm seven, cloistered and bobble-headed, we're taking the diesel train home having seen a flick in town. I have a large bag of coveted musks. And I ask you if you think the old man opposite us fought in the war. By this I mean your husband's war. (You've already met your husband.) And you're going to say: Why don't you politely go and ask him? And I do, and he was, and he eats most of my musks. This is going to be of defining importance to me. I doubt I can tell you why, but I'll briefly try. My curiosity, my intrepid urge requires bravery. And you supply it, and I realise as it's happening, as I'm talking to this old guy, that communing with strangers may be what it's all about – all of it.

I am going to be your favourite (I don't care if that's what everyone thinks). Your younger daughter has me, and my brother Rory. We don't reproduce like spot fires; we are still just ourselves.

The fairies change my life. You go whole hog with the fairies – tiny footprints in the sandpit out back, miniature bonfires still smouldering in the morning fog by the log, the glittering boy-sized pillow left on my bed by the Head Fairy to help with nightmares. This, needless to say, blows my mind, and my imagination has kittens all over its own face as a result.

I have written to you at the end of the war in the Pacific. You'll know this already, because you'll have found this letter, just now, with its odd typeface, in your pigeonhole in the Women's Auxiliary mess hall.

So you're elfin and prettily, toothily agape reading this.

Brian will marry you.

Things, of course, will change.

Brian dies, barely a fair innings, and you will continue to hear him whistle in the hall, and I will try and whistle like him in the hall whenever I visit from next door. Brian's brain stops around the time that the old man on the train, his mouth sucking musks, tells me he fought the Japanese in New Guinea, like Brian. It's the mosquitoes. The mosquitoes finish Brian in the end, but not before you work a family up with rules and ideas and love. You get time.

We will live next to each other my entire childhood. We will be perfect, perfect friends.

And you will change – how *much* you change is awfully impressive, bravery coming off you in waves. When you lose your lover, your flame, you reinvent and become a very hip, and very solo, much envied matriarch.

You become a shrink. Imagine that! Perhaps you can. There's all this liberation ahead, I'm a bit jealous. And you help these fascinating people, whom I will watch pressing your doorbell, some of them sobbing, from our kitchen window.

And in turn I will not just run over, sometimes sobbing, and commandeer the biscuit barrel – I will come over, commandeer the biscuit barrel and put my sneakers up on your floral couch in therapy mode. And I'll fill you in.

You refuse to accumulate chintz – instead you shed any semblance of time honoured Nana-ness. Doilies and drapes are struck off. Floral furniture is replaced with café au lait leather as the century closes, until, at the end, you're hosting your sundowner bridge game in a serviced apartment so sleek as to be Icelandic. Just three stainless steel-framed photographs on the laboratory-grade kitchen bench.

So. What's happened in the nine months since you shuffled?

Um, I'm doing *The Importance of Being Earnest* in Melbourne. You'd dig it. You'll see all my gags, don't worry, they're coming up.

You're a fan. Trust me, I'm right up your alley. I want you to laugh the most.

Mum's going out with this younger dude who came to tile the house. He's pretty hot but, as Rory says, he's a little too keen to unpack his acoustic guitar and crank out the originals.

Rory is slapping up graffiti on wheat silos in the Simpson Desert. Dad won't let us see his flat in North Perth.

My friend Travis just had a baby and today I saw him. I am godfather and it's lovely, you know, it's magic – it's a baby. While I was there, Trav's parents walked in straight off the plane and I watched their faces become grandparents. I thought of you so much I *was* you.

Thank you for taking Dad in. He's an odd Dutch-Indo with a handbag, and I am rather fond of him.

Thank you for taking me to Melbourne at a horrible cusp. We share a bed in a 1930s cold-water and you urge me to wander the town alone. You buy me a shrink-wrapped edition of *American Psycho* because I am not of age (I can't describe that novel to you, I doubt I can forty-five years from now), and you buy me the Elle Macpherson calendar because I am too embarrassed. You sleep soundly as I have the slowest, stealthiest wank a teenager ever squeezed out in a bed next to his maternal grandmother. Remember to sleep soundly.

Thank you for describing the ugly things my colonial ancestors did. It took gumption and character to paint relatives as villains for one so prone to nightmares. It was very postcolonial studies and bold of you.

I'm not so brave any more, I don't know why. It doesn't seem to happen to you: you start swearing, stripping back, baring more.

I get panicky, and gravity tugs around my heart – it's a new thing. And there's always the nightmares.

But thank you for the head start on all that. I am loved. As you read this, I am loved.

You get time. And although, as you know, life is not without its agonies, you keep them all from me, even Brian, so I just see luck and bravery, and for this good, long stretch, you pour it all on me. Thanks in advance; it makes me.

And you get to miss the open coffin, which is a complete fiasco.

Your last line is a zinger, though, don't you think? And closing lines are never zingers unless they are set up very well indeed.

You get time, Patricia.

And you *make* me.

Now tear this into quarters, turn around and put it in the mess hall grate.

To the things I never told my mother

LESLIE CANNOLD

32 C.E.

When I was five, you caught me, Mama, kneeling over a bird's grave. I had buried the creature myself several moons earlier, after discovering it while prowling about on hands and knees in search of animal bones in the forest behind our house. These I would give to you to carve into needles to mend our blankets and robes.

Back bent like a crone, I scraped and scratched at the earth of the bird's grave, which lay beneath the rough and fissured trunk of one of the many ancient poplar trees that carpet the hills of Galilee. Soon I sensed the hollow and, working furiously to set the dirt aside, laid bare the prize. Leaning in, I brushed the skeleton with a gentle finger. It collapsed in a jumble of bones and dust.

Sitting back on my heels, I considered. Would it be possible to put things to right? What if the bird could be made to live again? If the bones could be assembled and reordered, each rib and vertebra set securely in place, might she sing and beat her wings once more?

Suddenly, urgently, I needed to know.

I set to work directly, swiping a place on the dirt clean with the side of my hand, and reaching in again and again to the shallow grave. I extracted femurs, the delicate bones of the wings, the ribcage, and fit them into place. Working confidently from the image in my mind of the intact skeleton asleep in its earthen nest, the puzzle drew together and the creature began to take shape.

Then I heard the bark of your voice. 'Rachael! What are you doing?' Your pinching fingers bit my ear. 'Get up! Get up!' you cried.

Your eyes fell on the bird, my project, only half completed on the ground. You squinted at it, Mama, and chewed your lip. Then you turned to scrutinise me, up and down, for clues. 'What is this, Rachael?' you said at last. 'I do not want for needles.'

'They are not bones for needles, Mama,' I replied, my heart pounding, the words pouring from my lips, knowing I must be quick. 'I was wondering if . . .'

But you had heard enough. You grabbed my shoulders roughly and faced me towards home. You pushed me in that direction. You said, 'You have no business here, Rachael. You should be at the hearth, preparing the midday meal. Or in the fields with the other girls, fetching and carrying water. Not out here in the woods, alone, indulging your . . . your . . . *curiosity*.' This last word, as it fell from your lips, was laden with contempt. Beneath the weight of your indifferent sandal, Mama, I heard the bones of my bird crackle and snap.

I began to sob, my stumbling steps slowed by the burden of my grief. Soon I could not go on. Immobilised, I stood amid a tangle of pink rockrose and spiny evergreen shrubs, sobbing as if my heart would break.

'What are you standing there for, Rachael?' you said from behind me. Then, in a different tone, softened by unaccustomed compassion and pity, you went on. 'Nothing to be gained by wailing about what is done and what cannot be changed. You will survive, Rachael. All of us do.'

And so I have survived. Flourished even. But now, so many years from that day in the woods, it is you, Mama, who is failing. This is why you have called me here, to your sister's house in Bethany, mere miles from Jerusalem. Summoned me to the side of your death mat at the centre of this dank, airless room. I have travelled for days from my new home in the northern city of Antioch to kneel beside you, my body bent like a claw, my ear pressed to the tired purse of your once lovely mouth, to hear your confession and offer forgiveness. Only then will you be able to rest in Sheol, alongside countless generations and every caste of Jewish dead.

But I never told you, Mama, what the true source of my grief was that long-ago day in the wood. That day when your heel crushed my spirit with the same careless efficiency it deployed to vanquish the bones of a bird. I cried that day, Mama, because you made me feel like nothing. Like no one. I had not asked to be born as I was – curious, questioning – but that was my fate, and I yearned for you to accept it, to accept me, as I was, and to love me for it. But you would not. Instead, you castigated me for my failings as a girl, my inability to be a good girl, the right sort of girl, then scorned me all the more when I tried to be other.

What I never told you, Mama, was that I cried that day, as much from shock as grief, at suddenly knowing myself a failure. I could not earn your praise on my terms, nor shed the femaleness that made all that I wanted, all that I was, so wretchedly wrong. I cried because at that moment I knew that my desperate quest for recognition would never, never win me your love.

———

Your own confession is finished now. When you speak from your death mat, it is in the creaking cant of the crone. 'So, now you understand, Rachael. You understand my life, my story. What made me as I was. You understand now, and will grant me pardon for my sins.'

It is a plea, though you assert it like a command, Mama. It is like Bindy always said: the old are as they ever were, only more so. And you, Mama, are still Mama: demanding, withholding, afraid.

Perhaps it is only now, when the time for hope has nearly expired, that I will finally accept that you will never change.

But I can change. I can change because I am no longer just a daughter, but a mother, too. I can change because I understand the wicked choice you faced having birthed a daughter such as I. What mother would want to pass down such rules to her child, rules that – on pain of death – she must obey? But then again, how could a mother who wants her daughter to survive *not* pass such rules down, and school her about them well? I can change because I have lived long enough to know that you had your reasons, Mama. All of us do.

So I take up your wrinkled hands in mine, stroke them with my thumbs, move one towards my face and press it to my cheek. 'Of course I forgive you, Mama,' I say. 'Of course I do.'

CLEMENTINE FORD

Dear Mum,

The cigarettes were mine. I only told you they weren't because I knew you'd get mad. And, hey, I was thirteen. Looking back on it, I don't know why I expected you to fall for the old, 'Oh no, I *hate* smoking. I'm looking after them for a friend because she doesn't want her mother to know she smokes. And why do I smell like cigarettes? Well, it's *obviously* because I've been spending time down at the pub. But don't worry, I only drink coke because I *hate* alcohol.'

But let's face it – what else is a thirteen year old going to do in a tiny seaside town on the arse end of England? Look at a map of the United Kingdom and you'll see a bent old woman shuffling towards coupon day at the local Safeway. Sheringham, a town where throwing yourself off the craggy cliffs that line the North Sea seems less romantic and more inevitable, sits on the northernmost tip of that geographical bustle, and offers three activities for miscreant youths: smoking, drinking and fucking.

I certainly wasn't doing the latter because a) I had the approximate glow and girth of a Christmas pudding, and b) I was saving myself for Benjamin Pert, the golden totem who secured my unending love the moment he popped his cigarette into the corner of his lip and offered me protection from the chill in the form of his three-striped Adidas jacket, and who I hoped to secure romantically through active engagement in the first two outlets for entertainment, i.e. smoking and drinking.

Of course, to you he was just one of the nice young friends I'd made playing frisbee down at the local park, in between studying and putting on fashion shows with Anna Chesney. And you chalked any residual misbehaviour up to the fact that I was entering adolescence, that curious state in which the natural order of things finds itself suddenly reversed – once a beautiful butterfly, determined to wrest the most out of the world around her, your child had become a bloated, sullen larva, dribbling all over herself and shuddering with revulsion as you tried to draw near.

It was a Pan's Labyrinth of lies – but you believed it at the time. Or at least it seemed that way. Perhaps you had no choice. You were a woman trying to do the best with three newly metamorphosed larvae and a husband working in a desert half a world away.

From my spot on the stairs, where I'd recently taken to eavesdropping, I listened as you recounted the story of the cigarettes to my father over a crackling telephone line stretching 6000 kilometres – two rusty cans joined by a bare string woven of love, frustration and need. Back then, all I heard was that I'd got away with it. Now, listening across a chasm of fifteen years, the whispers of things not said have grown louder. And rather than hide behind the mantle of humour, I must be serious for a moment.

In a marriage often defined by distance, how many words travelled up and down that line over the years? How many declarations of love, how many threats of abdication, how many rudimentary shopping lists of the banality that makes up everyday life? While Dad cast his net across all the adventures life had to offer him, convincing himself it was a necessary part of supporting his family, you cast your eyes to the horizon, a modern-day Mrs Muir waiting out the tyranny of distance in her dilapidated shack by the sea.

I used to wonder if you ever wanted to take to that cord with a set of kitchen shears, severing once and for all the expectation that it was your place to stay behind and wait, with three children in tow and a plastic smile that slipped more often than it didn't.

Now that I'm old enough to question your life without fear of what I might find, I wonder why you didn't.

Everything I know about you has been cast through a prism of motherhood and marriage. I know that my father wanted to marry you the instant he saw you, because this story has been passed like a prayer around our dinner table throughout my entire life. But what of your other lovers? Who else held you against them and wanted nothing more than to breathe you in until some of your essence settled beneath their skin? Who else looked for a passageway into your heart, hoping to find a secret room to which only they had the key, and a window through which they might have seen the world from your eyes? And who did you, in your private moments, allow yourself to think on, wondering how things might have been different?

Before you became a wife and a mother, you were a woman with a history – a complex equation with unexpected variables and the absence of precise rules. You were an ocean of mystery, the undercurrents and swells dragging your mind every which way. You lived in a vast underwater cavern, full at once with wondrous colours and dark, impenetrable caves.

You never ceased being that person – but the parts which your husband and children had access to lay only on that ocean's glossy surface, a reflection of the woman as the world wanted to see you, and, eventually, the only side you had the energy to show.

I wonder sometimes if you forgot which was which, or if there were perhaps two of you – the woman resigned to the role life had assigned to her, and the woman slowly suffocating in the depths of those murky waters.

There was a macabre poetry to your death. Buried for so long beneath the crushing weight of the depression that had marked so much of your life, the clouds finally began to break and you started to embrace all the possibilities the world might have to offer you. But it was as if the cancer had hidden itself shrewdly and chose that moment to announce its presence, destructive, triumphant and so very final.

Soon the glow that had come to your cheeks couldn't be attributed to the very basic human right of happiness, but to the hours of radiation we knew couldn't save you but which we had to at least say we tried. As summer stretched across the southern sky, clothes gave way to dressing gowns, wake to sleep, and hope to resignation.

And then you were gone. The ocean of your existence withdrew from our shores for the last time, leaving the surface to slowly dry and be scattered by the wind. After your death, I spent a lot of time mythologising the woman I thought you were. I wrote endlessly about loss – not just mine, but also that of my father. I wanted to believe you were a perfect woman, and that yours was a perfect relationship – that everything you'd been forced to sacrifice was justified by this enormous gift of love you'd both been given. Perhaps I was trying to convince myself. Now that Dad's remarried, he can barely bring himself to talk about you, and I have been forced to turn you into a ghost.

You had been the glue that held us all together – without your energy to orbit around, I was worried we'd become stateless entities, drifting aimlessly without purpose or connection. I thought that in losing you, we couldn't help but lose each other.

Of course, the opposite was true. Your absence forced us to reach out across the emptiness that you'd left and find each other's hands. As the four of us – my father, sister, brother and I – huddled together in that absurdly bright funeral parlour, we took turns saying goodbye to a dead body in a box. I poked it. It was hard and unrelenting. It looked like you, but not quite. It lay not as you did when you were sleeping, a turtle curled into its shell, but stretched out flat; it wore a dress I didn't recognise, and its face bore the pinched, irritated expression of someone who'd been hurried to an appointment and then realised too late they'd forgotten to bring their purse.

There is a memory I have from when I was ten or so, of tearing into the kitchen to spend an hour eating my feelings from the cans of Pringles you kept hidden in the pantry. But the treat I was after, of licking the MSG off every chip individually before shoving handfuls of them into my mouth, was waylaid when I found you sitting in the alcove behind the fridge, crying. What was wrong? I asked. Had you hurt yourself? Did someone say a mean thing to you? You ushered me away angrily, and I was bruised and defiant. After all, I had done *nothing* wrong. Why were you such an angry *bitch* all the time?

It calls to mind a scene from another kitchen, years earlier, and yet another, years later. Both times I told you I hated you, and both times you took it.

We consider hatred to be the prerogative of children – words said in anger are dismissed as a natural part of youth. It's only now that I can look back and see that, although I thought the battleground of feelings, recrimination and blame was my domain alone, there were times when you hated me too – fiercely and passionately, and for reasons far more complex than not being allowed to go to a party. But this hatred had no outlet or voice. Like so many, you were a mother first and a woman second, and mothers are not allowed to view their children as anchors that have the power to drag them under.

Here is my confession to you, the thing I never told you because I didn't have the courage to admit it to myself, and the thing I can't say now because it's too late. I'm sorry. I didn't look for the woman beneath the waves, but I would give anything to meet her now. I think I would like her.

I would dive beneath that surface and drag her out, and I would offer her a raft that she could take wherever she chose, even if it was away from me.

I wanted you to live because I needed my mother, but that was all I ever allowed you to be. My punishment for helping to confine you is that I will spend the rest of my life looking for you.

You came to motherhood like an immigrant to an unfamiliar country. You neatly folded the precious parts of yourself that you didn't want to forget and you buried them in jars in the backyard, to be reclaimed at a later date and made glorious, just as you were.

With my little shovel in hand, I head out to that garden and dig, hoping to hear the clink of metal on glass so I can pull forth another clue as to who you really were. I know that the consequence will be a disturbed landscape of gaping holes, but the ravaged ground revealed will be more beautiful than perfect could ever be.

Clementine

GERALDINE QUINN

My family has never been great at the openness thing. Sure, scold-
ing children, criticising appearances or bitching about an in-law
– we're all over that kind of openness. But as for the intimate in
a family way – no, not that 'family way', the other one. Oh, this is
getting worse . . . Anyway, we rarely express how we feel about each
other beyond the above examples. Therefore, when I was informed
that my Women of Letters appearance was to be themed around a
letter to my mother, it was, frankly, a challenge. I consider my-
self more similar to my father, with his sentimentality, hot temper,
drinking, wordplay, overindulging, silliness and obsession with
melody and rhythm. While Mum's family is really good at sport.
Point made.

My solution was to perform a song that I wrote when my uncle
(Mum's brother) was ill. The constant road trips out to the country
to visit him before he passed away were reminiscent of the hours we
used to spend in my childhood pressed up against each other in a car,
trying with all our might not to a) be sick, b) rip out each other's
throats, or c) rip out each other's throats and be sick in them – all
while shouting country songs at the top of our lungs. So this song was
written for my mother, but in the most obtuse, indirect way possible.
Indeed, it is intentionally so indirect that hopefully she will never,
ever guess my intention . . . Oh, I guess I've buggered that up now.
I'm such an arse . . .

Long Way Back to Henty

I always get stuck on the letter 'L'
I've seen a hundred licence plates go past
My little sister's touching me as well
One more time I'm gonna kick her arse

The 'G', the 'E', the 'R', the 'A' are fine
Then a 'D', 'I', 'N' and 'E' go whizzing by
Yvette complains that she's got 'V' and 'Y'
But you only have to find six letters – I've got nine

It's kind of weird how some things never change
From the Kenny Rogers to the road trip games
The last time we were all stuck in this car
Was thirty years ago. Have we really got this far?

And it's a long, long way back to Henty
The air-conditioner vents still freeze our legs
We never stop to visit – one blink and you'll miss it
I wonder if we'll see this place again
Everything looked so much bigger then

Pull in mid-afternoon, the crickets ringing
The slamming of car doors, a violent sound
By now we're sick of all the fucking singing
The sun bounces back on us from the ground

Water from the tank with wrigglers in it
Gosh, we've lived in the city for so long
The funeral will start in forty minutes
We're still humming all those Kenny Rogers songs

It looks the same, and yet it's different somehow
The mantel clock is ticking loud and slow
Brothers, sisters, parents who are gone now
It must be really strange when siblings start to go

And it's a long, long way back to Casterton
The Boy Scout sign emblazoned on the hill
Grandpa's photo in the main hall
Fox skins on the shed wall
I wonder if we'll see this place again
Or doze off on the big verandah bed
Is that the pear tree where Nick cracked his head? Wow . . .
I thought that it was so much bigger then
Everything looked so much bigger then.

Geraldine Quinn [signature]

NADINE GARNER

Dear Mum,

The summer of 1978 was a scorcher. The Christmas holidays had been dragging on and I spent most of my nights alone, floating on an orange floral li-lo in the above-ground swimming pool, listening to the mosquitoes frying in the blue zapper Dad had strung up under the pergola.

I'd finished year eleven and was hovering in a safe, womb-like place of no commitments, no deadlines, no future. Year twelve was somewhere out there in the ether, but I had neither the energy nor the inclination to think about it. And aside from the growing tower of textbooks and reading material swaying on my desk, I was spared too many reminders. I was safely hidden beneath the dark, forgotten sky of the western suburbs. Our quarter acre block of brick and cement, an oasis where I wasn't expected to dream . . .

There were bursts of ambition that occasionally bubbled up through the black waters of apathy. One striking and persistent image punched through my dim, pubescent brain like a shampoo commercial on high rotation. The image was Miss Nichols. Miss Sally Nichols was twenty-one years old and my English lit teacher. We called her Stevie because she looked a lot like Stevie Nicks and we'd all OD'd on Fleetwood Mac the summer before.

Her hair was thick and golden and in the high-rotation vision in my mind it was falling around her bare shoulders. (Obviously she'd removed her sheer cheesecloth blouse for the full impact of the image.)

I was not the only sixteen-year-old student who had formed a fixation on Miss Nichols but I was pretty certain that mine had gone way beyond a schoolboy crush and was careering down a path of deep, unconditional love. It woke me in the night, tugged at my intestines and planted camouflaged landmines in my psyche. It was a lonely place to be.

You and Dad had gone on that trip to Thailand without Tom and me. Your first-ever holiday without kids. The kind of holiday you take to try to find out whether you still like your spouse or actually want to belt him over the head with a blunt object. (Your words, not mine.)

So there I was, home alone, with my jaundiced, lovesick, aimless longing.

Tom spent most nights at Gazza's joint. They were working together on their matching Toranas. It all seemed a bit homo to me, young men with their shirts off, covered in sweat, lying together head to head under the chassis ... You'd refused to have Tom's car spewing its innards all over the driveway any longer. The family's pride and joy and the envy of all the neighbours was the immaculate Holden Commodore, sitting regally in our double garage. Perfectly reliable and, from a teenager's perspective, completely undriveable. I'd sworn on my own grave not to drive the Commodore; I hadn't, however, sworn not to drive the other car. Dad's hobby car, the 1968 Mini-Minor, snuggled under its fleece-lined cover. It looked like a small child sitting there alongside the giant Commodore, but suddenly its true greatness revealed itself. How could I not have seen it? It was the sleeper, the secret operative that would become so integral to my love of humanity and my faith in the future.

Floating around on my floral li-lo, with the distant and comforting sound of V8 engines serenading me, I stared up at the one star I could find through the haze of the oil refinery. Suddenly it was blindingly clear: the Mini and I had to take Miss Nichols to the drive-in.

Saturday Night Fever had unleashed itself on a generation of music-crazed, sex-starved high-school kids, who all wanted to either *be* John Travolta or be *with* John Travolta. Tight white pants were spreading throughout the heat-bleached suburbs like a plague, and hair product sales had peaked. Everyone was walking around singing in high falsetto like the Bee Gees – even Miss Nichols had the soundtrack. I'd seen the cassette cover on the passenger seat one afternoon when I left some lavender under her windscreen wiper. It felt like the world was in the grip of a fever, the *Saturday Night* kind. Surely this was the answer to my endless, empty evenings of longing. Somehow, somehow, Operation Nichols had to be activated, and had to remain a top national secret.

The evening I peeled the Mini out from under its lining and rolled it down the driveway was at the end of another sweltering day. A northerly had been blowing the smell of rotting fish over from the tip since first thing in the morning. My head was thumping with the heat and the anticipation of having Miss Nichols in a seat next to me, all to myself.

Of course, the one time I needed him to be out, Tom was snoozing on the sofa. 3XY was crackling away on the breakfast bar but there was no way I could start the engine up without Petrolhead hearing it. So I chucked it in neutral, pocketed the tiny key and pushed her out to sea. I got a few houses away before I folded myself inside that tiny toy car and eased it the five streets to Miss Nichols' door. I had made an initial harrowing trip to her house a week before on foot, to leave a note requesting her company for the following Friday night. She had miraculously responded two days later in the form of a neat, simple note in my letterbox. It read: 'Yes, I'd like to. See you then.' And now I found myself in the completely surreal position of driving to her place to take her out on a date. My shirt was damp from pushing the car and my hair had already begun to spring out of place. A police car sped past me, siren bleating, and my heart pounded in my chest as I imagined having to explain to you and Dad what had happened. Then I pulled up outside Miss Nichols' house and prayed my gratitude up to the godless sky for being spared. I took a deep breath and noticed that a high white cloud against the blue looked like a crocodile chewing a marble.

As I was about to step out of the car and knock on her front door, a glamorous, tanned creature appeared in the doorway. Miss Nichols turned in slow motion towards me, brushing her hair away from her face. She moved to the car and I felt my heart thump so violently that I clutched my chest to try to stop it. As her hand landed on the car doorhandle, my groin jumped and I punched myself in the balls.

There's no synchromesh between first and second gear in a 1968 Mini-Minor, which means if you don't know how to use the clutch properly you can drag that box through a world of pain. We decided she should drive, given my close call with the cops. Needless to say, it was a particularly crunchy trip. Miss Nichols seemed to turn into a series of angles the moment she sat in the driver's seat, all elbows and knees, and her face reddened each time she ground through the box. But she filled the car with the smell of patchouli and her forehead glistened with moisture.

When our tiny car pulled into the drive-in, the place was packed. The sky had turned pink and there was a giant cloud baby smiling down at us, holding a rattle. She got out of the car and then poked her head back inside, saying, 'Come on, then. Blokes have to sit in the driver's seat at the drive-in.'

I loved her even more then, as I shimmied through the narrow space that was now left between our car and the Toyota that had pulled up behind us. I slid into the low green vinyl seat, and we waited for the sky to grow dark and the giant baby to fall asleep. While

Miss Nichols made her way to the candy bar, I struggled to hang our heavy, awkward speaker on the window. She bought two small tubs of Peters vanilla ice-cream and two Cokes. She wouldn't take the five bucks I offered her, which was just as well because that was all I had left in the world.

Our movie magically emerged from the white screen and carried us into the world of do-it-yourself disco, where for two hours we were glamorous, free and in love. By the time the Bee Gees finally sang 'How Deep is Your Love', I'd mustered the courage to slide my arm along her seat, and she turned to me and smiled, in the way that a woman smiles at a man.

The credits rolled. Engines started up. Laughter rang out, car doors slammed, someone screamed, 'Fuck you, Wayne!', and a bottle smashed on the ground.

We stayed staring at the rolling lines of meaningless names. Then she got out and stood by the driver's side.

We drove home in silence, except for the rasping sound of the box. She laughed at herself as she dragged the gearstick through, and I laughed along nervously, hoping she wasn't doing any long-term damage. When she pulled up outside her house, the Skyhooks were singing 'Balwyn Calling' on the radio.

She leaned across and kissed me tenderly, next to my nose, and said, 'I like you a lot, Glenn Slater, but don't ask me out again. I could lose my job.'

The next night, I was back out on the li-lo, staring at my one star, the sensation of her lips on my face still humming gently. The world looked the same, but it was changed forever.

I had let a woman know that I loved her without saying a word, and I knew – I just knew – that it meant something to her.

An apology letter

PARIS WELLS

Dear Wes Anderson,

Apologies – it's been a while since I've written to you. My journey shifted four months ago and I found myself busy with a process of personal healing.

This year I have been pondering the definition of class. What does it mean to have class, to have grace, to feel classy? Some days I don't have the answers, so I think to myself, What would Wes Anderson do? You use the same team, people you trust, to achieve your art, and you are unapologetic for taking the time needed to complete your expressions. No colour, sound, word or frame you use lacks meaning. Nothing is an accident, yet everything seems magical.

So I figured that in order to create a classy existence, I should eliminate all the things in my life that are not classy.

Yes, I owned two MC Hammer CD singles – into the bin.

Yes, I possessed huge pairs of underwear and various g-strings that made my ass look like a rolled cut of pork – bin.

Yes, I had a multicoloured beanie – bin.

Yes, I had a puffy Adidas jacket – bin. (Note: this is as opposed to my velour Adidas jacket, which, along with matching sweatpants, I like to call my 'leisure suit'. I try not to wear it with sneakers – more often than not I finish the ensemble with Italian Brunate flats and sheer knee-high stocking so that my ankles look smooth. I hate the look of 'shotti' ankles. I feel ankles on a woman are one of the most underrated tools of seduction, as are wrists. I talk more with my wrists than my hands, and I walk more with my ankles than my feet.)

Wes, where was I? That's right, eliminating classless objects. Unfortunately, objects are not all that need to be eliminated. There is also the controversial topic of classless behaviour. This is the era of the empowered female, where poor men are expected to make sure they have enough money to support us, while women are still in charge and independent – with the ability to purchase our own leisure suits if we so desire. And if a man wants to express his feelings, we women may listen, but we may also hold his vulnerability against him somewhere down the line when we parade more than ankles and wrists in his face. We expose our tits, hips and thighs, and then complain about misogynous retaliation in popular music and media. All the while everyone is *not* stopping to quickly ponder: *Would Wes Anderson find this classy?*

And I'll tell you, Wes, I too struggle daily in trying to live a classy life. My behaviour leaves a lot to be desired at times. Like in March when we toured Sydney. We sold out the Vanguard (a very classy cabaret venue). The gig was incredible – I was Annie Lennox reincarnated, even though she isn't dead . . . So I guess I was like her younger sister with an arse or something. My point is, it was a good show. The after party, however, crept up on me like some vodka demon, hiding in my handbag ready to attack me.

The next morning my task was to drive the band to the airport, and then to drop off the van and all the gear. I found myself vomiting into a used meat pie bag while battling Sydney traffic, gearstick in one hand, pie bag in the other. Not pretty, and certainly *not* classy. I figured the classiest way out of that situation was a quick nap after the airport, so I drove to Jodie's house.

Jodie and I used to have baths together as children and have supported each other through illness, death, break-ups and diets. She told her new housemates of my coming arrival but, as she opened the door excited to see her old friend, instead of saying hello I proceeded to vomit in her front garden. As I crawled into her bed to rest my aching liver, I heard one of her housemates whisper, 'Is that Paris Wells?' Before I could listen to Jodie talk her way around it, I was asleep.

I woke feeling guilty, and figured that the only way to redeem myself was to pick myself up, put on a decent pair of sunglasses and continue the day without making my liver everyone else's problem.

This was the other side of class: the ability to keep going, keep moving forward, no matter how you are feeling. Although my pain was self-inflicted, I began to think of the terminally ill, the disabled and the grieving, and how impressive it is that they can keep moving, to achieve greatness. Classy.

I thought of my friends who lost their child, and I remembered how at the funeral a friend of theirs removed a parking ticket from their car and paid it, never to mention it to anyone. Classy.

I thought of my mother picking me up from school when I was upset about puberty in general. She handed me a hammer in the kitchen and gave me permission to smash a plate into a thousand pieces. Then our tears turned to laughter, as we cleaned up and danced to disco music and ate olives. She made it okay to have emotions. Classy.

I thought about how you would appreciate these people, Wes.

So I guess nobody is perfect, and the definition of perfection is completely subjective anyway. The main thing I'm trying to do is to be better to others and true to myself. Last year I lacked the confidence to stand up for what I wanted in love and life. It wasn't classy to not say how I felt, and be who I wanted to be, and do what I wanted to do. The result was heartbreak. To be classy is to tell the truth, to feel the truth, and, in that truth, there is love. I should have said more because it would have meant I was being myself. And when you're yourself, it's magic.

Maybe I'll learn; I'm not sure. All I know now is that my under-wear usually matches my socks, my shoes stay clean, a pony is a horse (not a hairstyle), my mind is trying to listen to my heart, and if I stop to think, Would Wes Anderson find this classy, and will I feel classy doing it? – then maybe my life will turn out okay.

So once again I'm sorry I haven't written to you in a while. I think you'll be hearing more from me now that I'm realising joy is not supposed to overwhelm you, but that it's supposed to sit on your shoulders like a cashmere scarf, soft and warm. I hope I'm still writing to you when I'm eighty years old in my black pearls.

In the meantime – stay classy, stranger.

Sincerely,
Paris Wells x

LOU SANZ

This is a letter of apology to my nine-year-old self, pertaining to a series of events that happened in 1988.

Firstly, I'd like to apologise to you, Lou, for the birth of our sister. In my defence, though, short of flinging myself between the duelling genitals of our parents after the ABC's Friday night episode of *Taggart*, there was little I was really able to do, other than cry myself to sleep as our parents' door remained ajar that night.

And so she was born, and with her birth came the news that your ninth birthday party would be cancelled. But *why*?

It would've been a good party, too, a *Fresh Prince of Bel-Air*-themed birthday party if I recall correctly, as I often do. You were to be dressed as Will Smith, with Vegemite smudged on your face for that authentic touch, and adorned with a birthday sash you'd made in art class, which simply read 'Happy Birthday Me'. This showed an awful lot of flare and talent, which, for whatever reason, went unnoticed that afternoon. You did try and make things work, even going as far as to throw your own birthday party in the maternity-ward waiting room. After fashioning a birthday cake out of a vending-machine Mars bar and a used paddle-pop stick, you even managed to wrangle a guest – a young boy who had wandered down from the chemo ward. All afternoon he kept following you around, asking you questions like, 'What's it like to turn nine, Lou? The doctors say I might never live to see nine – is the air different there?' Even at such a young age, you had to face the reality that your burden in life might be to know the answer to everything, and for that I apologise as well. The heaviness of that burden on a nine year old is unimaginable. But you soldiered on, and knelt down to the boy and looked him in the eyes and said, 'Oh my God, today is not about you! It's my birthday! Christ, can't I just get one day . . .'

'Happy birthday to me . . .' Yes, happy birthday to you, nine-year-old Lou. You deserved so much more than that. I'm sorry.

But it's what happened only a few months later that still haunts me to this very day. I'll start by saying that the leopard skin-print bathing suit was never my idea. Mum had a thing for only letting you swim in tiny bikini briefs – yes, just the briefs – because, like she said, 'One day you won't have a bikini body anymore, so make the most of it while you can.' But surely I could've stepped in and said, 'Please, Mum, at least let me wear the matching top.' However, I chose to stay silent. I could tell you I was learning to pick my battles, but that would be a lie, and, although I may be prone to hyperbole, I never lie.

The swimming carnival was coming up, though, and, with the threat of your nipples being exposed to the world, you asked Mum for a one-piece bathing suit. You know, the type that most people over the age of five wear. To your surprise, she acquiesced, but you should've known better – it was a trap, a trap you walked right into. Were not your suspicions aroused when she said you couldn't go with her to the Myer stocktake sale in the city to help pick out the new bathers? Were you not suspicious when she denied you one of the few joys you had in life – walking in and out of the Bourke Street entrance to the store only to be greeted by that blow of hot air from the wall-mounted hot air blowers, which made you feel warm, wanted and even loved?

It was an unusually hot day when Mum returned with those

new bathers. A one-piece bathing suit, from the women's department, as requested – but with little foam cups where your breasts might eventually come in. Oh, and did I mention the leopard print? Yeah, I guess I did – but did I mention that the eyes of the leopard were perfectly fixed on top of where your nipples were? Again, you did your best that afternoon in your new bathers, using some gaffer tape wrapped around your chest to hide not only the glaring eyes of the beast beneath, but also your absence of tits. I won't apologise for that, as I think I've well and truly made up for your lack of breasts. You'll just have to deal, nine-year-old Lou.

And so, in your gaffer-taped bathers, you kicked back with your younger brother Michael in front of the air conditioner, drinking lemonade and watching *Pugwall*. Then your brother, in all his blond, white-pride poster-boy cuteness, laughed at you. Without thinking, without bothering to check for witnesses, you retaliated, tossing what remained of your Sprite back at him – a basic childish tit for tat.

It should've ended there, but no. Mum was watching and she saw you toss that Sprite in the face of innocence that afternoon, and so she grabbed you, marched you outside to the yet-to-be-renovated backyard. (Not that it matters, but we eventually got a pool to cover the spot of your shame and humiliation. I did request a remembrance plaque, but I was silenced by the current regime at the time.) There you stood, on the concrete, underneath the Hills hoist, your olive skin changing to 'lightly grilled' under the glare of the Australian sun. Then, without warning, your mother produced what remained of the two-litre bottle of Sprite you and your brother had opened that afternoon. She poured it all on top of you, declaring this your punishment for doing the same to your brother, who you were, and I quote, 'academically smarter than'. Little Lou, this was not the first time, and nor would it be the last time, you'd be persecuted for knowing everything, and again I apologise for the burden placed on you at such a young age.

Standing out in the sun, not allowed back in until you'd dried off properly, you wondered if this was how Joan of Arc felt in her last hours . . . It was then you heard it: a buzzing, soft at first, and then louder and louder, accompanied by a flicker of yellow and black, and then a more persistent buzzing. 'Oh my God, Mum, is that a wasp near Lou's head?' you heard your brother yell, showing the obvious signs of low-level autism. He then ran/waddled to get Mum.

'Oh my God, a wasp!' your mother cried – yes, she was definitely my brother's mother. Those words linger with me even today, every time I wake up naked next to a strange man whose name is of little consequence to me, thanks to hard liquor, Catholicism and shame.

'Quick, get Jono!' Jono was our neighbour who owned a hose. A hose capable of filling with water.

People often say that when they're facing impending death, everything freezes and their life flashes before their eyes. And so it was that day, nine-year-old Lou – your life flashed before you as your lungs filled with our next-door neighbour's hose water:

- The time you were cast as the only Aboriginal in your school's re-enactment of the First Fleet landing, dressed in the traditional Indigenous welcoming garb of Richmond Football Club stubby shorts and a *Neighbours* singlet top, and holding a set of rulers with streamers attached for the traditional welcoming dance, which was set to 'Down Under' by Men at Work.
- The time you were rejected from the Blondie club at school because you weren't blonde.
- Your being cast as Mary in the school nativity play year after year because you looked like you could've been raised in a desert. But come on, Lou, learn to take a compliment.
- Your short-lived career as a child star on *Double Dare*, and the glow-in-the-dark touch lamp you never did win because you

froze on the multiple-choice question asking how much water there is on earth. Your answer of 'It's subjective' didn't convince anyone.

- The time your *abuela* taught you how to iron men's underwear. (And I'm sorry, Lou, to tell you this now, especially as your life flashes before your eyes, but it's a life skill no one will ever give you credit for, no matter how much you think it'll save your relationship. If he's gay, he's just gay.)
- Those new tartan hotpants and the midriff-revealing lace bolero tie-up top from the Miss PTO collection you'll never be allowed to wear – and nor should you ever.

As you lie splayed on the concrete with water continuing to pour into your mouth, being attacked with a hose to save you from the sting of a wasp, your little nine-year-old arms flailing around, you realise you're not going to die, not just yet, that you will live to fight another day . . . Yeah, sorry about that, Lou, but it isn't your time.

And look, I really am sorry, because as you get older you will face a life that no one should be subjected to. Especially given that you'll grow up with an intolerance to pseudoephedrine, the key ingredient in speed, and also an especial sensitivity to opiates, which will see you one day lying in bed convincing yourself, at the age of thirty-one, that it's cool to wee the bed, because fuck it, it's your bed and you paid for it, and you'll be damned if anyone is going to tell you that you can't languish in your own urine.

But, most of all, I'm sorry for using you. Thirteen years on, your heartbreak and humiliation now pays my bills and my rent. It keeps me in the lifestyle to which I've grown accustomed, of Kmart shoes, packets of instant miso soup and flights on Tiger Airways.

But don't think you're alone in this. I offer you this, by way of an apology and to maybe help you feel better: a story from the archives of my life, a story of my 25-year-old self.

I was living in London and my boyfriend had once again left me for a man, forcing me onto a diet of Veuve Clicquot. A friend of mine wrote to me from Brighton, inviting me to come and stay with her. I decided it was a good idea, to just get away from it all. When I told my doctor I would be taking a train to Brighton, he prescribed me Stilnox as he was worried that being trapped in a train for over an hour might cause my anxiety to kick in, leading me to once again wee on myself. As I waited for the train, I popped a Stilnox so it would set in by the time I was seated on the train, but then they said the train would be early, so I popped another one – you know, just to hurry it up – and then they said the train would be delayed and so I popped another one, just so the first two wouldn't wear off. I only remember a few things after that last pill . . . Number one: a small Italian man kept trying to get me to eat his sandwich. Number two: finding myself in a rather heated argument with a lesbian over the merits of fisting. And, finally, number three: waking up in the hall-way of my friend's house, in nothing but my undies, with the front door slightly ajar, some chairs stacked neatly in the corridor which I was pretty sure weren't there when I arrived, and a Post-it note on my arm that simply read, 'Hi Tenille [the friend who had extended me the invitation], thanks for the lend of the chairs. I've just stacked them in the corridor. From, Toby, the neighbour. PS I didn't touch your friend, she was like that when I arrived.'

So, nine-year-old Lou, I know it might not make up for every single thing I've done – but hey, it's a start.

Lou x

JANE CLIFTON

Dear Justin,

I'm so sorry about the other night. I was drunk. Yes, again. So what?

I had the first wine on an empty stomach and by the time that one kicked in, I was on to my third and the entree still hadn't arrived. You, of all people, know how slow the service is on a Friday night.

I got such a shock when you walked in. No one told me you were back. It's been a long time.

That colour really suits you, by the way, and whatever it is you're doing with your hair is working a treat.

I should have left straightaway, of course, with Raelene, but I went all rabbits-in-headlights. Seeing you like that, with no warning, brought it all back in a rush: the way it used to be and how happy we all were. Was it only six months ago? Christmas, yes – that's when the shit hit the fan. Worst New Year's Day ever.

I should have slipped away, out the back, through the kitchen, but I couldn't take my eyes off you.

And then I saw her.

Listen, Justin, you and I both know that she is an evil, conniving, thieving, double-crossing fucking bitch. But I guess the whole restaurant didn't need to hear it, screamed across a crowded room, at quite that volume.

I am sorry about the language. You know my position on the use of the c-word. I absolutely never, ever use it as an insult.

I still can't believe I called her that, like it was a bad thing. Incredible how we revert to the Neanderthal under pressure. Under threat. Political correctness flies out the window when love comes to town.

Not that love is something that cow knows anything about.

Preening – that's what she was doing. Flaunting it. Oh, she saw me, don't you worry about that. Those vicious little peepers clocked me minutes before you did, make no mistake.

We locked eyes for just a second. And then she turned, ever so slightly, and unbuttoned her coat. The bump was there for all to see, outlined in pearl-grey cotton spandex.

It was like it had its own little neon sign, saying, 'Suck it up, loser'. She rested her hand on it, just in case I'd missed it, just in case I hadn't heard about the ring.

Is there anyone on Facebook and beyond who hasn't heard about the ring? How many diamonds, how many rubies. Justin, the Bling King – who'd have thought? Justin, who called flowers on Valentine's Day a monumental waste of money.

I know you won't believe me, but I did not see that waiter until it was too late. I didn't even know they did those flaming steak thingies any more. I assumed that particular culinary dinosaur had gone the way of the prawn cocktail and the slice of orange on the coleslaw.

You've got to admit, the damage would have been so much worse if the sprinkler system had been less efficient. Dominic was right to challenge you on that one. A few wet frocks and some soggy pasta is a much happier result than third-degree burns and a damage bill in the millions. You could tell the ambos were relieved. And the fireys.

I've reached an arrangement with Dom. He's not going to sue. He put two and two together as soon as he saw the two of you, but as far as the other witnesses are concerned, all they saw was an accident – an unfortunate collision.

They would have had no idea I was on my way over to slap that smug expression off her face and deliver a few choice words of advice concerning her immediate future.

All they saw was a dumpy, middle-aged woman stagger up out of her seat, a flying plate, and then the flames.

I always thought those butcher's paper tablecloths were a stupid idea. I told Dominic so from the start. One of those wanky concepts you saw in Brighton or South Yarra. And those pretentious little bowls of oil and balsamic ... Stupid. They're what did the damage in the end.

Them, and the tortured willow.

The important thing is, though, no one was seriously hurt. Not physically, anyway.

You looked great talking about it on the telly. Raelene always said you should've been an actor. Thanks for not mentioning my name. I was well gone by the time table five went up. I crawled under the tables while everyone was running for the door, then I hid in the toilet until it was safe to scuttle out the back.

Raelene says I'm being ridiculous, that I should forgive, forget and move on, like she has. But that's easier said than done now she and little Lisa are living with me.

Remember last Christmas, when we put the Barbie tent up for Lisa, and you promised you'd bring her back a special surprise from Thailand? Well, at least that was the truth.

I am sorry about what happened the other night, Justin, but I'm not sorry about the way I feel. I keep asking myself where I went wrong, how I managed to turn you into the person you have become.

I hate to admit it, Justin, but I'm ashamed of you. I feel sorry for you.

But you've made your bed. Now you'll have to lie in it.

Goodbye,
Mum

CATHERINE DEVENY

Dear everyone,

I'm sorry, but I won't be writing an apology letter to Bindi, Rove or the Anzacs.

Or to people who spend long hours working jobs they hate to send their children to private schools to feel good about themselves.

I won't be writing a letter of apology to women who change their surnames when they marry, or to people who drive four-wheel drives, or to fans of *McLeod's Daughters*, *The Footy Show* or *Two and a Half Men*, or to people who listen to 3AW, to readers of the *Herald Sun* or people who shop at Chadstone.

And I won't be writing a letter to *The Age* for supposedly offending people with bad-taste remarks, inappropriate language and being me.

And I'm not sorry that I won't be apologising to people who prop up sexism, homophobia, xenophobia or division by supporting religion, because I proudly say God is bullshit. Your faith is simply religion-approved narcissism, exceptionalism and discrimination. Sorry, yes, even you.

I won't be saying those things because I am not sorry. I have nothing to be sorry about. And, worse still, I'm not sorry I have nothing to apologise about.

I'm not sorry because I never, for a moment, thought about someone having sex with an eleven-year-old when I said, 'I do hope Bindi gets laid.' But others did.

And I'm not sorry I won't be apologising to people who twist things in their heads to offend themselves and then look to me to apologise so they can feel better by blaming me for something they created.

And I'm not sorry I don't feel compelled to explain to the tiny and noisy minority of fuckwits that I was simply doing what I do to draw attention to the fact every single female on the Logies red carpet was dressed to be sexually objectified. 'Who are you dressed by?' 'Oh, look, she's got her Logies body back.'

I never see the headline 'How [*insert name of high-profile man*] got his Logies body back.'

I tweeted 'I do hope Bindi Irwin gets laid' because she was the only female not dressed to get laid. And I'm not sorry if you think I missed the mark, that it wasn't funny or that I'm making excuses. You're wrong and I don't care. I'm not sorry and I will not pretend to be sorry.

Nor am I sorry for tweeting, 'Rove and Tasma look so cute, I hope she doesn't die too,' because that's what I meant. I'm sorry if you have some fucked-up notion of 'respecting the dead'. Rove and Tasma are both beautiful and I hope neither of them die. I think about death every day. Not my own but that of the people I love. Death is the sound of distant thunder at a picnic. And I'm sorry but I didn't write that – it's a line from W.H. Auden. But I did write this: 'You can only truly live with the thought of death at your side constantly tapping you on the shoulder.'

And, Anzacs, you're all dead. I don't have to apologise to you. But you wouldn't have wanted me to. You would have been cheering me on as I said:

'Anzac Day celebrations refuse to recognise the chest-thumping, dick-swinging and back-stabbing politicians who create the death, suffering, torture and poverty of war.'

Cheered me on as I said:

'Politicians should only be allowed to wage wars in which they're happy to stand in the frontline with their own children.'

Cheered me on as I said:

'Anyone who lived through war who is not a fucktard says no parades, no medals. Everyone who suffered and struggled should be remembered. Stop war happening again.'

Cheered me on as I said:

'Anzac Day. Fuck respect. Respect is just code for "support our selective narrative used to prop up our power that we use to oppress".'

Cheered me on as I said:

'Remember war. The whole truth. Not the selective version. All the heroes. All the victims. Not just Anzac Day. Let's move on and learn.'

When I sent those tweets, Anzacs would have held up their beers and said, 'Good on you, love. Where were you when they were lying to us, manipulating us and making us go to war? I was scared and I came home broken.'

And to you tragic losers who get your identity from the fact some old dead relative you never met shot other men and you've twisted it into something that makes you feel good about yourself, I am not sorry I said:

'I abhor people whose self-esteem is fuelled by nationalism-approved misogyny, homophobia, racism or cruelty administered by relatives who killed people because they knew no better.'

And I'm not sorry I said:

'Live your own life. Make your own mark. Stop feeling big because your dead relative killed people because they knew no better.'

I am not sorry. But I am sorry I didn't say it louder and more often.

And I'm not sorry about what happened at *The Age*. That they tried to gag the girl from the wrong side of the tracks for saying 'the emperor is not wearing any clothes' because no one was listening to them any more and they were overwhelmed by relevance deprivation, envy and misogyny. And still are.

And I'm not sorry to say that I miss my readers, I miss the column, and I'm not sorry those who felt validated by my weekly rants still miss the weekly rants. Those readers still grab me in the street and say, 'I miss you.' And I say, 'I miss you too.' I'm not sorry those readers may now feel marginalised because a voice they identified with is no longer being broadcast. *The Age* proved everything I have ever said about power, decisions, control, fear and the gatekeepers of information better than any column I could have written. And I thank them for their transparency.

And I am not sorry to say that I was not at all surprised when it happened.

I'm not sorry that when I sat down to write this letter for you all today, I thought long and hard and realised I have nothing I'm sorry about.

I'm not sorry that my house is grubby, covered in dog hair and full of people and visitors eating, swearing, laughing, messing and playing music. Badly.

I'm not sorry that I have never been even close to my ideal weight according to the BMI, but I feel unapologetically sexy, healthy, beautiful and forty-two.

Loving your body exactly as it is, is an act of civil disobedience. I'm sorry, I didn't write that. Joanna Macy did.

I'm not sorry I had an abortion. I'm not sorry I had an affair. And I am not sorry I like Brazilians so much I have one permanently.

I'm not sorry that I am no longer in a relationship with the father of my children but that I still care for him and we communicate every day. I'm proud of how we have gotten to the best possible place with the least amount of damage.

I am not sorry that all of us are better off and happier for it.

I'm not sorry the kids are better than fine. I'm not sorry that it clashes with your world order and assumptions that all family split-ups cause damage and that parents should stay together regardless. I'm not sorry that we are happy.

When we split up I saw many couples around us quietly smug and warm with schadenfreude. Then when I fell madly in love only five weeks later those same couples seemed resentful, angry and bitter.

I'm not sorry that I have sex almost every day. Beautiful sex with a man I adore and who adores me, who I have waited and wept for my whole life. A prince. Who calls me Princess Sparkle. And Baby Girl. You heard me. And I am not sorry that I love it.

I am not sorry I don't care what my mum, my dad or my nanna thinks. Or what you think. I've never had a husband, but if I did I wouldn't be sorry for not caring what he thinks. I only care what I think about what I do.

I'm not sorry that I feel good enough. That I look at those women's magazines and laugh, thinking how sad those in them and those who read them are.

I'm not sorry that I feel sad for you if you feel pressure to spend money you don't have to buy things you don't need to impress people you don't like

I'm not sorry I am happy. And I'm not sorry you're not happy, but I get no joy out of you being unhappy. It does not make me feel better about myself.

I'm not sorry I want us all to be happy.

I'm not sorry I am not angry and bitter. I'm not sorry I am happy and friendly and generous and, yes, also opinionated and passionate. I'm not sorry that I do not live up to some convenient stereotype of a woman with opinions and passions and a creative life being somehow unhappy and frustrated. I am not. I have a big, wild, messy, amazing life. I expect nothing less.

I am not sorry if it comforts you to think that what I say or do,

I do to provoke or offend you personally. I don't. It's actually what I think. I'm not sorry you disagree or feel offended.

I only do truth and passion. You can't fake passion. And I know nothing but truth.

I'm not sorry I don't care what you think. You can be wrong. I'm not sorry I just don't care. It's not my job to convince you of anything. I don't need you to agree with me to know I am right.

And I am not sorry that I say exactly what I think and that I'm happy for you to do the same. And even though I don't think the same, I have no intention of silencing you.

I'm not sorry I am telling the truth and not thinking, This is self-indulgent. That I'm not thinking I should be apologising to my parents, my children, my world or myself.

And I am not sorry I have escaped from a world of blame and mea culpa.

I'm not sorry I don't expect myself or anyone else to be perfect. I'm not sorry I never taught my children to say 'I beg your pardon' or 'Pardon me', but instead to say 'Can you please move?', 'I didn't hear you' and 'I just farted'.

Sorry, but I'm not sorry about anything. I feel no need to apologise or to be apologised to. If I cut you off in traffic accidently, I will give you a wave indicating that I realise that I have inconvenienced you. But I am not sorry. I am human.

I'm not sorry I don't feel the need to be perfect, and nor do I expect you to be perfect. Perfect is the enemy of good. I will not prop up a system that enables blaming and shaming and the default setting of perfect and the belief that anything other than perfection is a transgression needing forgiveness. There are no mistakes, only detours, and it's the detours that define us.

And I'm sorry but you don't need to apologise to me either. Ever. If you have done something to hurt or inconvenience me, don't apologise. Find out if everyone is okay, see if you can fix things or make things better, and change your behaviour so it doesn't happen again. Your apology means nothing to me.

I'm sorry but I'm just not sorry. Apologising is a get-out-of-jail-free card.

Doing the right things in the future is the best apology for doing the bad things in the past.

I'm sorry I'm not being funny, because I'm sure that's what some of you wanted. I'm sorry I just do what I like and refuse to lie down in the chalk outline drawn for me.

Never explain. Never apologise.

I hope you don't die, and I hope you get laid.

Dev x

ANDREA POWELL

Dear Derek,

How are you? Don't answer that – I know you're angry. Of course you are. And why wouldn't you be? You were just so wonderful and I ruined it all with those fateful words: I want you to leave.

I'm sorry our beautiful affair ended that way, because it started so well. When you suggested moving in with me instead of paying for a hotel, I thought, Great! I could do with some regular sex.

Oh, Derek, it's not your fault it got a bit expensive for me having you stay. I think I mentioned once or twice that I was a little short of money but perhaps you misheard me. Perhaps you thought I said, 'Let me pay for everything!' It's my fault, really. I just wasn't earning much money at the time. I'm sorry.

You know, I've always admired a healthy appetite. And the way you inhaled meals and chugged down bottles of wine was nothing short of astonishing! But do you know what really impressed me? That magic trick you pulled whenever a bill arrived. That was some vanishing act! Poof! You were gone! Step off, David Copperfield! Bravo, Derek!

Look, I understand why you didn't want to spend any of your *own* money. It's such a bore having to pull out a wallet and then search for the right note. And God knows our Australian dollars must have looked pretty funny to you. You probably thought it was toy money. Did you? Is that what you thought? Is it?

169

Anyway, you showed me, of course, that day you suggested we take a picnic. How romantic! I thought. I've been all wrong about this guy. He just needed some time to come up with his own ideas. To not be bothered with my preconceived notions of how a woman should be treated in her own home.

'Let's make it special!' you yelled. 'Let's get some really fancy food!' You thrust a list of your preferred gourmet imprudence in my direction and ducked off to Bakers Delight. I spent a small fortune at the deli and you returned with a couple of yeasty rolls. 'Oh, let's just eat at home!' you yelled bafflingly, like an oscillating moron. 'It'll be more comfortable!' As if the ludicrous picnic had been my silly idea all along. At home you made yourself a pretty fancy sandwich and then took a nap on the couch.

Wow, I thought, wondering if I could return the olive tapenade and the cheeses, if not the gourmet gherkins and mustard, that is clever. That picnic idea was quite the ruse. He just wanted some fancy groceries and didn't want to have to fork out. I mean, hats off, Derek, that was ingenious! You know, it'd be like if I wished you *all the best* but secretly wanted you to fuck off and die. Can you imagine? Can you? Try to.

But of course it wasn't all romance with us, Derek. Remember our sparkling debates? I recall you made some very interesting points about women. Such as that we're all crazy, and that we've been ruining your life since the day you were born. That was a bitter pill to swallow. Here I was, I thought, welcoming you into my home, feeding you, giving you love, but all the while I was simply a hysteric, fucking with your head and just spoiling everything. Who the hell did I think I was? I know, Derek, sometimes women just don't think. Probably because we're too busy screeching and ruining men's lives.

And let's be honest, you weren't too fond of my friends. You were subtle about it, but I gathered from the way you sulked in a corner for hours and were silent all the way home that you weren't that keen on spending time with them. 'I just want to be with you, for fuck's sake!' you bellowed, in your sweet, caring way, which was not at all controlling or creepy.

So where did it all go wrong? I believe the turning point for me was the night we went to the cinema. You paid for my ticket, which put me on edge from the start. You blew the cobwebs off your nylon velcro wallet, and we saw *The Departed*. Do you remember? How we hated that film! It's funny, you know, I've seen *The Departed* since then and loved it. But not that night.

I can't help thinking it may have had something to do with what you'd said during dinner. You probably think it's silly, but I felt disturbed when you told me that at the age of sixteen you'd punched your mother in the face. In your defence, you added, at the time your mother had been pretty annoying. It's not like you just walked into a room and punched her for nothing, in an unprovoked way. Like a madman. She was a nag! And I think you should just stop beating yourself up about it. Like you did your mother's face.

But I think the actual moment that ended it for me was the day you started screaming in my face. I don't know what it was about your foaming, beetroot rage that made me ask you to leave. I guess we'll never know.

Then, as I drove you to the airport, to make sure you didn't miss that flight, you said those memorable words: 'Hey, listen! You've done a lot for me and, well, I've left you something back at the flat. Something for you, to say thanks – for everything. It's in the fridge.'

'Really? You have? What is it?'

But of course you wouldn't say. You just winked. Bless.

I couldn't wait to open that fridge. What will it be? I nervously mused. Will it be money? No, why would he put money in the fridge? Although, who knows? The guy's a crackpot, he thinks women are the root of all evil. He punched his mother in the face. It could be money. Oh, please let it be money!

But of course it was so much more interesting than money, Derek. Because what you'd left me were not one but two slices of salami, in a plastic container. My first thought was, Well, this is too much! It's just too generous! I'll have to send one of these slices back to him, even if it does go mouldy in transit and then makes him reel and violently retch when he opens it. I'll just have to! And I would have too, except that suddenly I got very tired and just threw them in the bin. I know, you're right, women are crazy!

Oh, well. I just wanted to say sorry for all the hurt and that I wish you well in your life. Really. I mean this from the bottom of my heart:

All the best.

Andrea
PS Sorry about the herpes.

To a little
white lie

DI MORRISSEY

Dearest Gabrielle,

I've been thinking about the question you asked me in your last missive, of how I got published overseas. Let me tell you, darling, it brought back a lot of memories, not least of which were the teeny white lies I told Dr Ferguson.

It was some years ago now. I'd had a few books published in Australia but was keen to be published overseas. Do you remember, it was when I was renting a wood cabin in Byron Bay? I lived there alone, with just my adorable schnauzer Sheila for company. It was a bucolic setting – acres of tropical garden complete with a pond with blue waterlillies, all accessed by a horrendously steep dirt drive plunging down from the road.

One morning I received a call from a Dr Ferguson, who'd been given my name by a mutual friend. He said that he was leaving his local practice and was going to be a Flying Doctor based in Longreach. However, before he could leave, he had a problem to solve, and that was: Hannah, Harriet, Betty, Bobsie, Goldie, Marilyn . . . Oh, it went on.

'Who?' I asked.

'My prize orpingtons, guinea fowl and cochins.'

'Chooks, you mean?'

He shuddered down the phone. 'They might be prize breeding fowls, but they are my *friends*.'

It transpired that Dr Ferguson couldn't take his beloved flock to Longreach, so he was asking, nay, begging me to adopt them. I was moved, and I agreed. He sounded so desperate.

The parting was not pretty. I loaded all twenty-four girls into the back of my station wagon along with their luggage – boxes, bales of straw, feeders. I drove very carefully with instructions from the doctor on how I was to care for and love them still ringing in my ears. He told me that he'd be checking in with me on a regular basis to make sure I was doing the right thing and that all was well with his girls.

I'd arranged for a friend to come and build a permanent chook pen but at the last minute he begged off because the surf was up. So I made a flimsy corral as best I could.

The following morning, I was able to report to the good doc that all was well. The night had passed peacefully and the cooing and clucking and book-book noises the hens were now making as they scratched around my cabin as I worked were quite delightful.

On the second night, they seemed less calm. Something seemed to be amiss, but I ignored it. The next morning, as I was enjoying breakfast on the deck, there were shrieks and cries and squawks and suddenly I saw a hysterical mass breakout as the girls all flew at my flimsy fence, trampling it under foot and claw as they stampeded from – *oh my God, a fox*!

I hurled my cup of tea ineffectually at the fox. The girls flew into the nearby trees as creaky old Sheila tottered below. The fox fled.

The girls stayed in the trees for two days before venturing down. I found it impossible to round them up by myself, so they hovered close to my cabin.

'Hi, Dr Ferguson, I'm so glad you rang. Yes, they're fiiiiine . . . Enjoying the country air and scenery,' I said. 'And they put themselves to bed very well.' I didn't mention that they did it in the trees on my five acres.

But the fox returned. And what a cunning and wily bitch she

176

was. She'd circle the trees at night, seeming to hypnotise the girls, until one fell off her perch. I awakened to a screech as one of Dr Ferguson's girls was carried away into the night bush.

Each night the fox returned and it was awful counting beaks at rollcall each morning. 'Betty, Hannah, Goldie . . . Oh no, Marilyn is missing . . .'

And then the red menace began lightning daylight raids. This couldn't go on!

I rang around. A local shopkeeper came with a gun and a silent whistle, which he told me only foxes could hear. He crouched down by the garden dam, poised to kill, but to no avail. It didn't work. I mean, hell, the whistle was silent!

I was advised to ring National Parks. And to my rescue came an officer called Sam.

'You need the dog cage,' he said. 'We'll send it over. It's a big bugger.'

The cage arrived – a large iron-crate affair with a hook at one end for bait and a rod connected to the door at the other end. The idea is that the animal goes in after food, pulls the bait off the hook and, whammo, the door of cage slams shut, locking it in!

Very exciting. So I baited the trap and waited.

Nothing.

I rang Sam.

'Ah, you need rotten meat, nice and smelly.'

Righto, off to the butcher. I cautiously asked him about, you know, 'off' meat. He had some! And he charged me for it!

Rebait the hook. Nothing. Night after night.

The fox came back, ignoring the cage, which is perhaps not surprising as she had trees full of tasty meals.

I rang Sam again. 'Ah, I forgot to tell you, you mustn't touch the meat, they can smell humans, y'know. Use anchovy oil. On your hands and skin. Rub it well in . . .'

Have you ever tried to get the stink of anchovy oil off your skin? Not easy. I noticed no one wanted to stand near me in the supermarket queue. But still the fox would not take the bait. So I rang Sam again.

'Ah, pity she didn't go for the meat. Sorry, Di, I didn't want to tell you this . . . But really the only way to catch the fox is to use *live* bait. You'll have to sacrifice one to save many . . .'

'No, no, I can't do that. They have names!' Oh dear, what to do? Then I suddenly thought, Wait a minute – just down the road is a chicken farm and abattoir. I rang up and tried to explain my dilemma. I asked if someone could call me any evening when they had a chook that, you know, dropped off its perch, so I could race around really quickly and get it.

A nice chap actually said that he'd deliver it personally. 'Keep it warm,' I told him.

Now, at this moment my publisher rang from Sydney to tell me that the head of the UK publishing house was coming out and that they could arrange for me to have five minutes with him to try to persuade him to publish my books in England. Wonderful. I booked myself on the 7 a.m. flight to Sydney.

The night before this very important meeting, the nice man from the chicken farm rang me and said, 'One just carked it. I'll be there in a minute.'

So together we baited the trap with the still-warm chicken corpse. Thank goodness, I thought, there'll be no more little white lies to Dr Ferguson telling him how well his girls had settled in!

Very, very early the next morning, I tiptoed down to the trap in my Victorian lace antique nightgown to inspect the thieving, chicken-killing fox.

Ah, but the fox had ignored my bait! The trap was empty. I was so sure the still-warm but dead chicken was going to work. Maybe the bitch had been out hunting somewhere else and she'd be back tonight. I knew just what to do. I was flying back that night so I could rebait the trap. I'd get the chicken, wrap it in newspaper and keep it in the fridge – you know, keep it fresh – and then warm it up in the microwave and reset the trap.

Rather pleased with this plan, I only had to retrieve the dead chook. This meant crawling inside the cage and yanking it off the hook. Which I did, still wearing my antique Victorian nightgown. I pulled the chook off the hook. And bang, the door shut on my heels.

So now I was on my hands and knees in a metal cage, unable to turn around or move, face to beak with a glassy-eyed dead chook.

I told myself that I shouldn't panic. To just think about my situation. I am locked in a cage, alone, on five empty acres. I have told everyone that I will be flying to Sydney, so no one will call. Moreover, I will miss my flight and my meeting and I will never get published in England. And now it's starting to rain.

Now it *is* time to panic.

I started shouting.

But there was no one out there . . .

Time passed.

And then . . . I heard an engine at the top of my drive. It was the newspaper being delivered. Now, normally it was thrown from the roadway, as no one ever wanted to tackle my driveway. Oh no . . . But wait – someone's coming down – it's a new kid and since it's raining he has decided to drive all the way down and toss the paper onto the verandah. Glory be!

Halfway down the drive he spotted me in the dog cage on the front grass by the pond. Eyes popping, he rolled down the window. 'Are you researching one of your books, Ms Morrissey?'

'*No, I am not! I'm stuck. Get me out of here!*'

After helping me out, he couldn't wait to get back to town to share the news about the eccentric Ms Morrissey in a dog cage in her nightdress. I didn't care. I had seven minutes to dress and get to Ballina airport.

I didn't start to put on my makeup until I was on the plane. The hostess slipped me a glass of champagne. 'You look a bit frazzled.'

'Don't ask.'

I swept into my publisher's office and was ushered into the meeting with the English publisher who immediately asked me, in plummy tones, 'Exactly why should we publish you in the UK?'

I'd had enough. I stood up.

'Forget the books! Because I'm not going to lie! I've had a fucking awful morning locked in a cage with a dead chook, so the bloody least you can do is say yes. I deserve it!

He recoiled slightly – maybe it was the faint whiff of anchovy oil – but then he said, 'Oh, righto then. Jolly good. Let's do it, shall we?'

Thank you.

And that is how I got published in England.

Luv,
Mum

Di Morrissey

PS The fox never came back. The remaining girls lived to a ripe old age and I never had to lie to Dr Ferguson again.

ALICE PUNG

Dear Jaa'ni,

Thank you for your message. *Sua s'dei* and *Gam An* to you too.

I joined matchmaker.com because I would like to meet someone special and start a family. And this is the only site that has strong filters.

I noticed that you put down that you are Buddhist.

I wish I could enclose a photo of me on my knees praying to the Blessed Virgin in St Patrick's Cathedral, but unfortunately they don't allow cameras in church.

Much *metta* to you too, and I look forward to hearing from you,
Carnation

Dear Jaa'ni,

It is a good question but my parents did not name me Carnation after their favourite flower. They found the name on a tin of sweetened condensed milk.

May I call you Johnny? I am afraid I don't know how to pronounce your name.

No, my dad was not Vietcong, but I am glad the movies of Oliver Stone moved you in their showing of 'the stoicism of the other

181

side'. If you think that *Heaven and Earth* and *Platoon* gave an accurate depiction of life under American imperialism, I will watch them too.

And I am glad the portrayal of cross-cultural relationships between the GIs and the Vietnamese women warmed your heart.

No, my parents did not name my brother Charlie. His name is Anthony, after the patron saint of lost things. Oh, you were kidding. How funny. I am glad you have a sense of humour.

God bless,
Carnation

———

Dear Jaa'ni,

I am so sorry. How culturally insensitive of me to not realise that your parents in Daylesford named you Jaa'ni after the fourth level of Buddhist enlightenment.

Thank you for your two-page letter detailing your Buddhist epiphany in India. I am glad you resisted the temptation of Mara and her seventy nude dancing ladies while you were sitting under the tree. I am sure it was a Bodhi tree too.

How terrible that the villagers cut it down for firewood for the funeral pyre of their village elder. You are right. They have no respect for the environment or for their own sacred traditions. Lucky you got your epiphany before they cut your tree down.

Respect and God bless,
Carnation

———

Dear Jaa'ni,

Yes, I agree. This cross-cultural exchange is both fascinating and enlightening.

I have also changed some of my former bad habits. I now drink lattes instead of Nescafé from $5.99 tins. And if my mum sews me any new dresses, I will refuse to wear them because her garage is not Fair Trade-approved.

You have opened my eyes to the world.

God bless,
Carnation

———

Dear Jaa'ni,

Thank you for your recent photographs. Yes, I do love your shirt. I do not understand it but I am sure it is both ironic and meaningful.

And yes, I am also sure we would make plenty of attractive Eurasian-sensation love children if we ever met up.

But I am Christian and I hope you will respect my faith. And I would be happy if you sent me a promise ring.

Sincerely and God bless,
Carnation

———

Dear Jaa'ni,

Could you please tell me the place where you get your blow jobs? How and why do you get them for free?

My last blow job cost me $30 and it was not even a permanent wave. Just fifteen minutes under a Breville hairdryer. I could have done it myself at home. I will never go to Yvonne the back-garage hairdresser again.

Slightly annoyed,
Carnation

PS Please send that promise ring.

———

Dear Jaa'ni,

I am sorry about your insomnia but grateful for the long emails.

I don't do hand jobs either. But my friend Linh does.

Her place is called Happy Feet and Hands in Sunshine Plaza. It has a picture of a penguin out the front. It is named after the movie *Happy Feet*. The penguin is standing next to a sun, for sunshine. Is that the best use of irony and wit, or what? Haha.

But there is something you must explain to me, Jaa'ni, if you feel this is not too obtrusive a question. I don't understand why a man wants to get his nails done.

Or how this would help you get to sleep at night.

Sincerely,
Carnation

———

Dear Jaa'ni,

Nice of you to write that I must have soft skin because all Asian women have softer skin.

But how do you know?

Maybe you have a little Oriental petting zoo out the back of your house.

Carnation

———

Dear Jaa'ni,

Yes. The silence meant I was offended.

But because you apologised for not exercising mindfulness when you wrote, and assured me that you are not 'harbouring any menagerie of multicultural delights in a secret downstairs basement', I will forgive you.

I look forward to meeting you someday soon, too. But you still haven't sent the ring.

Sincerely,
Carnation

———

Dear Jaa'ni,

I'm sorry to have to break this news to you. I can't meet up on Sunday. My father has put me under house arrest because he discovered my online activities. And my folks recently found out that my first cousin Lam finished his degree at Melbourne Business School. So they've arranged a yum cha date for us then.

I am also afraid that the more I write to you the more I will fall in love with your *complex and sensitive and sacred personality*, so I can't continue this. I hope you understand.

It was nice to get to know you.

Much *metta* and loving kindness, and God bless you,
Carnation

Alice Pung

HANNIE RAYSON

Dear Nell,

Thank you for offering to have Christmas at your house. As always.

Everyone loves coming to Brighton. But Mum thinks it's time someone else did it. When you ring her tomorrow to check, she will say she doesn't mind, but really she thinks it's unfair that you always get lumbered with it. Especially since you are so busy with your Pilates and yoga. And even though you've got the nicest house – particularly now you've got the whole French provincial thing happening, and the lovely new breakfast nook – I agree with Mum. It's time that the rest of us, up here north of the river, stopped being such freeloaders.

The good news is that Molly's new kitchen will be ready and I'm sure she'd love to have the family Christmas in Coburg. Now, I know that means a big schlep for your lot. And I realise that Russell won't be happy because it will mean he can't drink. But the trade-off is that you won't need to do all the cooking or clean your house, although you do have that lovely Timorese woman to help. Does she still give you ghastly Christmas presents that you have to give away to the Brotherhood of St Laurence?

Of course, I'd be happy to have it here in Fitzroy, but I know your Russell would be reluctant after we had Mum's birthday and some smackhead scratched the Lexus. And anyway, ever since that *Four Corners* episode, I'm off meat, and no one wants a vegetarian

Christmas. Madeleine said that after seeing five minutes of that program, she couldn't put red meat in her mouth ever again, but I'm not sure of her position on turkey. The children won't eat tofu, of course, and Daniel won't eat anything.

I'll get Mum to buy the turkey, and I wonder if you'd ask Bonnie to bring the ham. But do make sure she doesn't buy it at Coles. She'll need to order it from Jonathan's in Collingwood. It's about time she put her hand in her pocket, and she'll listen to you. I'll do the vegetables.

I've told Martin that climate change is off the agenda this Christmas. No one wants a repeat of last year, of course. He really didn't mean to upset you when he said that the trouble with Middle Brighton is that it's protected from the rest of the world by other *types* of Brighton.

Mum thought Russell's views might have mellowed a bit, but then she said he had bought tickets to see Lord Monckton. Is that true? You know he's not really a Lord, don't you? The Queen has asked him to desist, which you have to admit does discredit him. But let's not get into another climate change argument. Did Bonnie ever replace that plate she smashed last year? She said she would.

I know that Russell doesn't really like these big family occasions. So if he decided to go to his sister's, we would all understand. We'd be sad, of course. We *can* all separate the person from his political views – despite our disagreements about the carbon tax, mining and private schools. As I said to Mum, I can see how happy he makes you, or at least how much happier you are than you would be if you were on your own, for example. And, as Bonnie pointed out, if you didn't have Russell you'd have to work and take the boys out of Brighton Grammar. No one wants that.

However, if Russell does decide to come, you do need to reassure Bonnie that Russell is perfectly fine about her *sexual orientation*. I remember you told me once that his mother had a fling with another woman in those wild Harold Holt days at Portsea. Is that a secret? If it is, I haven't told anyone. I just told Bonnie that the ruling class permit all sorts of debauchery among themselves.

On to the matter of presents. As you know, I am always happy to shower your children with gifts. I love watching them rip off the paper and throw my offerings aside so they can grab the next ones. But we need to discuss the adults' Kris Kringle. The year before last, I drew Madeleine and I bought her a set of Sheridan queen-sized sheets, four pillowcases and a valance. In return, my Kris Kringle gift was a tea towel. Then last year I drew Bonnie's name and I bought her a leather briefcase. My Kris Kringle present on that occasion was a copy of Burt Reynold's autobiography.

But since you organise the Kris Kringle, I was thinking that this year *you* might like to draw my name out of the hat. Since I've saved you the expense of putting on the lunch, which I'm sure must cost you at least $800, if you want a little gift idea, I'd like an iPad. I've priced them online and you could pick up one for about $540. That would make you roughly $250 up on last year.

So, if you're happy, we'll have Christmas lunch at Molly's. Do you think you could pick Mum up on the way? Of course, if Russell decides to come, that would mean you taking two cars. That's a drag, isn't it? I'll leave you to sort that out.

Hope this finds you fit and relaxed. Love to Russell, Tarquin, Chloe and Sebastian.

Your ever-loving sister,
Alison

Hannie Rayson

To the song I wish I'd written

KAV TEMPERLEY

Dear 'Umbrella',

The other day while waiting in line at the local supermarket, I glanced over at the magazine rack and quickly read the headline of some gossip mag: 'Rihanna spends $20 000 a week on her hair'.

I don't know why but it made me feel a little sad, and possibly a little jealous. I was concerned that since you'd 'ella-ay-ayed' your way to the top, creating the global megastar that is Rihanna, people may have forgotten what made them sing along in the first place. Blinded by the volume and cost of her hair, have they forgotten what a dark and mysterious world you created under your umba-rella?

Having just made the move to coiffing my own hair, I sympathise with the time and effort it can take to achieve the perfect 'do. But in my world, it only takes a $5 can of hairspray, a brush and a semi-decent hair dryer to create some pretty impressive results.

I came to you late. You had already been buffeted about on the winds of success before you came to rest in my ears. I remember sitting in a bar in South Korea while an acoustic rendition of you pushed its way through the crowd of foreign accents. I was struck by the dark, futuristic lyrics of your verse, describing a modern world of shiny cars and world wars, and then a chorus that lifted me up to tell me I would be sheltered if I just stood under your umbrella. By the minor shift at the end of the chorus, I was yours.

I was already imagining getting back home and finding the lyrics and chords on the net and working out how to play you over and over again. I was in love – but, like they say, 'Love is the ultimate outlaw, it won't adhere to any rules.' You were not a song born of late-night singalongs. You were a song born of beats and grooves and shiny flashing lights.

When I got home, I went to visit my brother, who worked at Billy Hyde Music, and asked him if he could sell me a drum machine of some description. He showed me a few until I finally saw what I was looking for. It was black with many buttons and, yes, flashing lights. He assured me it had all the latest, phattest beats. I didn't care – I'd found what I was looking for and I was ready for phase two.

I took it home and out of its box and switched it on. It lit up like a control panel from the Death Star, and after pressing this and that and scrolling through a thousand different menus, I realised I had no idea how it worked.

I spent the next few hours reading the instructions, and finally, when my will was almost broken, I managed to create some kind of beat. It sounded all right, so I put it through a delay pedal, then I put it through a distortion pedal, then I thought, What the hell am I doing? I just want to play you on an acoustic guitar with a beat behind it. So I picked up the ole guitar and started to strum along. It was all taking shape.

When I went to learn your words, I found I knew most of them already. Apparently you'd been playing in the background of my life for quite a while and I'd never even noticed. As I'd glanced at a thousand supermarket gossip mags, you were probably there 'ella-aying' around in my subconscious.

That weekend I played a solo show down at a little cafe in Fremantle where I live, and I played you on an acoustic guitar with my new drum machine keeping pace. Everyone sang along when I got to the chorus and they realised what song I was singing. By that stage they were all caught in your grasp too.

And it didn't matter that my hairstyle only cost me five bucks with a brush and a semi-decent hair dryer. My hair did nothing – you stood up on your own. All I could do was sign on as your accomplice.

KEVIN MITCHELL

Dear 'Not Fair',

I'm not sure I know exactly where to start. It's been a long time since I've written a letter of this nature, and I know that what I am going to write will hurt, although I suspect it will hurt me much more than you. Still, I have reached the painful conclusion that our relationship must come to an end.

For the last three years, I have been trying to figure out exactly what it is we have and where it is going. I think maybe at first my feelings for you were so strong that they blinded me to the fact that whatever we have together is ultimately doomed. I've only now begun to come to this realisation and I feel like I must mark an official stop to our affair so as not to string either of us along any further. I know that I need to move past you, as difficult as that is going to be.

I have to stop relying on you every time I need a bit of a helping hand. I can't go on just making what are, essentially, booty calls, because the undeniable truth is that you belong to somebody else and you will never be mine, no matter how many times people see us together in public, up on stage, performing.

You know, when I think back to how we first met, I realise that I should have known then and there that the relationship was doomed. I must admit, the first time I met you I wasn't even immediately taken with your beauty. In fact, if I'm going to be completely honest with you, I actually thought your older sisters were much hotter. But you, 'Not Fair' – you contained something that I thought I could use to my advantage, and that's what is killing me so much right now. From the moment you first fell into my arms, the lies began. My name isn't even really Bob – it's Kevin. Bob Evans is just a stupid name I perform under!

From the very first time we were together, I was using you for your wit and your charm and your lyrical qualities, all of which I know I don't really possess myself. You responded to my overtures so readily and easily, and to this day I doubt Lily Allen has ever known about us. Some might say that made you a bit of a cheap floozy, but it's me that is the cheap and desperate one. That first time we were together, you got me out of a real pickle when I had to perform a cover on triple j's *Like a Version*. We worked together, and not everyone approved. For every person who loved our match up, there was another who hated it! Many were made to feel so uncomfortable by our consummation that they felt compelled to cover a YouTube comment wall with nasty homophobic content directed at me. But that didn't bother me at all. In fact, it turned me on all the more! You see, they just didn't *get it*. Some people said I should have changed you, because it weirded them out hearing me sing your words. They didn't realise that you were beautiful just the way you were. To them, our relationship was wrong and taboo, but knowing that just made me want to have you again!

That's why I took you on the road with me. Sure, I enjoyed your company, but what I was really doing was using you, like a desperate travelling salesman selling someone else's art. When people started asking for you, I shamelessly hauled you out on stage, night after night, having my dirty way with you for the cheap satisfaction of a paying crowd.

I realise now that I'd fallen in love with you so much that I was blind to the reality of what was going on. Our relationship was not based on anything mutual. In the last three years, we must have been together more than fifty times. And while I was busy climaxing each and every time, I never once stopped to think about what you were getting out of it. It shames me to realise that I have been a selfish lover, more interested in how good you could make me look in front of others – taking your humour and using it as my own for the entertainment of a crowd.

So you see, 'Not Fair', it's time we put a stop to this charade. My feelings for you are still strong and they always will be. I'm not even sure how I'll cope without you. None of my songs are very funny. But in order for me to salvage some pride and self-respect, I've decided that I won't call on you anymore. If people ask, I'll just say we're no longer seeing each other.

Next time I'm playing a show and I need something funny to play – well, maybe I'll learn some jokes or something. I don't know, but that's not your problem. You'll be fine, I know. You have millions of fans. And you and Lily were meant to be. As for us, I guess we were just a bit of fun. If you have it in your heart to think of me, remember all the good times we had. I know I will. In fact, I wouldn't be opposed to one last crack, if you're up for it? I promise that everything I've written in this letter still applies. We are through! But maybe we could get it on one more time, for old times' sake, as they say. What do you reckon?

Kevin Mitchell.

HAYLEY MARY

To 'The Power of Love', written and performed by Jennifer Rush,

It was 1986. Hairspray and capitalism were A-okay, and, in Australia, where I was to be born the following year, you were number one. A more successful single by a female singer had never been seen in the United Kingdom. You were, as they say, the top of the pops. But the higher the climb, the longer the drop. People laugh at you now. They laugh at the concept after which you were named: they laugh at the power of love.

'Power of Love' (I'll call you POL for short), I'm not sure what it is that makes me wish I had written you. You're the epitome of crappy-ness, in many ways. You tell the most simplistic and false story of love. You're a liar, POL. So why do I love you and wish I had written you? Well, it comes from a desire to be naive enough to believe in you, or a desire to live in a world in which you were something worth believing in, neither of which is possible. I used to wish I could un-know the knowledge that makes you so hard to relate to these days. Then I could say something as simple as you say. But I am a complex, third-wave individual, in a world that is post-feminist, post-individual and post-post. Even the word post is a cliché. So what of 'The Power of Love'?

That's why it's so strange to write this letter. We've been dealing with words for so long, and if you say something too many times it loses meaning; it becomes absurd. Bottle, bottle, bottle, bottle . . .

Love, love, power of love. We avoid the arrow and throw it back at the dove. For the heart of today feels mirages of pain, and the ear of today waxes and wanes. It is sick of the sound of simplicity. Power of love? What a ridiculous idea. I've heard it so many times, I can't even hear it any more. Have sonnets killed the power of love? Has Hollywood? Has song? For you were a perfect concept, but became tainted when articulated, tainted when touched. Ruined, like any innocence touched too much. You grew up to be like a creepy paedophile, POL. Sung by Celine Dion, in Vegas, now.

I have a few bones to pick with you. I used to see you as the lighthouse, but I waded through an ocean of waves, and, struth! Every time one hits, it breaks down a truth. To start, POL. I am not a lady, and he is not a man. And, no, I do not do all that I can. Whenever he reaches for me, I think of my career, of how little time we have, and curl up in tears. When the man reaches for some of us, we torture his soul, strap up his balls, and smite him with coals.

I wish it was simple, but I am glad that it's not, for the sake of all the love that exists outside of your 'man' and your 'lady', POL. For everyone whose love has fallen prey to this simplicity, been thought of as loose, debauched, subversive, sick – even though it was often less sick than the idea that one man and one woman should own each other. I suppose it is this – your opposition to individual freedom – that makes you sort of appealing, though, in a world where one can become nauseated with one's own liberty.

POL, if things were as you say, I would speak to you in cliché. I would tell you that you're more beautiful than the world, and that I wouldn't give you up for all of it. I would tell you that I wouldn't change you for it – but I would.

Because perhaps I am *your* lady, POL, and you are *my* man. And I don't quite believe you, and I want to break you down. And I wish I had written you, because, in fact, you wrote me. You and all the others like you, throughout the ages. Sonnets of possession, idealisation and obsession not only shaped my understanding of love into something unsustainable and selfish, but trapped me with my brother, man. I thought he was drowning me. And, it turns out, he felt the same.

For the sake of harmony, I want to be free of you and I want to forgive you. But I don't want to forget you, because, like everyone, POL, I think part of what you say is true. We are heading somewhere we've never been, and, though it is frightening, I *am* willing to learn about the power of love.

Sincerely,
Hayley Mary

JOHNNY MACKAY

Dear Song,

I'm not sure this is the best way to get in touch with you. In fact, I'm not even certain that songs can read. It feels a little weird putting my feelings towards you down in this way, but I checked Facebook and there was no way to message you. Not even to poke you. I was, however, heartened by the fact that 31 470 people like you.

Anyway, I recently had an experience that has compelled me to communicate.

You see, song, I wish I'd written you, and here's why . . .

It was just this past June in Mexico City. Friends had convinced me to go to the wrestling and I was sitting there with an enormous bucket of beer, trying my best to join in the chanting of a rowdy group of Venezuelans I'd met that day. 'Rudos, Rudos, Rudos, Rudos!' we sang. Chanting for the bad guys.

Bout after bout, muscular masked men would gallop out under a hail of fireworks, through a pompom-armed salute of bikini-clad cheerleaders, ready to grapple with each other for glory.

At one corner of the ring, there was a midget dressed as a turquoise monkey named Che Monito, who the larger wrestlers would occasionally hurl at each other like a writhing little plush-toy projectile.

Anyway, each wrestler would charge out to a theme song. All the greats were there – 'Welcome to the Jungle', 'YMCA', 'This is How We Do It' by Montell Jordan. And then there was you.

Well, you and the large wrestler waltzing down the aisle like a gay truck driver in an invisible wedding dress.

I was told this fellow bouncing down the runway had been unmasked years ago in an infamous grudge match and now went maskless, as is the tradition. He had to be at least in his late forties. Big moustache, bigger gut, and a glint in his eye that gave you the feeling you'd be risking more than your sombrero if you got caught between him and his breakfast burrito.

I was told his name but had no luck pronouncing it, so I simply called him 'El Presidente', on account of his reminding me of some nameless South American dictator existing in the back of my ignorant mind.

I'm certain, though, that it was you, dear Song, who spurred him on to take control of one of the greatest demonstrations of guts, glory and man boobs I've ever witnessed.

'*El Presidente!*' I shouted at the top of my lungs, as he hurled Che Monito like no other had before him. And if he didn't knock his opponent down with the little blue hirsute dwarf, he'd simply thrust his giant belly (which would put Octomom to shame) in their faces, and they'd be left with a mouthful of sweaty bellybutton lint and the shame of being subjugated by El Presidente.

While I was witnessing this spectacle of grinding flesh, sweat and back hair, you continued to run through my head. Your rumbling intro, that unforgettable riff, the almost emasculating high-pitched vocal. You were driving El Presidente. I could see your name written across his face.

I thought to myself, That's the kind of song I want to be writing. A song that makes grown men prance about in a bouncy, roped-off square, wearing strange masks and drinking each other's perspiration, while thousands of crazy Mexicans cheer them on. I want to write that song. I want to write *you*. And for some reason I just had to put all that down in a letter.

Like, I'm not some weirdo who wants to meet up and hang out or anything. But in case you decide you want to drop in sometime, I've enclosed a small map showing where we keep the spare key and the side of the bed I generally prefer.

In any case, I'll never forget you, 'Eye of the Tiger'.

Thanks.

Love,

Johnny

Johnny Mackay

JAE LAFFER

'Where to, mate?' asked the cab driver, as I opened the door and got into the back seat, which was still warm from the passenger before me.

'Highgate Hill,' I told him.

'Funny, I just came from there, just now,' said the driver. 'Muso, are ya?'

'Yes,' I replied, as we pulled away from the Tivoli Theatre.

'The fellow that I just dropped off was, too,' said the driver. 'Local boy, nice guy. Name's Grant – you heard of the Go-Betweens?'

'Of course,' I said.

Wow. Wonder if he was at our gig? I thought, although I doubted it for some reason. Having an eternally romanticised picture of Grant McLennan in my head, I thought he had probably been writing another classic song on the side of a mangrove swamp somewhere . . .

Grant McLennan – the great thinker, the ultra-romantic of the Go-Betweens. I forget you're from Brisbane. Of course you live here, but you've been all over. England, Europe – all those achievements, however small, amount to a true success in my eyes, even if they don't in your own eyes. At least, that's how it comes across in the papers sometimes. They never sold a lot, people say, never fully appreciated in their own country. But it's funny, Grant – we've been talking about you and your band in my group for years, regularly. You're one of the handful of homegrown artistic benchmarks we look up to.

I bought your record *16 Lovers Lane* when I was about seventeen.

I hadn't even heard a Go-Betweens song before, I'd just heard whispers of your reputation, and I wanted in. I was hungry for new music and yours had a sticker on it that said 'classic Australian album'. Wow – who gets such a privileged introduction in a record store, Grant? That little sticker sums up my life goal!

Of course, from then on I had the great pleasure of discovering gem after gem of songs penned by you and your songwriting partner, Robert.

It's the small things in the songs, the atmosphere of them. You paint a picture of a scene, a conversation, something that resonates strongly, even if you don't know why. And when you get it right, they're always the songs that people quote when they stop you in the street. That's what I'm trying to do in my songs, and sometimes I think I get close. I'm still trying – they're elusive ideas – but they hit home when the feeling is just right. What is it about that line about your father's watch that you left in the shower that resonates like it does? Your songs made me think that maybe I wasn't from such a plain little existence in the hills of Perth after all – maybe being the kid who spent his time walking around in the bush dreaming of the wider world and making up songs was someone. Maybe that talent was special, something I could use.

I saw Robert in a bookstore in Carlton, signing copies of his new book and singing a couple of songs. I managed to get a moment with him. 'Good luck with the new recordings!' he said. 'I'm sure it'll be great.' His enthusiasm is always boundless.

But he might not have said it so flippantly if he'd known what a high standard you and he had set for the rest of us!

Not too long ago, I was leaving another gig when a young man stopped me out the front of the club. 'Great gig,' he said. 'New stuff's classic!'

Classic, I thought. Perhaps I'm still working my way towards that one.

'Thanks a lot,' I said.

He seemed genuinely happy to have my time, so we chatted for a couple of minutes while I waited for a cab. 'What have you been listening to?' he asked.

'Oh, all kinds of stuff,' I replied.

'What's your favourite song?'

'Got lots,' I said. 'I love Australian stuff.'

'What's the best, do you reckon?' he continued.

'Well, I'm not sure,' I told him, 'but I know a good place to start.'

And so I told him: 'If you haven't already, you have to hear a song by the Go-Betweens, called "Cattle and Cane".'

To the woman who changed my life

JULIAN BURNSIDE

Dear Jenny,

How I enjoyed having dinner with you. It reminded me of things I had forgotten. You are a bit younger than my mother, but you are part of the same generation, or near enough.

When you were in your teens, the Great Depression was crushing countless Australian families. At least a third of the population was directly affected. Many thousands of families were wiped out. Homelessness and the susso were a reality for a lot of people back then.

That might explain why people of your generation naturally notice someone who is worse off than they are, and why they offer a helping hand. Mum used to say, 'Fellow feeling makes us wondrous kind.' It was a sentiment you knew well. When you were growing up, you knew plenty of people whose lives had been blighted by the Great War. Later, you knew plenty of people whose lives were taken, or deformed, by the Second World War. Your generation witnessed the Holocaust.

So I guess it was natural that you looked for ways to help people who were trying to escape their own hell in Afghanistan or Iran or Iraq.

You were appalled that an Australian Government could revive its electoral prospects by holding off the Tampa at gunpoint. You were shocked by the idea that a small handful of refugees would be pushed off to Nauru, to languish in misery and despair as Australian politicians used them as pawns in a big, expensive political game.

How many letters did you write, I wonder? Not to the press – but to refugees on Nauru. One day each week you got together with your daughter and wrote letters to people you had never met, and they replied. Over the course of a few years, you built genuine friendships with refugees about whom you knew nothing except what they had confided in their letters to you.

And you gave them a sense of hope because, with each letter you sent, you let them know that not all Australians agreed with our harsh Government policies; that not all Australians shared the toxic views of the talkback reptiles, spreading terror but not pity. By writing to refugees on Nauru, you gave them hope. And when eventually they were brought into Australia to settle here – just as you had hoped and predicted – they embraced you as a mother.

Sixty years ago, my mother was a young woman driven by the same spirit. But back then Australia was receiving refugees cheerfully enough and they weren't really causing any trouble. Although come to think of it, back then people used to say the Greeks and Italians were too religious, and had too many kids, and didn't learn the language, and their women dressed strangely, and they didn't mix in enough. Still, it turns out that weird food like calamari, and spaghetti that hadn't come from a tin, made a welcome change from lamb and three veg, and most people reckon the reffos who came after the Second World War were pretty good for Australia.

Back then, Mum volunteered at International House and the Red Cross and the Institute for the Blind. The point was, there were people who needed help, so you helped them if you could. It was that simple, for your generation.

It is different now. I am not sure why. Maybe people are too busy now; maybe it is because your generation wanted us, the baby boomers, to have a life untainted by war and poverty and fear, and we all took it so seriously that we thought the world owed us something. For us, the focus was on our own welfare. We grew up the most spoiled generation in history.

I suspect that hardship taught your generation to care more about each other's problems than your own.

I remember when I first met you. Your daughter was about to leave Melbourne and move to Sydney. The two of you had spent years in Sydney when she was little. When I met you, she was getting over the trauma of having been stalked for eighteen months by some poor misfit who had seen her on TV and become obsessed with her. When the police eventually found him, it turned out that he lived alone in a rented room with nothing much except a mattress and some clothing and a computer and his obsessions.

Kate wanted to move to Sydney because she had been happy there. She must have been a challenging child, creative and headstrong. She had been expelled from school when she was fifteen for trying to organise a student representative council at her po-faced school. Although you would certainly miss her and she would miss you when she moved to Sydney, you supported the idea because you knew it would be good for her career and you knew the torment she was trying to escape.

It must have been incredibly hard for you, as a single parent, bringing up an only child in the 1960s. Not so many support services back then, when divorce was a dark, shameful secret and single-parent households were rare and unwelcome.

I still remember how shocked you were when your daughter announced that she had met some guy at an election party, the night Paul Keating lost to John Howard and Australia suddenly looked different. It seemed as though she might stay in Melbourne after all. Her career had already been on hold for a while because of past entanglements, and here it looked like her plans would be derailed again.

And worse than that, the person she had met was a silvertail – someone not likely to stick around for very long. You disapproved emphatically. You christened him 'Sir Valentine Dyall' – a casual reference to the sombre, forgotten British character actor from the 1940s and '50s.

———

I am grateful that, before too long, you saw that I was actually serious about Kate. When Kate and I married, I was acting for the MUA in the waterfront dispute against Patrick Stevedores. You were no fan of John Howard, so, by then at least, you thought that perhaps I had something to offer!

And then in 2001 the Tampa episode happened. Kate has always made things – jewellery, sculpture, drawings, paintings – pretty much anything creative. She makes art out of the most unpromising material. I didn't know it at the time, but you did: Kate decided she could make something of me. There I was, a conservative with a conscience who was being quietly remade as an activist, by your activist daughter.

They were pretty difficult years, after Tampa.

You and Kate spent countless hours writing to refugees, finding free accommodation for them, writing to newspapers and politicians – doing everything you could to bring this country back to its senses, to make it once again like the Australia you had known when you were Kate's age – generous, hospitable, concerned, selfless.

Meanwhile, I was making myself unpopular by criticising the wilful mistreatment of desperate human beings. Apparently I had become an 'outspoken critic' of the Howard government.

The consequences were surprising to me – I had never received death threats before this; I had never received hate mail before this. I used to have a lot of conservative friends, many of whom disappeared. The entire landscape of my life changed during those few mad, pressured, surreal years.

I couldn't have kept it up if Kate had not been so supportive, so encouraging, so convinced that here was something that had to be done if this country was to regain its soul.

And there you were during all of it – encouraging both of us, bemused as you watched Kate gently, persistently trying to reshape her country and her husband.

When you died in June this year, Kate was inconsolable. I never saw a mother and daughter so devoted to each other, so close.

You knew how good this country can be, at its best; you saw how badly it can behave when fear replaces hope, when decency is pushed aside.

Kate learnt all of this from you. You and Kate, between you, changed my life and made something worthwhile of it.

If my mother had lived to see this day, I know she would have approved.

ADAM ELLIOT

Dear Tracy Leahman,

Wherever you are on this grey Melbourne day, this letter is to let you know you changed my life, and I bet you haven't a clue.

I'll refresh your memory ... We were in grade four together at Pinewood Primary School in Mount Waverley, and I was *excruciatingly* in love with you. It was Easter, and just before we went into class for the morning, I hid an Easter egg in your little leather schoolbag hanging in the corridor outside our classroom. It had taken me many weeks to save up and buy you that egg, using my five cents-per-week pocket money, which I'd earned from picking up the dog poo in the backyard and burning Dad's old newspapers in the incinerator.

I bought the little chocolate egg before school from the Chinese man who owned the milk bar on the corner. His name was Ken and Mum said he had the breath of a thousand camels and hid coins up his bottom – but that's not important right now. I really liked Ken and told him the egg was for my *secret* girlfriend. He thought she was secret because we hadn't announced our love to the world; I said no, she was secret because she didn't know she was my girlfriend. Not yet, anyway.

Ken convinced me to buy one of his eggs covered in red foil, because in Chinese culture red is the colour of good luck. He also said red was the colour of the commie bastards who killed his brother.

I didn't know what a commie was back then; I thought they were people who collected comic books. Anyway, Ken gave my egg a special Chinese blessing before I handed over my pile of five cent coins.

I wrapped my precious cargo in my tartan hankie labelled with a little cloth nametag my mum had sewn on. Mum was always worried my brother and I would lose our hankies. I never lost mine, but my brother Luke was always losing his, so Mum sewed some string from the inside of his pocket to the end of his hankie. When the tough kids found out they flushed my brothers head in the toilets and wrote 'fuck knob' on his forehead with a big red texta. Mum said the tough kids were just jealous that they didn't have strings attached to their hankies – but that's not important right now.

Anyway, as you may remember, I also wrote a love note to accompany my love egg in your schoolbag. It was a simple note written in crayon on butcher's paper, which expressed my love and unceasing devotion to you. I remember every word I wrote on that note in my best handwriting. I even ruled up little faint lines so my words wouldn't be wonky. I chose purple crayon because I knew that was your favourite colour. You were always wearing purple corduroy skirts and that day you wet your pants in the library, I also sneaked a glimpse of your purple knickers covered in Smurfs.

As I said, I remember every word I wrote on that love note. This is how it went, in case you don't recall:

Dear Tracy Leahman,

I hope you like my red love egg. I think you have nice hair and I really like how you smell like toothpaste, not the boring white sort that smells like Grandma's mints, but the red and blue stripey sort that tastes like Hubba Bubba. Anyway, will you be my girlfriend? I know you like Smurfs, I like Smurfs too and have twenty-six. Maybe after school you could come to my house and play with my Smurfs. Anyway, I have run out of butcher's paper.

Lots of love,
Adam

PS Don't worry about always wetting your pants. My brother pooed in the bath the other night and he didn't even care. Dad hit him with a rolled up *National Geographic*.

Anyway, after I hid the love letter and the Easter egg in your school-bag, we went into class. Matthew Welch was making the other kids laugh by turning his eyelids inside out. You laughed the most. Even though I had seen Matthew's trick many times, I faked a big, loud laugh so you would notice and think I was cool. But you looked at me strangely and called me a spastic.

For the rest of class I became very nervous. I remember feeling like I had made a terrible mistake and was going to vomit. I started to wish I hadn't written the love note. I tried to find excuses to get out of class and retrieve my doltish gift from your bag. I told our teacher, Mrs Pendergast, I needed to go to the toilet. She said I was lying because whenever I told fibs my ears went red and that they were *redder than ever*. She made me sit down and continue my work, and said that if I did *really* need to go to the toilet, I should shut my eyes and pretend to tie my penis in a knot.

Before I could think of a new excuse to leave the classroom, the recess bell went and we all rushed out to play. I hoped you would race outside, but you didn't, you went *straight* to your schoolbag to get your playlunch: a packet of chicken Twisties and an orange Prima drink. You pulled out my red egg and started to read my note. Some of the other little girls noticed and gathered around like vultures. I stood nearby in the corner underneath the emergency fire alarm that I was secretly hoping would go off. But it didn't, and my worst nightmare became horrible, tangible, *real*.

You finished reading my note and burst out laughing. Not a happy, sweet, caring laugh, but an evil, sadistic, condescending laugh; the sort that strips self-esteem from a little boy's psyche; the sort of laugh so dark and cruel, its sound would cause a flower to burst into flames. You then showed my note to your heartless cohorts who read my sincere words and laughed even more cruelly. They held my little red egg up in the air and started to throw it around like a tennis ball. It landed on the ground and shattered into a red-foiled mess. My heart shattered as well and a little part of me died that very moment.

Mr Robinson, the art teacher, walked passed and skidded on my crumpled egg. It now looked like a giant skid mark on the white linoleum. To me it looked like a giant symbolic scar – a deep wound on my soul that has lasted until now.

Mr Robinson kept walking as you and your wicked friends suddenly spotted me hiding in the corner. The whole horrific event had caused me to wet my pants a little and a yellow blotch appeared on my cream-coloured slacks. You and your friends began to point and tease me as a crowd grew bigger and bigger. Your friends started one of those horrible chants: *Adam loves Tracy, Adam loves Tracy.*

I had to escape. I could feel tears begin to well in my eyes and felt like my whole body was leaking. I suddenly made a dash for it and ran aimlessly outside. The mob pursued me as I sprinted for the back of the oval under the industrial powerlines. There was a back gate I was hoping wasn't locked, so I could be lucky and escape and run for home. Alas, it was more locked than I could have imagined, with huge chunky chains and a rusty padlock with a red-back spider in the keyhole.

I was cornered and as I spun around with tears flooding down my cheeks onto my imitation Hang Ten t-shirt, I found the gang of chanting hooligans had grown enormously; the entire school had joined in. Back in the 1970s, there wasn't much to do at playtime, so such things as fights, random acts of vandalism, British bulldog or mob bullying were the unfortunate games of choice. Now I think of it, the word 'playground' seems a bit of a stretch. It was just a large, harsh, asphalted slab, similar to the grounds of a prison.

The only greenery was made up of a few large gum trees and, as the teasing mob approached, I decided to scramble up one. I was a good climber and knew I would be safe if I could get up the main trunk. A few months earlier, one of the grade sixes, a boy called Anthony Buttersworth, had climbed up the same tree, taken off his pants and tied a ribbon around his penis. He was eventually coaxed down and the principal dragged him away. We never saw him again and there were rumours he went into a mental institution. My dad said he was probably a fag and that an institution was the best place for him. My uncle agreed and said all homos should be chained together and dragged to the bottom of the sea – but that is not important right now.

I clambered as high as I could and clung to a flimsy branch that I was sure would eventually snap and drop me into the taunting clutches of the deriding mob below. I remember looking down, Tracy, and seeing you among them, laughing and pointing as well. I wondered then, and still do, if you meant it, or if you were just joining in due to peer-group pressure. Maybe you secretly *did* like me, but didn't have the courage to admit it, didn't have the gall to go against the crowd, to be an individual.

Anyway, as you may remember, the bell rang to announce the end of playtime, and the mob began to disperse. I eventually climbed down and went back into class, dishevelled and humiliated. Luckily, the attention spans of children are short, and everyone moved onto the next school-time amusement. Later that day, Matthew Welch turned his eyelids inside out one too many times and had to go to the hospital with a ruptured eyeball. The whole school watched as he was taken out to an ambulance with eyes so bloodshot he looked like the devil and made some of the prep kids cry. I spent the rest of the day trying to be as invisible as possible, but every now and then another kid would remember my gesture of love and taunt me briefly.

The next day, life for me at Pinewood Primary went back to normal and it was someone else's turn to be bullied. Still, I was never quite the same after that and became somewhat introverted. I spent a lot of time by myself, drawing and letting my creativity become a world where I could hide and be safe. I'm almost forty now and still remember that day so well. I often wonder where you are today, Tracy Leahman. I'd love to find you and catch up. I'd love to tell you I'm gay and that maybe you had something to do with it.

I believe sexuality is predetermined, like the colour of our eyes, but do sometimes wonder if that horrible, scarring day, when you rejected my little red egg, somehow pushed my psyche in a different direction. Your behaviour changed my life – but I now think for the better. That day made me stronger.

A few years ago, I saw a woman working at the checkout at Safeway who reminded me of you; maybe it *was* you. She had twisted blue varicose veins on the back of her legs and she had your beautiful green eyes but in a face that looked world-weary and tarnished. I hope it wasn't you. Despite your cruelty that day in 1979, I hope you are now happy and successful. I hope you have someone who loves you deeply, someone who writes you love notes and gives you Easter eggs, the ones covered in red foil, blessed by a Chinese man.

RONNIE SCOTT

Hi,

So when our hostesses first told me what our theme would be today, I actually just thought about straight-up lying. Because I knew straight away exactly who the woman was, and I also knew she'd be kind of a strange one to talk about. But, of course, I could not lie; I did not lie. And in the end I'm glad I didn't.

Because, dear Alanis Morissette,

It turns out I have so much to tell you.

You first influenced my life in small ways, mostly, as when my long-suffering father had to explain what it meant to go down on someone in a theatre. But when you released *Supposed Former Infatuation Junkie* on 3 November 1998, ten days before I turned thirteen, I was primed to move from the taste-based free-for-all of the pre-teen brain to hardcore teenaged super-fandom. I was going to love something, and the thing I chose was you. You continued to exert those influences. My half-arsed grasp of your vocabulary was the reason my team lost year-nine debating, when I argued that an asteroid striking the planet would lead to 'a very tumultuous time in our lives'. And baking you a cake for your twenty-fifth birthday, with your name in blue icing across the top, was how I learned I'm not a cake fan. Unwittingly, though, when I listened to *Junkie* and found it smart and thorny and totally beguiling, I was also letting you forever shape the way I think about music.

One working definition of music describes it as 'humanly generated sounds that are good to listen to, and that are so for themselves and not merely for the message they convey'. It sounds pretty obvious, but the more you think about it, the cleverer the definition is, since it excludes everything from poetry and speech to birdsong and the howling of the wind. With *Junkie*, then, it turned out you were setting yourself against the very definition of your medium. The friends of mine who called you 'Anus Morissette' were objecting to the idea that you were good to listen to. But even I could never have argued that your music was what it was 'merely for itself'. You were crafting sounds around great lists of lyrics; they were custom-made to house your thoughts on, for example, India. Worse, in that song, India was about as concrete as you were getting. In the main, you were just listing abstraction after abstraction: providence, clarity, consequence, frailty, silence – it went on.

You were also being bankrolled by Maverick Records, who were responsible for selling the red-hot mess you'd written. They even hired a company called Edison Media Research to help them with a sales strategy. 'Because of the nature of the business,' they reported, 'we knew Alanis had earned a "Free Pass" from radio and MTV – her first song would get massive airplay no matter what it was.' So they created sales projections for the album based on one hit single up through five. One of these was what they called a 'doomsday scenario' – no further hit singles after the first one. 'Sadly,' they said, 'we were dead on with this projection.'

Here's why *Junkie* didn't work, I think. It didn't work because it was self-helpy. It was authentic and personal, but in a really limited way – you weren't thinking too hard about pop or rock values, or listenership, or commercial savvy. Jamming these new songs onto FM radio was a bit like projecting your diary onto a billboard in Fed Square. Such an activity might have felt really good to you, Alanis, but it probably wasn't going to stay up there for very long. The emotional centre of the album was a song called 'That I Would Be Good'. You wrote the lyrics when you were hiding in a closet, while your house was full of friends, and you thought you needed some alone time. Oh, Alanis. (Incidentally, this is what your name means: in tribal Germany, when the black sheep of a family would run off and do something black-sheepish, the family would do a face-palm and say, 'Oh, Alanis.') Anyway, this was one of your listy songs: it suggested that you would be good, if you lost your hair and your youth; that you would be good, if you were no longer queen. And towards the end of the song, you got out the flute you learned to play in primary school – probably you found it in the back of that closet – and gave it a little tootle. Oh, Alanis.

The other day, I learned about this other possible way to explain why the album sank: something called centrality gradience, or the 'prototype effect'. I'll explain it really quick, because it's great, and because I just learned about it. Even though we definitely know what a bird is, some birds seem to be more like birds than others. Crows and sparrows seem more like birds than penguins or cassowaries. It's just about perceived averages: if you're a crow, you possess more bird-like features than a cassowary, and also fewer features that are crazy and extraneous. Thinking this way has heaps of benefits. It's just one of the ways our brains sort information so that we can think more quickly. And nowadays, you do fit right in the middle of a category: the lukewarm nuclear winter of adult contemporary radio. For the tenth anniversary of *Jagged Little Pill*, you recorded a defanged acoustic version and released it exclusively through Starbucks. But back then, you were uncomfortably distant from the centre of any category we could've drawn. You didn't belong in the stratosphere of alternative music, and you didn't belong on the Starbucks counter next to Jewel or The Corrs, at least not yet. Some of it was that you'd changed. Some of it was that we'd changed. Either way, you were the cassowary of all flocks.

Except mine. Even later, when I became a canvas satchel-carrying indie kid, it was all about you, Alanis, every time. I hid my Alanis Shrine, my detailed scrapbooks. I got a new email address that wasn't named after one of your songs. Even then – everything I listened to, everything new, was judged by how much *you* was in it. You were my sparrow, seagull, crow. Somehow or other, you're responsible for my mental centres of everything, from authenticity in music to the country of Cuba. Even this tiny thing! When you were twenty-two, you went on a trip to Cuba with Leonardo DiCaprio, and that's where you met Dash Mihok, your boyfriend at the time, who'd co-starred with Leo in Baz Luhrmann's *Romeo + Juliet*. To this day, when I picture Cuba, my first image is of Dash and Leo in their trash-bag costumes from that movie sitting around a cabana peeling fruit.

So you were my prototype for all music; my most musical musician. But, more than that, you were my prototype for life.

It was a source of humour for those who aren't fans of yours, Alanis, when you recently posed on the cover of *High Times* magazine calmly sniffing a marijuana leaf. You did this because you were dating a lobbyist for the legalisation of pot, and that is fine. We do these things. But you looked like a dickhead when you were profiled inside that magazine and you explained that pot smoking brings out your psychic powers.

The thing about you, though, is that you don't go in for coolness. You believe in the value of abstractions like 'providence' and 'clarity', and you expect listeners to think about these concepts.

In this way, you have something in common with the only other stranger who's so strongly configured me. You happened earlier, he happened later, but that stranger is David Foster Wallace.

Towards the end of his career, Wallace said this: 'In the day-to-day trenches of adult life, there is actually no such thing as atheism ... Everybody worships. The only choice we get is *what* to worship ... If you worship money and things . . . then you will never have enough . . . Worship your body and beauty and sexual allure and you will always feel ugly, and when time and age start showing, you will die a million deaths before they finally grieve you.'

He was speaking to a class of graduating college students; in the main, he was offering a warning. And I loved it when I heard it, but I also didn't need the warning. Because I was lucky. I got to worship *you*.

Let's go back quickly to that self-helpy list song, 'That I Would Be Good', the emotional centre of your album. It's not as eloquent, or funny, or outward-focused as Wallace. But the song acts as a kind of prayer that you might see behind the curtain of everyday worship. It's a request that you be happy without automatic worship – without money, popularity or cool. I mean, it's not a great song. It's essentially platitudinous, and you play the fucking flute towards the end. But what I always try to remember is that you wrote this song when you were *twenty-three*.

I, on the other hand, was not even thirteen when I first heard it – a pretty good age to have this song, and chew over what it could possibly mean. In fact, though, I never found a way to contextualise it until I read Wallace later on.

At first, I thought I was doing that thing where you conveniently assume a connection between all the things you like – the idea that since reality TV is fun, it must express intelligence as well. But then, last year, this journalist, David Lipsky, published a long account of a book tour he took with Wallace back in '96, when he was getting big, and you were getting big. Even so, I wasn't prepared for what I found.

But there it was. The journalist, when describing Wallace's apartment, mentioned 'the big poster of complaint singer Alanis Morissette on his wall'.

And that's it. That's all there is. Nowhere else in this 300-page book do either of them address this. I'll probably never know why it was there.

Meanwhile, when people are (reasonably) giggling about the thing in *High Times*, you're hanging out in California with your friends and fellow marijuana enthusiasts Alicia Silverstone and Woody Harrelson. You're laughing your arses off as you get stoned on a strain of marijuana that is – I am not joking – *grown from the ashes of Woody Harrelson's dad.*

[This is a thing! She talks about it in *High Times*.]

In other words? If part of the adult world involves picking one's battles, I believe you've picked some quite good ones to win.

Other than you, Alanis Morissette, I don't know what I worship. I don't think there's such a thing as heaven. But if there is one, I'm pretty sure it involves hanging out with you, because you're kind of a dickhead, and I'm kind of a dickhead, and we both know there are more important things. We'll spend the afterlife hanging out, probably sinking into a pair of disgusting beanbags. You'll play the flute badly, and make me read Alicia Silverstone's diet book, and we'll hang around mumbling boring platitudes to each other, like 'Whatever happens, happens, man', and 'The personal *is* the political', and 'What it all comes down to, my dear friends, is that I haven't really got it figured out just yet. But I've got one hand in my pocket, and the other one is giving a peace sign'.

Until then – thanks for everything, good luck with your baby, and take care.

HENRY WAGONS

I write to you without expecting you to break from your proud yet fragile poise for one moment. I would hate for you to budge a single inch to see me biting at your ankles with this little letter. After all, you are very busy. Busy holding the entire symbolic weight of a nation together. Your image has been on so many postcards leaving your home, heading out to foreign lands, but I think its high time we turn the tides of the waters that surround you, and send you a well-deserved postcard in return.

Dear Statue of Liberty,

Many people may find it strange that I am writing to you, given you are a colossal copper sculpture. But I've had no trouble emotionally connecting with massive inanimate objects ever since the Rockbiter in *The NeverEnding Story* came to life. Remember: 'They look like big good, strong hands.'

I'm writing to you because I want to tell you how fascinated, inspired, awed and entertained I am by you, even in your stillness. I am intrigued by the place you hold in your cultural home. I find you both supremely powerful and subversive. Wholeheartedly accepted and embraced, yet an alien, an outsider. You are an interloper that has slipped through a red, white and blue loophole. You were forged in France, French through and through, but today you are the beating heart of all-American freedom. You stand proud in the country that, inspired by French hate, changed the name of French Fries to Freedom Fries. I love that you're standing there. It's cheeky.

When many people are teenagers, they go on journeys of self-discovery. Many of us Australians go to the UK to get shit-faced and work in a bar; many to India for spiritual growth; and many go to sweat in temples somewhere in South East Asia. But I couldn't wait to go to the US of A. I could put it down to any number of things: watching Looney Tunes and Police Academy movies, listening to Kiss and Elvis, or reading Zane Grey Westerns, Bukowski and Hunter S. Thompson. I have always been fascinated by America. By the best and the worst of it. It seemed like a place where the good always comes with the bad. All the best and worst of Western civilisation, all at once. All in one big mouthful – in a big gulp of an Elvis bacon and peanut butter fried sandwich. In a bite of a pretzel M&M, or a bacon and maple syrup-flavoured donut. Or perhaps in a sip of a bacon-infused whisky cocktail? All so wrong, all so right.

Statue of Liberty, you left your mark on me unexpectedly at first, when I saw you in a rare moment of weakness. I was taken aback when I first looked into your eyes. I saw you during the 'Wild West' phase of my self-discovery US trip, during a week-long stay in Vegas. You got my attention at the New York-New York Casino in the thick of the Las Vegas Strip. You were perched on top of a slot machine, slowly rotating, in a Marilyn Monroe pose, with your dress being blown up. I couldn't stop looking. Standing on the casino floor, I didn't know what to make of you. I thought it was gross, and offensive, and yet one of the most awesome things I have ever seen. Should I feel sorry for you or should I giggle?

Unbeknownst to me, that contradictory feeling was one that I would have on many more occasions during subsequent visits to the States. I now realise this feeling is the thing I love the most. I thrive on it. It's my creative muse. It's as if I can only feel the utmost joy when there is also a tinge of evil to remind me to fully appreciate it. You represent all that and more for me, Statue of Liberty, you evil minx.

My dear Statue, I don't know what it is that makes me like this contradictory vein, both good and bad at once. Why can't I just love something fluffy and nice, or something unquestionably refined and beautiful, or skilfully intricate? Why must there also be a hint of the kitsch or the gauche, doses of liquid chocolate or saturated fat, always with touches of Mahoney or Venkmann in the mix? When it comes to most things, even in my professional life in mu sic, I love the artists that are wholeheartedly respected and appreciated but also have ample hints of gross. Fat Elvis is a prime example. What an amazing singer and entertainer. What a sweaty and amazing man.

Statue of Liberty, just so you know where I am coming from here, I studied philosophy for a long time at Melbourne Uni, while my music was first starting to bubble away. Even in my studies, I always searched for explanations for my love of the double-edged. I fell in love with the Heideggerian concept of *dasein*, which may explain things. *Dasein* describes the concept that you can only get the most insight into the workings of the world when something you use every day breaks. You go to work, doing the same routine, for months, even years, without a second thought. Then one day your front door handle screws up and you can't get through the door. You are never given the opportunity or insight – or, some might say, the privilege – to allow yourself to think about and reflect upon your routine, until that broken moment. I think there are plenty of things very broken and wrong about the United States, but, like a moth, I'm drawn to the flames – I guess in the hope of insight.

Though our shows in the US are still humble, it's a dream come true to play in your shadow every now and then. Since my very first unspiritual journey of self-discovery to the US, I have visited New York City quite a few times – even, many moons ago, falling in love with one of your minions for a brief time. I got to hang around your backyard for six months or so. It was an amazing and artistically formative time in my life. Thank you for that. I think I soon realised I was more in love with you then her. I find your city to be over-whelmingly and relentlessly inspiring. The sheer number of people all battling to be on the world stage, bumping shoulders with each other, sometimes butting heads, sometimes kissing, sometimes cre-ating, sometimes just eating and laughing. Everyone is there to win, all at once, in the one place, at the one time. It's so fucking stupid. It's so fucking amazing.

I just wanted to tell you, my dear statue, that I appreciate what you're doing. Your arm must be sore. Maybe I don't appreciate you in the same way as your average gun-toting, macaroni and cheese-loving American, but I love you. In a way, I want to be like you. You are a fully embraced outsider in the US. You, a French maiden, are the beating heart of US freedom fighting. Your image is on every crappy US souvenir in every airport. You've somehow slipped in and taken over. I don't know if I'm speaking out of turn, but for me, you are not a guiding light for Americans, even though they think you are. For me, you are a beautiful goddess, holding the flame for foreigners, shedding light on how ridiculous her home is, from the inside out. You are the welcome beacon, the lighthouse, for naive Australians like me. I think the French knew what they were doing when they plonked you down there on Liberty Island. You are my favourite double agent. You stand as evidence that my hopes and dreams in the States just might come true one day. You give me a glimmer of hope that I may one day be sipping cocktails from a hammock in my Vegas penthouse, living next door to Celine Dion or Wayne Newton, with my own Statue of Liberty slot machine in the reception room. I can only dream.

Wish me luck in my attempt to leave a tiny mark on the US over the coming years. Even if I end up in a gutter in Omaha, at least

I will have enjoyed hanging out with you a little more, and for that
it's worth it.

Much love and see you soon,
Henry Wagons

SHAUN MICALLEF

Dear Her Majesty, Queen Elizabeth II,

I apologise for writing to Your Majesty out of the blue like this but Marieke Hardy insisted. She, like you, is a very powerful and charismatic woman and one dares not defy her. Anyroad, I write to share a memory my father says he has of the two of you meeting, many years ago, when you first visited our country back in 1954. He tells this story often, but, as he has for many years been quite senile, we've always had our doubts about its authenticity. So we wondered if perhaps you or an equerry would be kind enough to write back and confirm whether or not it actually happened (a stamped, return-addressed envelope, with 'true' or 'false' boxes to tick on the back, is enclosed herewith).

(Please don't think me presumptuous, but as Your Majesty is quite elderly I have taken the liberty of writing this letter in 54-point Helvetica. I know you still make proclamations and sign Acts of Parliament and so forth – and must therefore read a lot of normal-sized typing – but I thought I would try and make this whole process easier for you. You have a special place in my father's heart and the memory I am about to jog may well move you to tears – so it'll be difficult enough for you to read this letter anyway without having to squint as well.)

My father describes, with great fondness, the day you met. Your Majesty, newly crowned, had just arrived here to open the

Commonwealth Games with your young husband, Prince Philip. My father's rheumy eyes mist over still as he recounts how radiant you looked in your Norman Hartnell wattle-motif dress. Melbourne Town, too, had never looked so beautiful, with its Houses of Parliament ablaze with fairy lights, the trains at Flinders Street Station a'gleam and a'sparkle at smart attention, and even the Town Hall, festooned as she was in the flags of all nations and home to several regimental pipe bands, was more than equal to the occasion.

According to my father, there was dancing and singing at the old Royal Exhibition Building, and he and my mother won a prize for being the happiest couple on the dance floor – and then, just before midnight, they all rode down Nicholson Street on the W-class tram to Spring Street, past Alcaston House and the Houses of Parliament, all the way down to Flinders Street to see the fireworks in your honour on the banks of the Yarra River.

Your Majesty and Prince Philip, of course, were transported not by tram but by a beautiful carriage pulled by six plumed horses. Father still remembers the clastic sound of hooves on the cobblestone in the warm night air as Your Majesty drew up, and how you swept past, laden with flowers and in a cloud of scent, onto a punt to take you across the water to where a speech was to be made.

But halfway across, as my father tells it still with a tremble in his voice, Prince Philip somehow elbowed Your Majesty in the mouth and you fell into the river. There was panic and screams from the citizenry. The police ran every which way. Several children were trampled. My father, though, says that without a moment's thought for his own safety, he immediately stripped down to his underwear and leapt in to save you. With a few powerful strokes he was at Your Majesty's side, and within precious moments he was carrying you in his rippling arms, dripping and unconscious, to the riverbank – where he laid you down carefully in the mud and administered the kiss of life.

There was cheering and general jubilation when you were re-vived. Men of importance pumped my father's hand with great zeal and women of high society pressed around him to kiss his cheek in gratitude. Prince Philip was so grateful that he took my father to one side, clapped him on the back and offered to grant him whatever royal favour it was in his power to bestow. My father thought long and hard, and eventually, with the self-effacing country-boy way that still charms many to this day, he asked the Prince if he might be allowed to spend the night with you at the Windsor Hotel. Such was the Prince's appreciation that he magnanimously agreed.

'The most torrid night of lovemaking I've ever had with a human woman,' is how my father often describes the experience. In fact, such was the impression Your Majesty apparently made on him all those years ago that, even now, well into his ninetieth year, whenever he hears 'God Save the Queen', he rises unsteadily from his wheelchair, and tries to remove his trousers.

I look forward to hearing from you regarding the veracity of this tale. (There is another one he tells about you, Robert Menzies and half a brick of ganja, but I don't believe that one. I can't imagine you in a caravan at Dromana, for a start.)

I remain your obedient and loyal subject,
Dictated but not signed by . . . etcetera.

 . P.A.

KAMAHL

I'm an incurable romantic and an eternal optimist, and I've always believed in love at first sight. But it is one thing to believe and another thing to experience, and I never truly thought it would happen to me.

Then, one Saturday night in 1965, after having supper with some friends at the Mandarin Club in Goulburn Street, Sydney, I was playing the pokies. There was a mirror in front of it, so I could see what was happening behind me. I saw a group of Asian students walking past, and among them was a lady in a green sari. As soon as I saw her, she took my breath away.

Despite my shyness and insecurity, I stopped the young lady and asked a couple of questions: 'Are you a model?' and 'Are you an air hostess with Air India?' Inane questions like that, to which I got monosyllabic answers: 'No. No.' Then she and the others drifted away to another room and I went back to playing.

I was just about to run out of money when the group came back and, as they passed me this time, I was determined to speak to her properly. I said, 'Look, I know you're not an air hostess and I know you're not a model. Do you mind telling me what it is you do?' She said, 'We're all nurses – we've just graduated.' And I asked, 'Is there any chance that we could meet again? Where will I find you?' She said, 'We are all at the Crown Street Women's Hospital.' I tried to appear cool and said I'd call her in a couple of weeks, but I actually wanted to call her straightaway. Her name was Sahodra and I was smitten.

But I waited, as promised, for two weeks. We arranged to go on a night out, to see a movie. On our date I discovered she was an Indian from Fiji. She was hoping to go back after graduation – or at least her family were expecting her to go back with a degree and to marry a boy they had already chosen for her.

Then she asked me, 'What about you?' I said I was made in Malaysia but the parts came from Ceylon, or Sri Lanka, and my parents had similar wishes for me to go back to Malaysia to marry a Sri Lankan girl.

Sahodra and I kept seeing each other, and kept falling in love, but I never revealed to her the serious problem I had with the Immigration Department. Back in 1958, I had miraculously escaped deportation because a very kind immigration officer, for some reason I couldn't understand, had not followed orders from Canberra to deport me. That same year I met a man in a nightclub called Rupert Murdoch, who became my saviour. To cut a long story short, it was he who brought me from Adelaide to Sydney and he even gave me sanctuary in his home for a couple of years – in 1962 and '63 I was a boarder there.

I always thought that, sooner or later, immigration would catch up with me. On the second week of June in 1966, I got an urgent telegram from the Immigration Department demanding I attend their offices immediately. When I arrived, I was shown to the office of a lady who didn't seem very friendly. She opened a file and said, 'I see you've been here since 1953. What have you to say for yourself?' Then she took another piece of paper and started reading: 'I've been advised by the government of Australia . . .' With that I became psychologically deaf – I was sure my days were numbered. She must have repeated whatever she'd said a couple of times, and then she stopped and said, 'Would you please listen to what I'm saying! I have been advised to give you, Kandiah Kamalesvaran [that's my real name], permanent resident status in Australia.'

As she said this, that unfriendly lady looked to me as beautiful as Ingrid Bergman. Immediately I rushed out and called Sahodra at the Crown Street Hospital. I said, 'What are you going to do with your life? Do you want to get married?' And she said, 'When?' I said, 'What about next week?'

We were married within two weeks – my family heard about it two years later in a *Woman's Weekly* magazine.

And that was forty-five years ago.

I love her now more than ever, and I will not stop loving her. This beautiful poem by Bengali poet Rabindranath Tagore perfectly describes our relationship.

Unending Love

I seem to have loved you in numberless forms,
    numberless times . . .
In life after life, in age after age, forever.
My spellbound heart has made and remade the
    necklace of songs,
That you take as a gift, wear round your neck in
    your many forms,
In life after life, in age after age, forever.

Whenever I hear old chronicles of love, it's age-old pain,
It's ancient tale of being apart or together.
As I stare on and on into the past, in the end you emerge,
Clad in the light of a pole-star, piercing the darkness of time.
You become an image of what is remembered forever.

You and I have floated here on the stream that brings
    from the fount.
At the heart of time, love of one for another.

We have played alongside millions of lovers,
Shared in the same shy sweetness of meeting,
The distressful tears of farewell,
Old love but in shapes that renew and renew forever.

Today it is heaped at your feet, it has found its end in you,
The love of all man's days both past and forever:
Universal joy, universal sorrow, universal life.
The memories of all loves merging with this one love of ours
And the songs of every poet past and forever.

MAX WALKER

Dear Miss Yeates,

We always have a choice, and it's my choice to write about you. Well, here goes, Miss Yeates, with my chunky black Mont Blanc Meisterstuck in hand, an extension of my mind. It leaves bold, black words on the geometry of a lined page – so old-world!

I first became aware of your notoriety during my two years in middle school. You were a teacher extraordinaire, but also somebody to be fearful of, as we prepared for our transition into the senior school classrooms.

At first sight, you frightened the living suitcase out of me! Pillarbox-red lipstick painted on pursed lips, rouge-powdered cheeks supporting a penetrating set of eyes too often zooming in and out of a distant preoccupation. Was it, as school folklore suggested, a constant thought of 'what may have been'? The terrible loss of your fiancé, a pilot tragically shot down during the Second World War? I guess I'll never know.

Loss is never easy, and life is neither fair nor an even, flat straight line. With death, there is no sense of timing. My dad died in my arms, and I remember thinking, Death is like a huge set of library doors slamming shut, never again to be opened – padlocked and chained against time. No more taking for granted the love, wisdom, mischief, laughter and friendship.

Maybe this is why you appeared so confronting and *blunt*?

If I shut my eyes and journey to the theatre of the mind, I can hear your reaction to my recital of, 'Friends, Romans, countrymen, I come to praise Caesar, not bury him.'

'Walker, see me outside my office at four o'clock and don't be late! Maybe then you'll get it right!'

I had momentarily forgotten, paused and stumbled over the opening words, primarily because I was intimidated and scared. My heart was pounding against my rib cage, and my throat was as dry as the Nullarbor Plain. As you know, I did eventually get my lines right, in the solitude of your office, after school hours!

Some people come into your life and change the way you think, act and speak forever. You were a lighthouse beacon to me, helping me to explore uncharted language. You taught me that imagination plus association equals a great story.

You focused my attention on the page and on sentence structure, giving me a frequency of language to pursue a different way of describing events. Storytelling has become part of my DNA.

I treasure the feel of a chunky black ribbon of ink on rice paper. The creative gates open as a page is brought to life in painted words and word pictures.

Your public criticism of my choice of words in delivering a weekly football score stung! All I said was, 'With a minute to play and three points behind, Scotty Grant kicked a miracle goal off his right boot, over the shoulder. The sealer! Like banging six large nails into the coffin lid . . . Hutchins was dead and they knew it. We earned the right to sing our team song again, and loud!'

'Don't you ever use language like that again in The Friends' School assembly hall,' you firmly said.

So I was constantly in search of different sets of words to deliver the score the next week and the week after that – less colour, and a more conservative tone.

Back in your English classes, I would gaze out the windows and dream of playing cricket for Australia, and of becoming an architect, and getting a kick in VFL football on the hallowed turf of the MCG.

Your shrill voice at mega-decibels and the slamming of books never failed to drag me back into the world of David Copperfield and co. Six hundred desperate pages of small text – a marathon, sleep-depriving read for any student of my age. But, thanks to you, we persevered, and came to understand construction and the ebb and flow of story, conflict and wisdom, good and evil.

Today, I love bookshops. I like nothing better than immersing myself between the covers of captivating books. I am saddened by the sudden loss of Borders and Angus & Robertson stores. Less places to visit, hang out and browse. Where is the contemporary publishing world heading? Paper versus digital? Can we bridge the gap between the real and virtual worlds? I'm working on it.

I secretly knew you loved cricket, too. No one else knew this about you, but I figured that anyone who had the ability to throw pieces of chalk, end over end, with the accuracy of Viv Richards or Ricky Ponting, had to have a passion for the game. The number of times you nailed me with a direct hit was outstanding – yes, communication is a contact sport!

It was not until I had bowled tens of thousands of 'inswingers' and 'outswingers' that I gravitated to writing, because no one at Channel 9 could write like I speak. It is much easier to regurgitate your own words than someone else's – straight down the barrel of a camera, red light on, audience in the millions. No need to be nervous, eh? I knew you would agree. My opportunity to write back then was limited, scarce. We only watched black and white TV in the sixties.

Only the now-defunct *Australasian Post* would acknowledge my potential talent – or lack of – among the Weg cartoons, the Etta-mogah Pub and the crazy array of tattooed people. Nevertheless, the experience worked – I became a writer.

I passed through the portals of the Quaker school for the last time in 1966. But I do remember one special school reunion. I was invited to speak. Not singling out any of the teachers was a serious part of my brief – but how could I not? Other teachers were good: Headmaster Bill Oates; Wilfred Asten, who introduced me to a cane named Excalibur, was unforgettable; Tony Hill was a maths guru and became a teammate; 'Dogsy' Forsaith forced me to taste hydrochloric acid after I suggested that several messy desktop droplets were merely water; 'Ninty' Nightingale made physics cool; and Noel Ruddock, our sports master, was a brilliant mentor. But you were the one. The most indelible, terrifying, tormenting figure, who would have an impact on a major part of my life. So, yes, I did mention you. Remember, I said, 'Without your influence I would never have summoned the courage to be able to pen books.' You made me believe I could write titles like:

How to Hypnotise Chooks
How to Tame Lions
How to Kiss a Crocodile
How to Puzzle a Python

You blushed at my verbal testimonial like an embarrassed young schoolgirl.

Afterwards, you hugged me tight and left a pair of shocking red lips on my cheek. The impossible had happened! Not a dream or a fantasy, but nonetheless a significant experience – to be kissed by your English teacher, in the prime of her seventies, was a moment to lock into the memory bank.

So: *thank you*. We all seek reassurance, support and feedback, and for me this kiss was the full circle. You triggered my journey in writing, and the passion continues daily.

Miss Yeates, what would you make of life in the 21st Century? Cyberspace, internet, email, talking books, podcasts and Kindle, buying from Amazon and using Google search. I've no doubt you would embrace the technology, embrace the iPad and be excited by a classroom with no boundaries. To be able to go global – *wow*!

In fact, I would like to think you would create your own website and app – with my help, of course. You'd engage with a massive following on your vlog and blog, have a virtual classroom on Facebook, encourage feedback in 'live' time, and demand learning DVDs. Your personalised QR code on printed material would turn your pixelated crossword puzzle and school logo into streaming video with the rapid scan of a smartphone. Yes, you would come to life, 100 per cent to camera, anywhere, anytime, with the subject matter limited only by your intellect and imagination. That's what I wish for – you to continue to encourage a new generation to love the page and to appreciate the possibility of word pictures in manifesting a compelling life.

I feel so much better having shared my thoughts here today.

Love,
Your humble, slightly unhinged, unordinary, yet captivated student,
Max Walker

HAMISH BLAKE

Somewhere in Africa 2 million years ago, there was a female of the species Homo erectus. Homo erectus eventually evolved into Homo sapiens, who evolved into modern man, of which I am one. This female was my ancestor, and some 2 million years later, I still carry parts of her DNA.

I have decided to write to her.

Hey . . . you,

Sorry for not being able to address this letter to you personally – you are my relative, after all – but details of the family tree are sketchy at best from around when you lived, so I hope you forgive me. Given your age, my first instinct would probably be to guess your name is 'Bethel' or 'Glenda', but popular scientific thought has it that you probably even predate the first 'Bethel'. Still, it would be nice to know what to call you, in relation to me.

Here's what I'm thinking: if my grandmother's mother is my great-grandmother, and her mother is my great-great-grandmother, then we're going to be here a long time doing all the 'greats' for you under the traditional system, since about 90 000 generations have passed. I reckon 90 000 'greats' equals an 'incredible', and hence you are my Incredible Grandmother.

Obviously the elephant in the room is that you're dead, which is a bummer. I suppose it did happen 2 million years ago, so you might be over it, but I still wanted to offer my condolences since we're family. And I just want you to know you haven't been forgotten. Well, that's not true – clearly you have been thoroughly forgotten – but I'd like to 'un-forget', or, as we say these days, 'remember' you.

I should introduce myself. My name is Hamish. I'm part of your lineage 2 million years into the future, along with approximately heaps of other people on Earth, possibly including Antonio Banderas, which would be cool. Earth turned out to be round, by the way, which is a little fun fact from the future. I have other facts too, but I don't want to freak you out too much. Okay, one more: *It's a Knockout* is rumoured to possibly return next year. I know, how old is that show? You were probably too young to remember it! Hahaha.

Great jokes aside, I guess the reason I'm writing to you is to really say, thank you. At some point 2 million years ago, you chose to mate with another Homo erectus (that's actually what we call you guys – I'm not just saying that because he would have had an erection), and from that child you created the lineage from which I eventually sprung. It's crazy to me to think that one decision you made, 2 million years ago on a sunny African afternoon, can directly be traced to my existence and very ability to be here now, writing these words. If you'd decided to go for a walk that morning or, less likely, play bocce, I would never have come into being. You didn't just change my life, you enabled it. Just from choosing to mate with whoever my Incredible Grandfather was.

Do you remember him? I bet he was a real catch, huh? He probably wooed you with a few wildflowers he picked and a cheeky wink, didn't he? Then majestically took you down to a meadow by a stream? Actually, from what I've read, it was probably more akin to what nowadays we would call 'sexual assault', but I understand times were different back then and you can't really go applying our rules. Otherwise you'd have all been thrown in jail for indecent exposure, due to your pant-phobic ways. Still, without technically condoning the ethics of my Incredible Grandfather's actions, I suppose I have to be grateful to him too, and whoever he clubbed to death to win you as a mate, as they were also both players in the chain of events that led to me.

Those were probably crazy times for you guys, huh? You had just figured out axes and tools, which must have been a lot of fun and totally revolutionary. Did the guy who invented the axe for you do a big presentation in front of everyone wearing a black skivvy? We had one of those guys, too, until just recently – say hi to him for us if you see him.

You had Neanderthals hanging around as well, didn't you? The gossip these days is that they were being killed off around about the time you were alive, and I don't want to give you and your mates a big head, but it looks like you guys won. You may have even knocked off a few yourself. Again, I'm not judging. They were different times, and it sounded like a bit of an 'us or them' situation, so your actions once again ensured my eventual existence. Way to crack a skull or two, Incredi-Nan!

Speaking of skulls, wanna hear something weird? We have this thing called 'the internet' now, which is basically like a very big cave painting but with less yaks and more boobs, and it has some actual pictures of fossilised skulls from around your period. It's not impossible that one of those skulls is *yours*, especially if you died and fell into tar. Do you remember falling into tar? I understand if it's tough to remember. But anyway, I might have actually seen your skull. Creepy, huh?

I haven't seen anyone in my family's skull, except our pet rabbit Bugs, when I was a kid, whose grave we accidentally dug up when we put a new veggie patch in. I don't think he minded, though, as the veggie patch went on to sprout a lot of vegetables, and I get the feeling that if he cared about us desecrating his grave he would have come back as a ghost rabbit and eaten the crops at night, which he didn't.

I guess you've probably been wondering what happened since you checked out? Wow. Heaps. Let me see . . . We figured out kaleidoscopes; we have a lot of different types of cheese; we accidentally got rid of dodos but invented pug dogs; karaoke boomed for a bit and is still kind of popular. I'm not really going to be able to fit it all in, and I didn't even pick the best examples just then, but it's been a pretty hectic 2 million years.

In case you're wondering, I turned out great. I assume you can't check up on this, so let me just say I am basically this awesome, athletic warrior-poet who is King of Earth now, so that's been a pretty nice development.

But I really want to thank you. Alongside becoming King, I wouldn't have got to do anything without you. I wouldn't have been able to see a sunset, fall in love, burn ants with a magnifying glass – any of that. I'm not saying those are my favourite three things I like doing, I'm just saying I'm very grateful to you for making it possible, although the ants probably aren't.

So – thanks. Thanks for enduring the probably unpleasant tryst you went through with whichever bloke is my Incredible Grandfather, and whatever else you did to set the ball in motion that got me here. If I see a Neanderthal around, I'll give him what for for you! Bloody Neanders! Stand up taller, morons! No, I'm not racist, but I know how old people love a bit of racism, so I just put that in there to try and connect with you.

Take care, and write back if you can. Seriously, that would be amazing.

Love,
Hamish
Your Incredible Grandson

WALEED ALY

Dear Mum,

I think you'll be proud. I just marked an essay and underlined every single split infinitive. No explanation, of course. Just an underline. My fantasy is that that's all they will need; that they will know why it's there; that they will note the marking, then instantly exclaim, 'Of course! How could I have been so careless!'

Clearly, that won't happen. I know they will probably think the underline is there as a mark of admiration for their phrasing. I could write the words 'split infinitive' next to such obscenities, but they'd probably think it was an instruction. At least until they rushed off to Wikipedia for enlightenment. Alternatively I could just write 'SI', but that would almost be self-consciously obscure. I'd be like one of those people with teased hairstyles: expending conspicuous effort trying desperately to look like I've put in no effort at all.

You might think I should do whatever most helps the student. But let's face it: when it comes to grammar, I'm not a teacher. I'm a snob. It might seem that I am enraged by every misplaced apostrophe, and every redundancy – but the truth is that if everyone got this stuff right, a little piece of me would die. What is a pedant without an object of derision? These days I hear that split infinitives have become so common that some grammarians now hold them to be valid. I simply cannot abide this. I have no choice but to resist. It's not about grammatical integrity. It's about me.

That's the difference between you and me, Mum. Your precision with grammar was always about the grammar. You did it out of love. I just enjoy the sport. I don't deny your motivations are nobler. You were a high school teacher. I'm a university lecturer. How does that saying go again? 'Primary school teachers do it because they love the kids. Secondary school teachers do it because they love the subject. University lecturers do it because they love themselves.'

Undoubtedly, you love the subject. When I write an article, you text me, identifying your favourite phrases. When I finish a radio broadcast, you send me a grammatical report: 'Waleed, you should not say "the reason is because" – "the reason is *that* . . ."'

That's probably why your reminders were so constant. Remember that holiday at some beach town in New South Wales? Merimbula, I think. It's a holiday I'd describe as relaxing but grammatical. It was there – over dinner at some Italian restaurant or other – that I first became resoundingly aware of the evils of redundancy. I can't remember the offending utterance, but I remember the response: 'Around and about mean the same thing. Either is sufficient on its own. Combining them is ugly and redundant.' That was around about the last time I ever made that mistake.

I'd just finished grade three at the time.

At that age, it never really dawned on me how remarkable all this was. You were a boat person. Months of seasickness brought you here from Cairo. Now you are about forty-five years into a two-year stay. Sure, you came for educational reasons, but plenty before you with mountains of academic qualifications ended up in factories. I know I've asked you this before, but I can never get my head around the answer: How does a young Egyptian woman, upon migrating to Australia, end up teaching English and Australian history at secondary school? Not English as a second language, either. English. As in poetry and essay writing and that. And Australian history? Really?

Maybe all this is because you actually learned the language properly. I'm convinced that 90 per cent of the people left on Earth who speak the Queen's English have brown skin. Only someone from the Indian elite would open a conversation with 'felicitous greetings to you'. Maybe it's something to do with colonisation – you'd know a thing or two about that. And maybe I inherited this nerdiness as a way of proving myself. I still remember when I was a law student, reading some horribly dense, lifeless tome on the train – only to be stopped by a very impressed-looking woman who declared, 'You must be very clever to be doing that in your second language.'

But I think you just derive a particularly rich joy from words. You often say to me that whatever else I'm doing, in your mind, I'll always be a writer. And fair enough, too. None of that work was possible without your influence. Neither was my previous legal career or my current academic one. You made all that happen.

As I descend ever so accidentally into broadcast, I detect a lot of pride, but a modest level of accompanying disappointment, too. Sure, your support is unwavering and you always gush even when I know it's undeserved. But broadcasters can be scandalously promiscuous with language, and you seem to get a greater thrill when I've written something. I must have given a thousand speeches, and your favourite is about the only one I've ever read from a written script. It's no coincidence.

But, Mum, I wrote this. I checked the grammar. If there are no split infinitives, that's thanks to you. If there are, feel free to underline them, and send this back. There's no need to explain.

Love,
Waleed

251

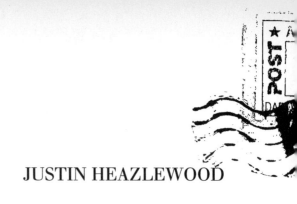

JUSTIN HEAZLEWOOD

Dear Nan,

Thanks for the birthday present. Just to let you know, it was the complete series of *Family Guy* that I asked for, not *Family Ties*. But it doesn't matter because I loved that show when I was ten.

I'll be able to make it over for Christmas this year, which is exciting. I can't wait to see your garden in the summer. It's festival season for flowers and your backyard is the Big Day Out. Deep Purple, White Stripes, Simply Red, they'll all be there – supported by The Bees. It's been a busy year for me, burning the midnight oil at both ends. My eyes are still hot from checking emails, so it'll be good to take a break from screens. That said, I hear you bought a new plasma TV! Lawn bowls was made for widescreen, not to mention *Gardening Australia*. But it's Gardening Tasmania I'm most excited about. I need to stand barefoot in the warm grass and breathe in your lemon verbena. To be taken with a dose of pineapple juice straight from the tin.

Let's have some barbecues while I'm there. Have you got the gas bottle worked out yet? The Rubik's Tube. I'm looking forward to chilling out on the swing seat – my childhood throne. I have fond memories of sitting with you in the late afternoon. You'd nurse a glass of home-brew and say, 'I'm just starting to relax.' We'd rock back and forth watching the birds flirt, our thighs scorching like almonds. You would share your backyard philosophies, planting a row of seeds in my head.

'You have to have a dream.'

'Only the strong survive.'

'There's always someone worse off than you.'

'A problem shared is a problem halved.'

'The greenies are going to ruin Tasmania.'

Not so much the last one, though.

I'd hang on your every word, once you'd had a few. You'd rile Pop about why he didn't become a carpenter. I found you more hilarious than anything on *Hey Hey*. I'm sure you haven't forgotten how I'd plant my ghetto blaster behind the couch and hit record. You'd spot the red light glowing from under a cushion. 'Have you got that thing on again, you bugger?' you'd say, entering a silent protest. My tapes were better than photos because they captured the whole atmosphere. I've still got one of us all playing Yahtzee – the sound of dice clacking on the table overhead. During the Boxing Day test of '93, after David Boon had taken a classic catch, I came screaming in.

'Boony took a good catch!'

'Oh, good on Boony, well done, David Boon!' you cheered, before breaking into:

Boony took a good catch, wow wow wow wow

Boony took a good catch, yow wow wow yow

You weren't like the other Nans. Or the other humans. You worked full time in your garden and loathed housework. You took 5 a.m. walks where you'd gaze up at the sky and mark out Mars and Venus, later reporting back to me because I had an interest in astronomy. I remember when we were caravanning at Bridport, you and I set off for a night walk along the beach. The sea air was fresh and the sand was glowing. I was so excited to be out on an adventure. We were stepping over some rocks and you said, 'One day after I'm gone, you'll be able to look up and I'll be the brightest star in the sky. I'll be Jupiter. You'll be able to say, "There's Nan, looking down on me."'

I've realised this year how much I miss nature. I spent so much of my childhood seeing Tasmania with you on bushwalks. I'm still honoured to have done the Overland Track with you at seventy. (You, not me.) I remember being torn from my dreams at 6 a.m. by your cold finger poking me in the cheek. And getting too cocky coming down Barn Bluff and getting trapped on a ledge. You were down on the ground, going out of your mind.

What are you reading at the moment? I just finished *The Songlines* by Bruce Chatwin. It talks about how humans are genetically predisposed to wandering. Some days I feel pretty stagnant in the city. The older I get, the more I sense there's an important part of me still there in the bush. Next year I might clomp out and find my version of a songline. Even if it does only play 'You're the Voice'.

Just to let you know, I haven't forgotten about the loan. I will pay it back, one day. You really are Nan & Pop Records, even if it is just Nan now. I'm so glad Mum's well and can be there to help you out. You were always so generous to us, even when Mum got bad. I remember the worst day when I was twelve and had to hold her back from attacking you. Mum was all wide-eyed at my strength. You told her I was no longer a boy and had become a man. That made me feel proud. Later on, I found you huddled down by the hothouse and I didn't know how to comfort you.

Remember your favourite saying, 'a place for everything, and everything in its place'? One of my favourite bands, Radiohead, has a song called 'Everything in its Right Place'. I think I had it on once and Pop asked if the CD was skipping. You said you liked the beat and you could see yourself doing the housework to it. I think that's what inspired my song 'My Nan Really Likes Radiohead'. I haven't played that one in a while.

How's Zoey? I tell everyone about how you run a piece of wire up and down the back lawn and attach her leash to it. So she can have some freedom of movement but not attack your birds. They find it hilarious – a cat on a leash.

Well, I'd better go – I've got to buy some ladies' wigs from the $2 Shop for a film clip I'm making. Yes, this is a real job. I had a thought the other day that Uncle Ken and I aren't the only artists in the family. You're an artist in your garden. Your plants are like a living painting you can step inside. Paper fireworks to celebrate each day. You've spent your life growing children and flowers. One day, when I look up at the brightest star in the sky, I'll think of passion and strength and vegetable soup. It's a comforting thought.

Say hi to the budgie, but watch out because there's something about him. He just has this . . . seedy underbelly.

Love,
Justin

Justin.

To the best decision I ever made

ANGIE HART

You think you're it, don't you? The best decision I ever made. You told me no one would ever love me again. You were wrong.

Not like you did.

You were right about that.

It wasn't deciding to sleep with you on the first night of our national tour of Canada together. Duh.

No, the vodka gimlets made that decision. I was out of the office for that one. Or was it the two dozen longneck beers? I don't know, I just read the reports the next day.

Apparently, on our way up to your room from the hotel bar, I told a stranger in the elevator that you were my husband. Embarrassed? No. Presumptuous? Turns out, no. Psychic? Sure. But I was heartbroken when we met and I ran out of credit on my ESP broadband connection shortly after we consummated. So I couldn't see it coming.

It wasn't my best decision, but it was one of the most monumentally life-changing actions that my body did without me, in its potent, distilled-potato-induced state.

I am only able to share this with you now. Now that I have an unlimited cap on perspective, and hindsight! I was able to roll both into one plan, and I am happy.

That night, when I didn't make the best decision I ever made, I really should've been looking where I was going. Because somehow, through the course of my bucking and wailing blindly under and over you, and over and under you, and so on (and now that I have that valuable hindsight, I suspect you were not the slightest bit in-ebriated, but we don't need to talk about that, because that's creepy, and the rest, as they say, is. . . anyway) – somewhere along the line was the start of a long, long, long, long, long line.

Of dominoes.

And that night I knocked down the very first one.

Whoops-a-daisy!

I married you. Even after the eye and ear hospital assured me that the ringing in my ears was not tinnitus, I ignored the deafening alarm bells.

You wanted me to move away from my friends and family to America, to be alone with you. How romantic. I might've mentioned I was nursing a broken heart at the time. You never let me out of your sight and that was flattering, to say the very least.

Did you know that my sister took me aside that day? The day before I said 'I do', to what I didn't know, but I would have to have been made of wood to not have sensed. She gently reminded me that I didn't have to go through with it. You must've made such a sweet impression on her!

The way you treated my mother and sister, when they arrived for the wedding, was nothing short of appalling. You barely talked to them. You acted as if their presence were an imposition.

We were in Austin, Texas, an hour out of town, and you refused to drive them or me anywhere once they'd arrived all the way from Melbourne, Australia, so we could do the pre-wedding cheeky lin-gerie shop. (A waste of time anyway, as on our wedding night you passed out on the hotel bed as if dropped from a great height, arms and legs spread out like the coyote looking up at the roadrunner from the base of a steep cliff face, but in an x-rated episode, wearing only my diamante choker. Meep meep.)

In a series of less-than-best decisions, we'll call this one number twenty-five. It was little more than six months in and I'd already lost track. I was twenty-five years old, so it seems a good number for this particular fork in the pudding.

I've met some very wise twenty-five year olds, so I know they exist. That day, I proved that I was not one of them. My sister handed me this golden ticket from a place of unconditional love, a genuinely concerned offer to help me to disappear the friends that had flown from around the globe to witness number twenty-five take place. She offered me a hand, reaching out to ease the shame of what would have been a very small mistake in the scheme of what was to come.

I saw it as an affront and dug my heels in further. I knew what I was doing, I told myself, like the actress I would never be.

I don't need to remind you at this point, but I will anyway. That deal I got with the unlimited hindsight came around eight years after that day.

We split our money straight down the middle. Rent, food, gas, the lot. Which was good for you, seeing as I wasn't making any. We even split the coins for the laundry to an exact three dollars and two dimes each. I got a job that started at six dollars and twenty-five cents an hour, which helped me pay my way.

You were very busy with your session work, which paid in actual money, so you probably didn't notice that I didn't have any means of driving myself around Los Angeles to look for new friends or a better job. That's okay. Eventually someone donated a car to me. A Dodge Colt, hatchback, with every panel a different colour.

You upgraded your Honda to a brand new one, of the SUV variety, which I was not allowed to drive. As a passenger, I was not allowed to bring food or drink, or to apply my makeup in the car. I didn't like being a passenger, anyway. Road rage was your mood du jour, sometimes even when you were driving.

Like I said, it wasn't just all those things.

I also married you because you were good-looking and you smelled different. It's true.

I thought being with you elevated my worth and hopefully I'd even see myself in a better light.

I thought my animal instincts had led me to a different kind of mate by scent. That in your odour, which was alien to my kind, I'd be rewarded with a different and better life, and of course healthy children, as was the Darwinian genetic code.

I wasn't entirely wrong. I mean, one out of three. Come on.

Out of 'different', 'better' or 'healthy children', I got 'different'.

Better?

Things were never worse. I had quit my highly successful band, Frente, moved countries and married a man I didn't know. We were self-employed, sharing a one-bedroom apartment and a problem.

Children? I made sure we didn't have any.

We started a band together. We called it Splendid.

I'll just let that hang there for a moment.

There were other things, too. Good things. That was confusing.

We made beautiful music together. Not a metaphor.

In a strange and complex turn of character, you never censored anything I wrote. So I wrote songs about us. You believed in our art and our music. I wrote thinly veiled songs of misery and struggle. I wrote about self-loathing. I wrote about spinning like a bird with one wing. I wrote about not being able to control anything in this world but my ability to cry. I wrote about trying to love you.

We were artists. We drew pictures together, listened to NPR, went to street art exhibitions. We modelled in a fashion show for a local up-and-coming designer. We dressed up for each other. We ate good food and befriended chefs. We even laughed.

There were good times and they were very good. But the bad times were very bad.

Every day, from that first tipped domino, was about trying to complete some picture in my head, some story, so I could be sure that I was done with this kind of narrative forever, and that I would be free. I wanted to stare into the fire, stick my hand through the flame, face my darkest shadow, and be unmoved.

It doesn't work that way, but there did come a day when I knew I could walk away.

You couldn't have written a screenplay with a better ending than ours. After a dinner out with friends (I didn't have many left by that stage), where, once again, we stiffly pretended that we weren't not talking, where we laughed from our sad faces and told silly anecdotes that held grains of truth, while you squeezed my hand hard under the table, as you did when you thought my behaviour was inappropriate or you just wanted to go home and I had better snap to, we ended the dinner with one of our lame excuses that any close friend could see through.

On the way home on the 110, we flipped a coin and decided to exit the freeway early at the edge of Hollywood. There was a sake bar that we'd kept saying we would go to, but never did. We sat down, ordered a premium cold sake imported from Niigata, and stared at the table.

We stared at each other.

We said nothing.

The sake came.

We touched glasses and said, 'Kanpai!' which I believe is something like 'cheers' in Japanese.

You looked at me and said, 'I think we're thinking the same thing.' And with those seven words you set me free.

I nodded.

We finished our sake and left.

The next day you reneged and wanted to give it another try. I was powerful and resolute for the first time in eight years.

I didn't want to do anything with you.

The divorce was not nice. Who cares. I made a joke on the escalator at the courthouse about my not really being dressed for the occasion. Irreconcilable wardrobe differences. You didn't laugh.

I asked for some money to help me get back home. You called me a cunt.

I knew I wasn't a cunt.

Was that the best decision I ever made?

As I sit here writing this, I'm on the balcony of a hotel in Bali, the place where we were once engaged because we found a cheap ring and we weren't fighting that day.

It's seven years since the divorce from an eight-year marriage, which I can only write about now. That's fifteen years since that first domino fell.

The line is long and eventually the numbers changed; the odds are now in my favour. I think about all of the great decisions I have made, numbered or otherwise.

I am happily ensconced in East Brunswick, married to a man who loves me, never raises his voice even when I do, is generous and not just with his money, because in the end that doesn't matter either.

I don't have children, but I also don't have a bi-continental family with someone I never speak to, and I couldn't be more grateful for that.

I am a solo artist. I write more than just songs, although the songs would be plenty.

I have a wonderful sister and mother. I even made peace with my father before he died.

So you might have guessed by now that you were not the best decision I ever made. You might be thinking that you were the worst, with everything that I have had to say. You weren't. There are no worsts, or even any bad decisions.

I may sound at times like I have regrets, but I don't. I treasure the time we shared, fraught and fragile as it was. I am glad I'm not there anymore, and I am happy that we don't talk. I like who I am in spite of, or because of, everything that happened. I'm proud of myself and

I'm proud of us for giving it our flawed best. I know we tried and we even became better people, with plenty more to learn.

The best decision I ever made was to only live in the pursuit of happiness. I veer at times. Sometimes I sink way below the bar that I've set. But happiness is my north, and I come back to it like a magnet, whenever I drift.

It's not only myself that I have to thank for that.

KATE HOLDEN

Dear Best Decision I Ever Made in My Life,

We haven't properly met.

I'd like to introduce myself and explain why I've got in touch. And to apologise for what may have appeared like inappropriate contact in the past.

I'm sorry about the times I phoned you and didn't say anything. Heavy breathing down a phone line can be disconcerting, I agree. Though you didn't have to blow that whistle into the phone at me; it hurt.

I regret that day last week when I walked past your house several times and hid in the bushes. I know you saw me, but I was too embarrassed to wave. The police officers who took me away were very understanding. I still wasn't sure I'd found you, I had to do reconnaissance, I explained.

The twelve postcards have all, you'll be glad to know, been safely returned to me. Though I think it was a little hostile of you to put 'not known at this address'. I have spent the past month trying to get in touch with you and I am almost certain this is where you live. My research has been diligent and thorough. But I have to hand it to you: you're very private. This public event is the only way I can think of, now, to draw you out.

Let me explain why I've been so determined to get in touch. The best decision of my life is important to me. I don't want to seem ungrateful. Perhaps it's like a haunting, like an injury, that we've become so estranged. I'm not sure we ever did meet, or, if we did, perhaps it was in a crowd. We passed in the night, as they say. Maybe we shook hands. You've never known what you did for me, and so I have been chasing you, Best Decision, I've been chasing you all over Melbourne and the world, and now I think I have you.

It's true that there have been false leads. Many paths have led me nowhere. I even thought you were someone else. You should see my lists! (I can post them to you, they're covered in notes and phone numbers and diagrams, each colour-coded, with lists of dates and times; my boyfriend said it was a bit frightening but I think it just shows how careful I have been in my pursuit. You should be flattered.)

There was the time – I know, it seems silly now – I mistook you for the decision to get off heroin. You'd have thought that was definitely it, wouldn't you? Getting off heroin: generally applauded. Saved my life. Probably the best thing in terms of getting my resume back on track. Etc, etc. But I'm not sure there *was* a decision. I don't remember meeting it. In fact, it was one of those things that worked best without a decision – just tricking myself into it with a lot of denial and pretending it didn't hurt like hell. I just remember that it happened, and to this day people ask me how, and I have to say, It was more like a ship-board romance, we never exchanged names, that decision and I. Sometimes the best romances are like that. You're just left with the memory, and the result, and the ship coming into berth with your family waiting nervously on the quay, and something precious and mysterious letting go of your hand.

I tried thinking more laterally, and I thought – I did – you might be the decision to take heroin for the first time. Ha, that was a funny one. I know it sounds weird. But you might understand why I thought that: because heroin gave me the hardest five years of my life and nothing but trouble and sorrow and nearly killed me; but you see, it was also a blessing. It took me out of my cocoon and taught me a lot. I met extraordinary people and discovered a lot about myself. And let's face it, hard narcotics are tasty, at least in the early days before it all goes to shit (it always goes to shit). We had wild times. It was a hell of a relationship we had, heroin and I, and meeting it was something that has stayed with me. I don't believe in regrets. Fate works in funny ways. Where would I be now if I hadn't walked into that bedroom in Irwell Street in 1996 and stuck out my arm for the needle? Where would my life have taken me instead? But when I wrote to that decision, I got no reply.

What about the day I joined a creative writing program which ended up with me being a published writer? Well, yes. I think it was the sappy priggishness of that decision that made me hesitate; just as well, as it only giggled when I called its home, and it said, Oh, you sad thing, there's no one of that name here. You don't decide to be a writer, after all! God knows, your tax accountant has tried to talk you out of it often enough. The hours are great but, god, have you read the hate blogs about you? And remember the terror of the blank page? And how about the way a writing career is 10 per cent actual writing, 80 per cent admin and filing, and 10 per cent worrying about the fact you have no superannuation and can't get a mortgage?

Then again, you get to do cool stuff. You get to come to Women of Letters.

So you weren't that decision, snorting at me down the line and making me listen to its smug pride. And meeting that decision might only have made me blush. As I found out in a former career, some things are best left in the brothel, and a writing career, where you're paid to sell your soul on a page, is one of them.

Recently I finally got my driver's licence and bought a car. This decision is still in contact with me, we speak daily when I hop in the car and tell myself in a loud firm voice that I do really know how to drive, just start the car, put your hands on the wheel, Kate, and – oops, the handbrake! So far it's working out well for us, I'd wanted to meet that decision for a long time and we have great times. Just the other day I set out for South Melbourne to buy a filing cabinet and two hours later – after mistaking which lane I should be in, being swept variously onto Kings Way, Wurundjeri Way, through the badlands of Port Melbourne and into the city where – white of knuckle and wild of eye, I only just escaped death at the front end of a speeding tram – I ended up in Elsternwick, trembling. We're going to have great times, my decision to learn to drive and I. I know it's terribly nineties to drive, and yet it's opening up whole vistas to me: like, I can go to Ikea and buy anodyne crap I don't need! I can go to Gippsland! But I do wonder. It might be the *worst* decision I ever made as well. Every time I get in that car I think I might get out dead. We're taking it slowly.

But I want you to know, I look after my decisions. When I can find them. Mostly they like to go unnoticed, blending in with the crowd, hiding modestly behind the mass of life and mistakes and destiny and humdrum and ambition: but with a bit of attention *they're* all easy to find, after all. Once you coax them out they positively throw themselves at you!

But you, Best Decision, you're quiet. You're private. Look, actually, I think I'll send this and leave it there. I don't want to embarrass you. It's okay, I'll leave you alone now. I only wanted to say to you, whoever you are, whatever sweet spirit you represent, whenever we met: thank you.

Hang on, maybe I don't mean thank you. Now I think of it, you're an uppity bitch. Fuck you, Best Decision, I've got on fine without you.

Kate

DEBORAH CONWAY

I have a substantial amount of money in a Nicaraguan bank account which for very complicated reasons I can't access without the help of a perfect stranger who just happens to have your email address. I dearly hope you can help and for your trouble you will be richly rewarded with 50 per cent of the funds due, totalling ten million pounds. Just send me all your bank account details and your password and you will be amazed when you open up your account later today.

Dear reader,

I did not respond. But occasionally one does do crazy things against all better judgement. No doubt if I had responded to the letter above my amazement would have been at the swiftness with which my bank account was emptied and at my own stupidity. But not all crazy decisions have obvious ends.

Let's call this a letter about the best decision I ever made although I didn't realise it at the time. I'll paint the picture. My eldest daughter needed pyjamas. I picked her up after school on a rainy Friday afternoon and drove through crazy traffic to the Bonds discount shop on Claremont Street. We ran in and, after twenty futile minutes of searching for a pair that she liked and that fitted, we gave up. The sun went behind the clouds, and I'm not talking about the weather.

I felt for my daughter, don't get me wrong – she simply hadn't been on the planet long enough to have had the 'I'm going shopping but there isn't anything I want to buy' disappointment that the longer lived have experienced and muddled through.

We got back in the car and headed to the next store, where I was hoping we might get lucky. I should mention at this point that we were not travelling alone. The entire family was along for the expedition, and pretty bored at this point, I must say, as it had taken a long time, what with traffic, rain and general Friday afternoon mayhem, to get a relatively short distance. At any rate, we were committed, so on we ploughed. The trip, however, was close to being abandoned, as the mood in the car had stretched to breaking point with teenage and middle-age hormones having drawn swords and about to lunge. The rain was relentless, quite a thing in the middle of drought-ridden Melbourne, and the traffic was almost at a standstill. Then suddenly, directly in front of us and conveniently across the road from our next shop of destination, a miraculous thing happened: a parking spot, a parking spot where no parking spot should have been. It was too much like fate and the shopper within me overrode the mother with an undeserving child within me. 'Park here,' I barked at the poor hapless father of the annoying teenager. He slid in to the spot and, leaving the other three in the car, I took the teenager over the road to see what we could find to purchase.

If there had been pyjamas at Bonds, if we had already started the fight, if we hadn't found a parking spot, if the other three had found something interesting to listen to on the radio and if the parking spot hadn't been right outside Pets Paradise, things might have been different. But a perfect storm is where all the elements are leading to one unavoidable event.

It took long enough that by the time we came back across the road with a fine pair of green flannel pyjamas covered in monkeys the rain had eased somewhat. The husband was calling me: 'Come here, come

271

here, come see this.' I could sense with every fibre of my being what he wanted me to see even before I knew absolutely what it was.

Our family liked to window-shop in pet stores. We had a few of them close to where we lived and it was something we liked to do: hang around and look at greeting-card-cute puppies and kittens that we'd never buy. As a family we had never had a dog, though we had had a couple of very unsatisfactory cat episodes in our lives.

Like Yasser Aracat. A tabby terrorist through and through. He would lurk behind the door for the three-year-old to walk past before springing out, wrapping his paws, with claws out, around her ankles and sinking his teeth into her flesh. His other cute trick was to hang out at the end of our bed in the morning and, when he had decided it was time for us to wake up, he would play at finding our toes, claws out. After waking up like that often enough, even his winning dietary predilection for fresh cucumber could not persuade us to hang on to him. He remained with our old house when we sold up, a house-and-cat package.

And then came Purrball, an oriental blue, cross-eyed with a long nose and bat-like ears and his own fluffy dog that he used to chase when it was thrown. Purrball had many endearing qualities but road sense was not one of them. Blue-grey cat, blue-grey road, blue-grey day, red car (actually I don't know if it was red but they – whoever they are – say the red ones go faster). No good.

It had been almost a year since that traumatic incident and the visits to pet shops had just recently started to ramp up.

Dear reader, are you still with me? We went back across the road and joined the others in Pets Paradise. And there was our future paradise: a rather substantial brindled puppy with massive paws and a great deal of skin which didn't seem to serve any immediate purpose except for the accommodation of future occupancy. He had been allowed out of his holding pen and the staff were engaged in a game with him which involved him trying to get through some kind of maze, but he was doing more tumbling over his four oversized paws than anything else. 'Boy, he's going to be big when he grows up,' I said to anyone listening. 'American bulldogs grow to somewhere between 40 and 55 kilos,' I was told.

I realised my mistake immediately: I had appeared to be asking a practical question. Practical questions were not part of the window-shopping experience and, with my casual comment, I had crossed the line. Four pairs of eyes were suddenly fixed on me very purposefully – five pairs if you include the large brown ones of the bulldog.

I looked around from face to face, including that of the husband, and understood that if I wanted a different outcome from bringing home a dog I would have to take on the role of killjoy. The sniper against happiness. The sign on his cage read '$1200' but this was crossed out and '$700' was written on top. A bargain!

There were so many reasons not to buy a dog. Picking up the poo, the expense, the responsibility, the walking, the feeding, finding him a place to be when we went on tour and the children stayed with my parents, picking up the poo, actually toilet training in general, and the smell, and picking up the poo! I mean, how large would the poo of a 50 kilo dog be? I was starting to think about shovels.

We were about to renovate our house as well, which meant we'd be moving out and finding a rental property – how many of them would let us have a pet? 'I'm not lying to a landlord about having a pet,' I said, lamely. Who was I kidding?

When we left the shop twenty-five minutes later the staff were in tears. It might have been because of the further $100 they had to knock off the price (I'm a hard bargainer) or because they would really miss the bulldog. Certainly the tears looked very genuine. I felt a bit like crying myself, but I held back.

I drove the car while the rest of the family walked Buddy home. Buddy: it wasn't a particularly original name but his sister had been called Holly and the symmetry was appealing.

That first walk home took quite a while. Buddy would just sit down, apparently too exhausted to take one more step, and have to be dragged along until the husband relented and carried him.

I was already home and drinking tea when the husband and children walked in with Buddy. They gave him a guided tour. He pissed on the floor upstairs, then he pissed on the floor downstairs, then he pissed on the stairs. Jesus, what was this, a pissing machine? Male dogs – honestly. 'Outside,' we all yelled.

I dived for rags to mop up. Buddy looked perplexed.

No good? he questioned silently, with his head cocked to one side, looking uncannily like Gromit. No good, I responded.

He kind of got it. Kind of. Of course, then there was the poo and that had to happen inside the house a few times so he could be disgraced and understand the difference between in and out. After forty-eight hours of being on constant rag-and-bucket call, I succumbed to tears. What had we done? It hadn't been so long since I was wiping my children's bottoms; did I really need another baby in the house? Especially one who would never get past the mental age of two!

He went to bed that night in the bathroom, which was perfect considering he was constantly needing to use it.

The following morning, the middle child came into our room. 'I'm too scared to open the bathroom door, Buddy sounds like he's going to bite me.' It was a period of readjustment. I came downstairs to hear the sounds of a puppy getting excited about his imminent release from his bathroom prison, though I could imagine how, from a perspective closer to the ground, that might have been interpreted as a slobbering, savage wolf about to maul whatever was behind the door. I opened the door and he fell over his paws to greet me. No biting or mauling involved.

To celebrate our new family member, my brother-in-law gave us a book, *The Intelligence of Dogs*. In the back of it was a table of dogs rated in order of intelligence. Top three on the list were the poodle, the collie and the alsatian, closely followed by the labrador and the golden retriever. I had to get to number seventy-seven out of the list of eighty before the American bulldog was mentioned. Still, how much of a difference could there be between the smartest and the dumbest?

After a few more days of ineffectual toilet training we called in an expert. The dog-training professionals turned up and my world shifted on its axis. It was a whole new paradigm of relationship between dog and human. I wondered if I could train my children to behave so well with a similar approach. In no time at all Buddy had the hang of sleeping, eating, peeing, pooing and basically living outside, with occasional forays into the house to be cuddled.

Everything seemed to be travelling in the right direction until we had to move out and rent a house. We found one we liked direct from an owner. Great, I thought, I won't have to lie. But it was a false dawn. The forms came out when we went to have a look at the place. As the husband and I hadn't made a prior plan we both left question six – do you have any pets? – blank. I am a bad liar. The owner looked at the form and said, 'So, do you have any pets?' I paused for long enough so that the husband could leap in and answer the question. Dead air. 'Do you?' he asked again. 'No,' I said, supremely unconvincingly. 'Good,' he said. 'Dogs are smelly things that dig up the garden.'

We moved in with our smelly dog a week later. Sometimes he smells like a fish shop with faulty air conditioning on a summer afternoon. And sometimes he smells, as my sixteen-year-old said the other day, like testicles in a pair of underpants that haven't been changed in ten days. (Not sure how she would know what that smells like.) Though back when he was a puppy it was more like five days.

He hadn't shown any interest in digging up to that point, but after we moved into the rental he suddenly became an archeologist on the most fascinating dig of his career. Every morning there would be another hole in the lawn and another fresh piece of history unearthed, usually in the form of a faded plastic piece of a tea set or something like it.

It's an ancient story: resistance, acceptance, capitulation. He had started to weave some kind of magical spell upon me and I was falling in love. I bought the whole 'man's best friend' deal completely, with his pure, in-the-moment, uncomplicated joy and his unconditional love. Buddy was a gentle soul but looked and sounded like he might tear a ne'er-do-well apart. It was about then we started leaving our children alone for the first time, feeling comforted that our trusty watchdog would make them feel safe. And he did.

He also gave them a sex education. He is all man, with everything intact. We were told early on that we should neuter him but he was so relaxed already that we thought he might actually turn into a carpet. And someone else told us that if you neuter a big dog too soon their heads stop growing and they look like Zippy the Pinhead. So we left him alone and put up with his teenage masturbating, with him never reaching climax but clearly enjoying trying.

Buddy became a father a few years ago, with nineteen puppies born in one litter to an American bulldog bitch. I'd take care packages over to the mother and owner; they were both overwhelmed. The puppies were unbearably adorable but despite them being darling and the attendant pleading, I would not succumb to a second one. At least I have that much sense.

And that was the best decision I ever made.

Yours sincerely,
Deborah

SAMANTHA LANE

Dear Sally,

I haven't had many memorable moments wearing latex gloves, but as I spun dishes in my kitchen sink, with that musty warm-rubber smell puffing out of the oversized fluorescent fingers, I realised that seeing you was the best decision I'd ever made.

The direction towards you came from my GP, who I'd consulted out of fear that my friends might disown me if I kept up my long-term effort to unpick a conundrum of the heart. And it eventually led me to a most eventful 1 November, 2005. Makybe Diva won the Melbourne Cup for a third time. I was twenty-six and broke up with my first true love after four years.

Before I'd come to you all confused several weeks before that Cup Day, Sally, I'd asked dear Tom (not his real name) to give me two weeks to work things out, once and for all. It sounds ridiculous as I record it six years later, but discussions had become painfully inconclusive. I had serious reservations about where we were at, but couldn't imagine, and didn't want to live, life without him. Nothing was wrong in the macro frame, but there was trouble in the micro. The prolonged period of indecisiveness prompted me to call a deadline.

I don't suggest for a minute that these circumstances were unique to me. But when they were weighing on my heart and weaving through my head, the issue felt as vivid, perplexing and important as anything I'd ever contemplated.

The question that hung as heavily as any was: What if this is it? And by that I meant: What if this is love?

With Tom, I could see a lifetime. Kids. Living somewhere with things that appealed to our similar tastes. Agreeing with each other about what was right and what mattered. But what I couldn't see was how we were going to get there.

More than once I wished he'd offend me, do something so wrong that it couldn't be made right, or just book an extended overseas trip. Something like that would take the decision-making out of the decision.

I recounted these feelings, years later, to a man I very much enjoyed kissing, in a back booth of my favourite restaurant, and he asked, 'Haven't you ever been the bad guy?' 'Not by choice,' I replied.

But back to you, Sally, and that seminal dish-washing session, because it was over that stainless-steel double basin that clarity arrived at last. It was in this moment that the prompts you'd provided in our first meeting seemed the work of a genius.

I've checked the notes I scribbled down afterwards. 'Conflict' was the first heading. Under it I'd written, 'We don't have conflict.'

Headline two – 'Mystery, admiration, intrigue' – was followed by this annotation: 'Tom rolls along thinking that if we just hang in there, it will all be okay.'

The last headline was 'Smell'. No notes here – the pointer was enough.

Sally, you had asked me to close my eyes and think about Tom's smell. I haven't carried out a more revealing test since.

In the beginning of love, all aromas are heavenly and heady. In the end, they aren't. I'm not talking about superficial smells, but rather human, instinctive scents.

Although my conclusion was reached, Sally, it took several more sessions with you to arrive at a point where I could follow through with delivery.

Then, at the end of that sober Cup Day, I sat on a couch, looked into Tom's face, knowing it would be the last time we would be so physically close, and sobbed.

'I could spend the rest of my life with you, but I have to end this. I needed you to be more demanding of me. It's about dynamics.'

Typically bigger-picture, he countered, 'I think that's a separate matter to love.'

On a black street in Richmond that night, I kissed a turned cheek.

'I feel empty,' I said.

'I love you,' he replied.

Then, a final kiss on the lips.

'I'm sorry.'

The clarity I'd found in dish washing deserted me then, and all that was left felt sick and lonely.

With this night in mind, I made an appointment to be back in your comforting consulting room, Sally. The bubble couldn't be re-entered rapidly enough.

I returned, and returned. You reassured. Gradually, I left our sessions with fewer pieces of crumpled tissue stuffed into my sleeves, and increasingly confident the line could be held. I remember gripping the arms of the chair when you told me, very gently, at the end of our final sitting, that you thought it could be our last. It was the last time I saw you, but not the last time we spoke. Your number has been a comforting entry in my address book for years, and recently I called it.

You said you couldn't help a friend of mine who was in need because you've stopped counselling to put all your energy into writing. You told me you'd had some work published.

I told you that you'd changed my life.

I also told you that I am in love again. With none of the commentary that used to debilitate and paralyse. But on occasion I return to that list of yours.

Conflict?

Well, yes. The pub dinner last night was delicious, but the ride home wasn't the best. His stubbornness – it couldn't possibly have been mine – was what started it.

Mystery, admiration, intrigue?

It has been three years now in this new love, and I don't know nearly enough.

Smell?

In bed this morning, I inhaled deliberately and deeply.

The scent was impossibly good.

With eternal thanks, Sally.

Yours,

Sam

LAURA JEAN McKAY

To the best decision I ever made (with a special dedication to my new face),

Autumn. The trees haven't turned yet but they will. They'll look like they're dying but really they'll just be starting anew.

I had ten thousand dollars of arts funding money and a dead friend. So I made the best decision and took them to Cambodia.

I couldn't bear anything else sharp from outside and begged the doctor not to give me needles. 'If I get bitten by a dog again, it will just have to not be rabid,' I said and signed a declaration waiving his responsibility.

On the plane I threw my face into the seat and sobbed into the weave. I took photos of my deformed features in the Singapore transit hotel. Everything leaned to the left: hair, eyes, mouth. But to the right of me was my friend. 'Where am I?' I asked her. 'Where's my face?'

When I arrived at Phnom Penh airport I realised I was in good company. Everyone in Cambodia has a dead friend. Two million people and 95 per cent of all artists were killed or died from starvation or disease in the four years of the Khmer Rouge regime. In a tiny country of now fourteen million, two million dead friends plus my one made for quite a crowd.

I had been to Cambodia before and would come back again. To the bland, mine-punched flats of the west. The dark, dark heart beating at the Mekong vein. The choking dust of chickens and children, the Hummers, the staring, the dirt. The collective face of national grief wasn't my face, but this time I recognised something in each battered smile: that the best decisions are sometimes made on the slopes of the skull-fucking hills of sadness.

I rented a stunning apartment for the price of a damp sharehouse back room in Preston and sat on a balcony over the Tonle Sap river. In the mornings I went down to the water and taught students how to write character and voice. The students were kids from the city rubbish dump – a place they called 'Smoky Mountain'. I'd been there. It was like some fairytale nightmare, columns of smoke rising from the combusting waste, the children eating from it and living on it. In the clean schoolroom by the river I sweated heavily, transfixed by the whiteness of their shirts as they gathered around me for each class.

In the afternoons I dodged the rats in the alley and sat inside under air conditioning in my apartment, reading the last words I'd written in my journal before she died: *Autumn. The trees haven't turned yet but they will. They'll look like they're dying but really they'll just be starting anew.*

In Phnom Penh the rainy season started. Children dropped things from the roof above, to watch them slide into the street below where cars sped by with all their doors ripped off to accommodate chickens. The plucked birds stared at the ground with dead eyes. I found myself a quiet lover and didn't notice that he'd just been released from a mental institution. His teeth-grinding silences matched mine. In contrast, many of the Cambodians I met vocalised their grief in long tirades that had me at once envious of their vocabulary for it and guilty that I'd been given the choice to just take off to another country.

I saw footage of evacuated 1975 Phnom Penh, the empty catacomb of streets. I wrote about a woman paralysed by fear of landmines. I met Madame Migraine and couldn't get out of bed. I took photos of my face as it fell into decay. My arts funding dribbled away but my friend was still there to the right of me. And when I drank I knew I wanted to die too.

An ex-lover emailed – sussing me out to see if I was a little less broken. I wasn't.

'Do you have to live your life like a Gabriel García Márquez novel?' he wrote.

I wrote back, 'I'm coming home.'

But I didn't have time to act on that decision before my next teaching job with the kids from Smoky Mountain. I rearranged my wonky features and went down to the river.

'Let's make a character, a face,' I told them. 'What does it look like?'

'Black hair.'

'Black eyes.'

'A girl.'

'A boy.'

'She lives at the dump.'

'She lives at the dump with her mother because her father died when he was crushed by a rubbish truck . . .'

'No, no, she lives with her *grandmother* because her father gambles all the time and her mother drinks . . .' They were describing their lives. The room filled with their story.

'Have you ever made up a whole story before?' I asked. They shook their heads. 'Well, congratulations, you're writers now and you've made your first story together.' The translation from English to Khmer took a while to come through and I rose to leave – to book a plane, to pack my case, to get out of Cambodia. A boy flung his arms up, like an umbrella caught in a sudden wind.

'I'm so happy!' he shouted. It stopped me. I gaped. One by one they all started doing it. 'I'm so happy! I'm so happy!' It spread like a schoolyard cough. I looked to the right for the face of my dead friend but in its place was the lively face of the librarian from the school, once a boy from Smoky Mountain. He smiled.

There are photos of me on that day. I'm dancing in a circle with the kids, looking like a bit of a dick, as foreigners do. But the new gouges and shadows are settled in a face thrown back, laughing. As if all of life, all my stories, true or not, might be behind me. As if I might, at any moment, yell and fling my arms in the air. Like an autumn tree that hasn't turned yet but will. That looks like it's dying but, really, it's just starting anew.

I decided to stay.

Thanks.

Laura Jean McKay

To the life
I could have
lived

VIRGINIA GAY

The Life I Could Have Led: Myth, Folklore and Analysis

[Imagine this italicised first section as coming from a stuttering, bespectacled speaker – all nervous tics, endless meandering clauses and poor timing . . .]

Epistolary form – 'epistolaris', from the Latin – of or pertaining to letters. Pertaining to – also from the Latin, 'pertinere'. Coincidence? Perhaps. The most significant defining feature of epistolary form is the total lack of an omniscient narrative voice, which acknowledges – in fact, draws attention to – the specifically myopic ('short-sighted' – Greek) view of the world that a story, written by a single author, a single mind, a single voice, must naturally stem from, and yet which the indication of omniscience attempts to negate. Letters create the appearance of a more personal engagement, but are delivered in the flawed voice of a character – much is more often revealed by what is left out than by what is included. This, of course, asks something of the reader or audience, complimenting their intelligence, asking them to 'come to the party', rather than reinforcing a passive arrangement made with a silent partner. From Les Liaisons Dangereuse *to* Carrie, *from high art to pop schlock, the epistolary form has endured, to this very day. Literally, this very day, Marieke Hardy and Michaela McGuire's* Women of Letters *being a shining example . . .*

High school was hard. I'm sure it was for us all. Bookish girls with unapproachable haircuts don't peak then. We wait. But please, travel back in time, if you will, to a performing arts high school, in the mid-to-late '90s, almost entirely populated by young, sexy hippies and artfully created outcasts. Boys and girls and everything in between trying to get into each other's hemp gym shorts, in a flurry of dreadlocks and inconveniently placed piercings. They would then sing about it in one of our many school bands.[1]

Enter Jinny Gay: 5'10", at *thirteen years old*, with an ill-advised crew cut, and cursed with a psychotically damaging, although of course unforgettable, name. A singer, sure, but only good enough for choir; an actress, yes, but too tall and with too much of this magnificent jaw at thirteen, to play anything but maiden aunts and poorly adapted male parts; and sporting the build of an aspiring shot-putter. This is actually true – I was regional champ for a year. This metre and a half of shoulder is not just ornamental, my friends.

I swiftly realised that I was never going to win roles from these effervescent ingenues, these lithe Lolitas, these future guest stars of *Entourage*.[2] What could I do, that no one else could do? How could I excel, when all around me my limelight was being stolen? How could I exert control in a world increasingly spinning out of my flimsy grasp?[3]

How could I involve myself in stories if not to perform in them?[4]

---

1. *Sex Death And Rock Enroll: High School Counter-Cultures*, NSW Board of Studies Review, 1996.

2. *Competitive Instincts in Unusually Tall Adolescents: The Jo March Syndrome*, Luisa George Catha, 2005.

3. *. . . And Other Half-Baked Teenage Thoughts: A Nation Remembers*, Volume 12. Ed. Jeramiah Souzeman, 2008.

4. *Circuitous Ways to Role-Play [Non-Sexual]*, Collected Essays, Ed. Josephine Campbell, HarperCollins, 2002.

'O Captain! My Captain.' Walt Whitman, 1865

[This is clearly a subheading. Can you subdivide a letter? I mean, I know you can, but is it stylistically appropriate? Discuss.]

Enter an inspiring English teacher, who offered witty comments as a reward for a finely weighted sentence, a correctly referenced foot-note[5], and adored my consistently commanding control of comically conducive alliteration. An accelerated course and a university entrance followed, applause of a kind through a parent's delight – my path was set.

Ah, the corridors of academia! The musty scent of ill-cared-for carpet, the carelessly cracked and decrepit walls – because what of the trappings of a literal building when the architecture of the mind is what matters? The vine-covered exteriors created the unapproachable air of briar roses keeping the harsh realities of the outside world at bay. The stories, the roles, I now knew so intimately. These characters, these authors – these were my friends, my confidants. The cloying smell of stacks in Fisher Library and the sound of creaking book trolleys, reminding me in equal measure of Edgar Allan Poe and the opening scene of *Ghostbusters* – so daringly postmodern of me. Finally, people who cared where a plural possessive apostrophe went! Who understood the fine line between a hyphen and an en dash! Here was a little corner of the world where my total inability to look up a single word in the dictionary without being distracted by sixteen others on the way there (and don't even *start* me on the bliss of anticipating a correct derivation) was considered an asset!

Here I begin work on my thesis. A companion to *Possession* by AS Byatt. Each allusion in her highly dense, highly rewarding prose, is identified, indexed, itemised and cross-referenced. I begin to imagine

5. *Footnotes and Their Correct Application in Academic and Other Writing,* Second edition, Sir Alfred Hyatt, 1996.

the inspiring but poorly attended lectures I would give. The David Lodge-style rake I will briefly and misguidedly consider myself to be, as I take up my tenure at the university, with 'my table' in the local cafe, where I set my famously sadistic First Year Reading Lists, and cap and uncap my red Sharpie in the crisp winter sunshine. Here I have my affairs with waiters and students alike, who are drawn to my sharp-as-a-steel-trap mind and my uncompromising moral code when it comes to the sourcing of material, and my surprising and much-whispered-about perversions when it comes to the act of physical love.

Perhaps I will be the much sought-after injection of young blood, setting pulses racing through the department with my reckless, tinkling laugh, my slightly too low-cut jersey tops and my scintillating knowledge of the early works of Donne.

Perhaps – and this I only whispered to myself on dark days – I am more likely to become the sexless, crumbling, cliché of fawn-wearing, comfortable-shoe'd Professor Gay, just because 'it's easier to get the work done this way, and the work is what matters.' I become prey for some oversexed American scholar who briefly admires my brain but more lingeringly my legs, with whom I have a torrid three-week conference-motel-room romance, who lies to me and breaks my heart and makes me swear that I will never love anything alive ever again. *Thou, Language, art my goddess!* Not because it is quantifiable and controllable, but because it is constantly rewarding, and my intricate probing will be appreciated, not rejected as 'frightening nagging' or 'endless, inappropriate phone calls'. True, it is a one-sided intimacy that I have with literature, but it's more intimate than that sham of a relationship I had with you, Leo! (I have called the American Leo in this other life because of his faintly Nordic white-blonde mane of hair, which gives him a leonine appearance, and his Old World name, which he has shortened – 'abbrieved', as the young people say – indicating his lack of respect for language.)

He is the crushing Leonard Woolf to my misunderstood and self-destructive Virginia. I take an early walk into a river one morning, pocket full of stones and head full of dreams.[6]

And so my unlived life panned out, and ended abruptly, in front of me. It was no small relief not to take this route from high school, not only to me, but also to the endless number of students who I didn't teach, the guests at the interminable dinner parties I didn't breathlessly preside over, and the bodies of water that I studiously avoided.[7] All of this was undoubtedly going to happen, if I hadn't once stepped on stage at uni, palms sweaty – and with half a brain thinking, I must get that essay in by two – only to realise that this height and this face could see me cast as the Kooky Best Friend, and that the kooky best friend gets all the best lines, and that suddenly all of Allison Janney's back catalogue was open to me. Hearing a hundred people laugh, on cue, at something you have painstakingly set up and delivered, is the greatest high that I have ever felt, and I have been unashamedly chasing it ever since.

The frightening, embarrassing, humbling truth is that I'm living the life I could have led. I'm living the thing that I never even dreamed I could have, as a cripplingly self-conscious, bookish tomboy, because it seemed like asking too much of the world. Longing for too much. If I ever acknowledged how much I wanted to be an actress, a real grown-up-lady actress, it would mean acknowledging how much it would hurt if I didn't get it. So this still feels like a dream, a magical parallel world, from which the real Virginia will wake up and then have to return to the real world, where I never had the courage to try out for drama school, or I got kicked out for that terrible thing I did, or that one, *one* audition that never got seen by the right people. Then I'd be back to the lukewarm kettle and the

---

6. *Half-Baked Clichés – Volume One,* Herald Sun Compendium, 1999.

7. *Half-Baked Clichés – Volume Six: Road Metaphors,* Herald Sun Compendium, 2007.

flickering fluorescent light of the interdepartmental tea room.

I am inexpressibly, shiveringly grateful – to whatever mad storyteller there might be in the sky – that I have had the chance to play at drama, rather than to catalogue it, however enthusiastically I might have gone about the cataloguing. I know it all might end. Soon, if a show gets cancelled, if Australia votes me off the island, or if those photos of Kerry Stokes at *that* party get destroyed in a poorly timed house fire; or later, as my heavily Botoxed face slides off my bones in a wet sludge, as I try to squeeze out one last tear at the age of eighty-five. But to have been – *to have been* – a contender, however briefly, is more than I could ever have hoped for.[8]

Dear Mad Storyteller, thank you, thank you for letting me be a mad storyteller.

Love, the unapologetically named,
Jinny Gay

8. *Marlon Brando's Impact on Unformed Teenage Minds,* Stelllllllaaaaaaah DuBois, Belle Reve Press, 1956.

ITA BUTTROSE

Dear life I might have had,

I'd almost forgotten all about you. How, I do not know. There was a time when you were all I thought about.

And now, because of Women of Letters, I've been reminded of your influence and my love for you.

It's a strange feeling at this point in my life to be asked to write a letter to the life I could have led.

What would my life have been like, I wonder, if I'd chosen you instead of journalism?

What if I had followed that early dream of mine to become an opera singer?

Would I have sung at Covent Garden or with the Paris Opera? Or at La Scala and the Met? How wonderful that would have been.

Music was very much a part of my upbringing. Mum was an accomplished pianist who played with well-known orchestral groups in Sydney. Dad studied singing at Adelaide's Elder Conservatorium and had a splendid tenor voice.

He and I often sang operatic duets together, usually after dinner parties. *La Bohème* and *Tosca* were two of our favourite operas. I don't think the neighbours thought much of either though, and once a neighbour knocked on the front door and asked us to be quiet.

Dad and I were quite miffed.

My grandmother Ita (she was Mum's mother), after whom

I was named, made her professional debut as a contralto when she was nineteen.

She and my aunt often argued about my voice. My aunt would insist I was a soprano, while my grandmother was equally adamant that I was a contralto.

I reckon I was a soprano – a mezzo-soprano, in fact, although these days I probably am a contralto.

I'll never forget the night Dad took me to hear the celebrated Australian soprano Marjorie Lawrence at a concert at Sydney Town Hall.

I'd never been to an evening concert before and was in a state of high excitement as only an eight-year-old could be, especially as I had been allowed to wear my best dress of yellow and brown embroidered wool (which sounds pretty ghastly but I know I loved that dress back then).

Marjorie Lawrence was wheeled on to the stage. She looked beautiful, like a princess in her long evening gown of voluminous pink tulle.

Then she sang. My spine tingled. It's rare when that happens but when it does it's fantastic, isn't it?

Did you notice I mentioned Marjorie was wheeled on to the stage? That's because she contracted polio on a concert tour of Mexico. She never walked again but she had a special platform on wheels made so she could sing standing up.

It was also feared she'd never sing again but Marjorie was back singing in eighteen months.

Dad used to say that on the way home from the concert I asked him if opera singers made a lot of money and when he said yes, I told him I was going to become an opera singer.

Dad trotted that story out on numerous occasions.

Singing gave me so much joy though, that money didn't really enter into it. I don't think I've ever been driven by money actually. When I was an adult and well along in my journalistic career, Dad often lectured me about the need to take money more seriously. That's why I probably never believed that tale of his.

Singing allowed me to escape into another world and what a place that is. It's just you and the music and you can scale the highest of heights.

Marjorie Lawrence became my role model. If a girl who was born on a farm at Dean's Marsh near Winchelsea in Victoria could make it to the stage of the Metropolitan in New York, so could a girl who was born in suburban Sydney.

At the end of the Second World War our family moved to America where we lived for six years. Dad met Marjorie through his work as a journalist with an Australian media company.

They hit it off and he ghosted her autobiography, *Interrupted Melody*, which Hollywood later made into a movie starring Glenn Ford and Eleanor Parker.

Marjorie was renowned for Wagnerian roles. Dad was an aficionado of Wagner's too and every Sunday afternoon, after the traditional roast lunch, he would stretch out on the couch in the lounge room and listen to Wagner's *Ring Cycle* at full volume.

We kids were not allowed to make any noise. Consequently my brothers and I know Wagner's operas intimately. I think Wagner's music is sublime. I loved singing it.

I always admired Marjorie's gutsy spirit. It seemed to me she'd have a go at anything.

She notched up a notable first at the Met when, as Brünnhilde, she rode a horse on stage into the flames in *Götterdämmerung*. It was an extraordinary feat. The audience couldn't believe their eyes. Dramatic sopranos did not ride horses at the Met. They walked the horse into the flames. Is it any wonder she was my role model?

I joined the choir at school, sang in all of my school's Gilbert and Sullivan operettas, took singing lessons and discovered the incredible acoustics of the bathroom.

Life was good.

My three brothers and I all learned the piano. Mum started teaching me when I was five. My eldest brother, Julian, also studied singing. After dinner, Mum would play the piano, which was conveniently in the dining room and we'd often enjoy family singalongs.

Our favourite song was about Oliver Cromwell:

Oliver Cromwell lay buried and dead
Hee-haw, buried and dead

There grew an old apple tree over his head
Hee-haw, over his head

The apples were ripe and ready to fall
Hee-haw, ready to fall . . .

I can't remember all the words but I think an old woman came along and gathered the apples. Why we sang about Oliver Cromwell, I do not know.

I dreamed about making my professional debut just like my grandmother.

Then when I was fourteen I did a vocational guidance test at school – everyone did them when they were fourteen in those days. I was asked to put down my first two career choices.

Well, of course becoming an opera singer was my first choice; becoming a journalist, my second.

When I went in for my assessment no one even mentioned my opera singing choice. It was as if I hadn't written it down at all.

I was told I had the potential to become a journalist and that was that. I felt somewhat confused. Singing was my passion; surely someone could have talked to me about my first choice.

And then, in the way that life so often does, everything changed. My parents separated and later divorced. It was a sad, bitter time and family life, as we knew it, came to an end. There were no more singalongs after dinner.

By now I was fifteen and therefore able to leave school and I decided that I should do that: get a job and support myself and become responsible for me, dependent on no one.

And so I became a copygirl with *The Australian Women's Weekly* and this year, more than fifty years since I started work, I featured on the *Women's Weekly*'s cover. What a thrill that has been – almost something to sing about!

All the good things that have happened to me have occurred because I became a journalist. I have been very happy with my life. But writing this letter has reminded me of another life I once thought I would lead. So many memories have stirred in me.

And last night . . . Well, I dreamed I was singing at the Met – as Brünnhilde in *Götterdämmerung* and, in the best Marjorie Lawrence tradition, I rode my horse into the flames. The audience went wild.

How I did this, I do not know. I'm petrified of horses. I only like the ones on carousels. But that's the power of singing for you. Anything's possible.

The life of an opera singer – a successful opera singer that is – would have been an amazing life but it wasn't to be. Fate chose otherwise. I am content with my lot but delighted that the writing of this letter caused me to visit a world I once dreamed of as mine and last night in my dreams, for a brief moment, I was actually there.

Thanks for the memory.

Ita

MONICA DUX

To my better self,

It will be fourteen years this summer since that afternoon when I finally turned away from you, and, after all this time, I thought I ought to write to clarify something.

People often talk about the life they could have lived if only they'd chosen differently at some decisive moment. You know what I mean: a *Sliding Doors* moment. In that film we see two different versions of Gwyneth Paltrow's life play out. One where she misses her train, gets mugged, stays with her worthless, philandering boyfriend, miscarries, etc, etc. But, oh my God, it could have all been so different, because we also see that if she'd caught the train, then she would have dumped the bad boyfriend, and ended up with not just a better man but also a way better haircut.

Ending up with a better job, a better boyfriend or even just a better fringe is all fine and dandy, but there is also another kind of life-changing moment: the type that might have made us better people. The moments when we step up, or down, as the case may be. And you and I both know that they do exist. And yes, I am talking about that unfortunate business at Tamarama.

I know you'd probably prefer to forget all this, but let me talk you through it.

It was 1997. I was in love. I mean, *really* in love. You could measure the size of my love in frequent flyer points, because my man was

298

a restless spirit. A wanderer. An adventurer. He had to keep moving, he told me, so I moved too.

I met Dave on my first day in London, and we clicked immediately. Then he was off to Miami, so I went to Miami too. We drove across the United States together, camping wherever we stopped, even when there was clean, budget-priced accommodation nearby. Because Dave loved the outdoors. So we camped in the desert, in the snow, in the mountains. They warned us that it was bear country, but that didn't stop Dave. Dave laughed at bears.

Eventually we ended up in San Francisco, finally in a hotel. I'd run out of money, and time. Back home in Sydney there was a PhD scholarship waiting for me and I couldn't afford to let it go. I begged Dave to come with me, but restless Dave still had so much travelling to do.

I pined for him, and he must have missed me too, because he unexpectedly changed his itinerary and turned up in Australia shortly afterwards. In typical form, he got off the plane jetlagged but ready for action. I knew that Dave loved the sea. He loved swimming. He loved taking his shirt off. So we dumped his backpack and headed straight for the beach.

Dave took one look at the wild Tamarama surf and stripped. His lily-white back glimmered in the midday sun. I offered him sunscreen; he refused. I tried to offer him advice about beach safety: swim between the flags, arm up if you get in trouble, watch out for rips. He just smiled, amused at my womanly attempts to corral his wild-stallion spirit.

So he dived into the surf and I sat on the beach, reading my book.

Fifteen minutes later, I looked up. Scanned the beach. There was no sign of Dave. But there was a commotion beginning – swimmers getting out of the water, lifesavers running in, just like in a Nutri-Grain ad. There were ropes, and a raft. And they were wearing those funny caps, so I knew it must be serious. A small child was pointing. His mother scooped him up, hiding his face in her shoulder.

A crowd was gathering now, as crowds will when there's a whiff of catastrophe. Then someone pointed. A dot on the horizon, way out past the flags. It wasn't a shark. It was a person. It was Dave.

My insides became heavy, like my stomach was going to drop out of my bum. Could he be dead? My wild English beau, a man I'd followed across continents, a man to whom I'd offered endless love. A man who'd travelled around the world to see me, now drowning at my local beach.

And as this catastrophe dawned on me, what was my first thought? What can one think at such a moment, when your entire future is about to be washed away? Well, what I found myself thinking was: If he drowns, what will I do with his body? I don't think he's got any travel insurance.

But then I saw, they were dragging him out. Alive. He was okay, and the potential difficulties of coffin transport were banished from my mind.

He stumbled up the beach, unsteady, waterlogged, confused, vulnerable. The crowd was pointing and smirking. I wanted to run to him; believe me, I really did.

But instead I found myself thinking, Shit. This is really, really embarrassing. What if somebody recognises me?

So, instead of running to him, washing his face with my tears, then drying it with one of the handtowels he'd stolen from our hotel in San Francisco, I just sort of mingled. Blended. Backed off into the crowd.

People around me were speculating now about who Dave was. 'A tourist, a Pom by the looks,' said one bystander. 'A reckless idiot, more like,' said another. I joined in: 'Yeah, who'd swim way out there? Crazy.'

Internally I was planning, thinking that perhaps I could slip away, get us ice-creams, return when the scene was over. Pretend that I'd missed the whole thing.

But then the couple in front of me stepped suddenly away. My human shield was breached, and Dave saw me. Going to get gelati now probably wouldn't have the desired effect. So I stepped forward instead, trying to look worried and relieved for Dave, but at the same time neutral and distant, like a well-meaning stranger, a good Samaritan helping this naive idiot who'd dived into the treacherous Tamarama surf, obviously not listening to his girlfriend's advice, whoever she was.

'Wow,' I said to Dave, softly, maintaining my best Samaritan face. 'I'm so glad you're okay.'

Dave looked straight at me. 'Were you hiding behind those people?'

What could I say? I gave it to him straight. 'How could you even suggest such a thing! What kind of person do you think I am?'

Sadly, he now knew exactly what kind of person I was.

Needless to say, that was a turning point in our relationship – and not for the better. But it was also a turning point for me. As you know, I've always been a blusher, a person who hates a scene. I am the one who dances very aware of who's watching. Who sings only when absolutely nobody is listening. Who loves, well, only men who never wear clothes that might attract negative commentary from my friends.

I see now that this moment on the beach was my best chance to change. To put love and decency before shame and embarrassment, and perhaps to become that better version of myself. After all, if I couldn't do it then, at that tender age, for my adored Dave, then I never could.

Instead, I embraced the Bad Me, the lesser self, who would rather die, or in this case watch someone else die, than feel embarrassed.

But realising all this about myself now leaves me facing a kind of paradox. Because hindsight has taught me another important lesson. Dave was actually a total dickwad. The camping, even in the snow, even in fucking bear country – it was all because he was as tight as a wasp's arse. The freewheeling sexual experimentation that he prided himself on – what it really amounted to was hours, and hours, and hours of porn.

So if you, my better self, had exerted yourself back on Tamarama Beach, where would I be now? With Dave, perhaps. I see the money I could have funnelled into his travels. The weeks spent shivering in tents, the bear maulings, the tedium of watching him parade around topless. The hours of philosophical debates regarding the bourgeois hypocrisy of commitment and fidelity.

In one of his early movies, one of the funny ones, Woody Allen says that he doesn't want to get rid of his guilt, because it's guilt that stops us from doing terrible things.

Well, shame and embarrassment have had a similarly beneficial effect for me.

So you know what, better self? I'll settle for my lesser self. After all, you didn't even want to see *Sliding Doors*. You wanted to drag me along to the cinematheque instead, to watch a three-hour snore fest by Andrei Tarkovsky.

But I had the money, and I got to choose. So I know how it ends. I know that the better-self Gwyneth, the one who didn't miss the train, who ended up with good hair – she also walked out in the middle of the road at the end, and got mowed down by a runaway car. So who's laughing now, hey?

Yours without regret,
Monica

LALLY KATZ

Dear Life I Could Have Lived,

I came really close to living you. This is when and how:

I was in New York earlier this year. In January, the middle of the New York winter. I was there on a Churchill Fellowship, to meet with theatre companies and to learn more about American theatre.

I also happened to be there for a series of very big blizzards. These city-stopping blizzards made New York a quieter, softer place than the New York I remembered. Snow has a way of doing that. It makes everything look like a childhood we all remember, even if we ourselves didn't actually grow up with it.

If you were standing outside when these blizzards fell, it felt as if you were in a silent hurricane. I would stand just outside the doorway to the apartment building I was staying in and watch the street get painted in white. Someone would walk by holding a useless umbrella and we would look at each other, look at the umbrella and laugh. Extreme behaviours of nature seem to do that – put people on common ground.

Being overseas, especially spending a lot of time alone in a snowed-in apartment, gives you a chance to reflect on your life. And on the choices you are making. I had been alone for a long time. I didn't know how to be anything else. Even when I fell in love, I would fall in love alone, the other person always being far away, and more some sort of myth than a sweetheart. I wanted to break this pattern. But I didn't know how. I looked out the window, into the new-looking world, the reinvented New York, covered in snow. Perhaps I could change too.

This particular night in New York was clear. A cold but clear night. At about 9.30 p.m., I went out onto the street in my snow boots and thermal clothing and sleeping bag-style puffy coat. I thought that while the blizzard had stopped, I might as well go for a walk.

I didn't bring my wallet with me in case I got mugged. I just brought my credit card in my pocket. No ID, just my credit card, keys and some cash. It crossed my mind that if I was killed, there would be no way to work out who I was. This worried me, but not as much as the thought of losing another passport.

I walked through the still empty-ish streets. The snow had been shovelled from most of the sidewalks by now and ploughed on all the big streets. But most people still hadn't come back outside, and as a result, it felt isolated and kind of dangerous. I walked across the East Village and onto 14th Street. It seemed more populated and so maybe the safest option. The air was colder than it had been when it was snowing. It was biting my hands and face.

As I walked up 14th Street, I saw a sign in a store window that said 'East Village Psychic'. I looked through the window and there, sitting in an armchair, smoking a cigarette (hardly anyone smokes any more in New York – especially not inside), was a woman, maybe my age, with dark hair, and dressed in loose-fitting garments. She looked like a gypsy. She caught my eye, leisurely, through the glass. She smiled. I walked in.

'I knew you'd come in,' she said. This impressed me. Her fortune-telling office was heavily heated, like everywhere in New York. It felt warm and thick-aired.

'How much is it? To hear my fortune?' I asked her. I knew I had $84 in cash in my pocket.

'Depends how you want it,' she answered in her thick New York accent. 'You want your palm read, it's $45. You want tarot cards, it's $55. Or you can get the works for $80.'

'I'll take the works,' I said.

She sat me down and put a crystal on my heart. She kept her hand on the crystal and then looked into my eyes. Her eyes had a sort of casual, hypnotising feel. They were clear and hazel. 'Your heart's lonely,' she said. 'It's been following your body all around the world, and now it's lonely.'

'How did you come to be a psychic?' I asked her.

'My mother was one and I inherited the gift from her.'

'Do you have children?' I asked.

'I have a five-year-old daughter.'

'Do you think your daughter will inherit the gift too?'

The fortune teller smiled and said, 'She already has.'

She rolled up my sleeve and looked at my palm. 'You will have a long life. No serious health issues. Just one that will happen ten years from now, but you will overcome it.'

'Oh no – should I do something to stop it?'

'You can't do a thing. But you will overcome it when it comes. You will have a long life. A healthy life.' And then she took out her tarot cards. 'Do you have any questions you want to ask the cards?'

'Yes. I guess so.'

'You can ask two questions.'

'Okay. How will my career go? And do you think that I'll . . .'

'Romance?' she asked knowingly. 'You want to know if you'll find love?'

'Yes. I want to know that.'

She began to sort the cards, holding each one in front of me and then speaking. 'Oh, that's good. That's very good. Your cards are good. Your work is going to be very successful. I can see great things for your work. And yes, here is a man. He is your soulmate. You will meet him in the next year, you will get married, and you will have three children.'

'Three children? That's a lot.'

'You will have them.'

'But I'm thirty-two now.'

'There is time. This is what I see.'

'Can I really still have my career and have three children?'

'Yes. You will have it all. A family, your career, wealth. Yes, you will have wealth. A lot of wealth. And your health. Everything you've ever dreamed of is yours. I can see. You will have it all.'

'Wow, that's really good news.'

She maintained eye contact. She could feel me getting dismissive about it. Playing it down. But she knew, and I knew, that I had come in with questions. With longings. It was too late to play cool.

She leaned in and smiled at me, sadly. 'But there is only one thing that is standing in your way. One thing that is stopping you from having all this happiness that you are meant to have in your life.'

'What is it?'

She put her fingers back on my palm and her eyes held mine. 'There is a darkness around your soul. Do you feel this darkness?'

'I don't know.'

'You know. Can you see this darkness?'

'I guess so.'

'You know what I mean, don't you?'

'I don't know.'

'It didn't used to be there when you were a child. Did it?'

'I don't remember.'

'It has only been the last few years. Right?'

'I guess so. Yes.'

'In the last few years, this darkness has trapped your soul. It is stopping you from living the life you should be living. It is standing between you and all your dreams. If you get rid of this darkness, then all of these things – a family, your career, your health, wealth, happiness – are yours. But if you don't get rid of this darkness, you will remain where you are. Nothing will change.' She leaned forward to me, her eyes going deeper into mine, her hand holding mine firmer. 'Are you ready to do what you need to do to get rid of this darkness and live the life that I saw for you?'

'Yes. I think so.'

'Are you ready for the life I saw for you or not?'

'I'm ready, I think.'

'You need to do it for your family. For your soulmate who will be your husband. Your three children. For your career and your health. You owe it to them. You owe it to yourself. Will you do what it takes to get rid of this darkness so you can live this life?'

'Yes. Okay. I think so. What do I need to do?'

She smiled, reassuringly. 'That's the good news. You don't have to do anything. It is so easy.'

'It is? It's easy to get rid of all the darkness that's surrounding my soul?'

'What if I told you that I can get rid of all of it for you – tonight? That after tonight it would all be gone and there would be nothing standing between you and all your dreams?'

'Wow, that would be great.'

'I can do that for you. I'd like to do that for you. And I can do that tonight – get rid of all your darkness – for only $1400.'

'Oh. I can't afford $1400 . . .'

'This is your life you're talking about! You can afford $1400 to live the life that you should be living, that you are destined to be living, but which is being stopped because of this darkness.'

'No, I'll be in big financial trouble if I spend $1400 tonight. I really can't. I'm sorry.'

'Don't be sorry. It's just that I want to see your soul lifted from this darkness. I want to see you happy. Don't you think your happiness is worth this? Don't you think you deserve this?'

'Well, I'm sure it's really great, but I just can't spend $1400 in one night.'

'$1100. I like you. I want to help you. I'll do it for $1100.'

'That's so kind of you, but I still can't afford $1100. I'm sorry.'

'This is your destiny, your dreams we're talking about. This is the life you should be living.'

'I know. And I would like to do it, but I can't.'

'Okay, for you, I'll do $900. But I can't go lower than that, because it's a huge amount of work and I have my daughter to think of. She's the reason I charge money. If it was just me, I'd do it for free. But I have to think of my daughter.'

'I really appreciate that, and I do want to get rid of the darkness surrounding my soul and live the life I should be living, but I really can't afford $900.'

'Well, what can you afford?'

'I'm sorry, but tonight I really can't go higher than $200.'

'Make it $300. This is your soul.'

'Okay. $300.'

'How are you going to pay?'

'Do you take credit card?'

'No. You haven't got cash?'

'No, I didn't bring my key card out of the apartment with me. I only brought my credit card. So you don't take credit card?'

'No. But we can go to the Duane Reade pharmacy on the corner and you can buy some credit card vouchers. American Express. I accept them as payment.'

We walked up to the Duane Reade pharmacy on the corner. She lit up a cigarette as we walked. When we got there, she said, 'I'm going to stay out here and smoke my cigarette. You go in and get the vouchers and then we can begin work.'

'Okay, see you in a minute.'

I went into the Duane Reade pharmacy and went to the credit card voucher section. I got three $100 American Express vouchers and took them to the counter. I handed them to the young man working at the cash register. He looked confused. 'You want all these?'

'Um . . . Yes, please.'

'I'm sorry, this is a lot. I have to get my manager to authorise these.'

The young man left, returning soon with his manager, a very short, Pakistani man. The manager looked at the vouchers. 'You want all these?'

I nodded.

'And how are you paying?'

'Credit card.'

'Do you have ID?'

'No,' I answered, 'I left it at home.'

He looked a little bewildered. 'I can't let you pay credit card for these without ID.'

'Oh, really?' I said.

'What do you want these for?' he asked me.

By now I was speaking to the manager, four other Duane Reade employees and about ten customers who had come over to listen.

'To pay the psychic. She doesn't take credit card.'

The manager suddenly looked angry. 'Where is she?'

I pointed out into the street, where the psychic was partially hidden, smoking. 'There.'

'Her! She is very dangerous. She is banned from this store. Why are you trying to give her your money? No, I definitely won't sell you those vouchers. She is a very dangerous person.'

'Okay. I understand. But what should I tell the psychic?' I looked at him and the other employees and the customers.

Everyone shrugged nervously. One of the employees offered, 'Just tell her you weren't allowed to because you don't have ID.'

The manager said again, 'She is a very dangerous person. Do not go back to her place. Stay away from her. Why are you giving away your money like this? Go back out there and tell her no. And get away as quickly as you can. She robs foreigners all the time.'

'Okay . . .'

'Good luck,' called out some of the employees and customers in Duane Reade. I walked back into the street. There was the fortune teller. She'd finished her cigarette.

'Did you get the vouchers?' she asked me.

'No. They wouldn't sell them to me because I don't have ID on me.'

'How come you don't have ID on you?'

'I don't know. I guess I should have been carrying it.'

'Of course you should carry ID.'

'Sorry.'

'But look, don't worry about it for now. Walk back with me.' We began to walk back to her place. She started smoking again and then she said, 'Listen, what we can do is this: you leave me something of yours, something of importance, of value, and I will keep it close to me tonight, and that way I'll be able to begin work, and then you can come tomorrow and pay me the money. It's okay, I trust you.'

'I don't think that's such a good idea – because I'm busy tomorrow . . . I'm going to New Jersey for the day. And I don't really have anything to leave.'

'You must have something.'

'What if I come back on Monday?'

'Okay. What time?'

'Four o'clock.'

'Okay.' She looked me straight in the eye. 'I'll be waiting.'

'Okay.'

I felt bad that I had lied to her. I wasn't planning on going back to see her on Monday. I was leaving for Chicago on Monday. I hoped that she wouldn't put a curse me when I didn't return. On my way home, I walked past the Duane Reade pharmacy. As I was passing, I saw the manager outside, smoking with another man.

'Hey,' he called out to me, motioning me over. 'Why are you seeing a fortune teller? She can't tell you anything about your life. You have to make your own decisions. There are no easy answers. Don't you know that?'

I shrugged, sheepishly. 'I guess. It's just that she seemed like she knew stuff.'

'Everyone seems like they know stuff. But only you can know about yourself. What do you think she's going to do? What do you think anyone's going to do? It's not meant to be easy. That's the journey of life – to work this stuff out for yourself. You've got to start making your own decisions. Be your own person and find your own answers. Only you can do that,' said the manager of Duane Reade. 'You're the only one who can live your life.'

'Thank you,' I said. 'You're very kind. And wise. Thank you.' I waved goodbye to the manager of the Duane Reade pharmacy and I continued home.

As I rounded the corner back onto East 2nd Street where my apartment was, it started to snow. By the time I reached my building, it was another silent hurricane of snow. A couple walked by me, holding out a useless umbrella, and we looked at each other and laughed. We were in it together. Nature. New York. Life. It was a happy moment.

But sometimes I can't help but wonder what would have happened, if I'd spent the money, if they'd sold me the vouchers, or if I'd returned the next day, and followed the fortune teller's advice. Would my life be different now? It only would have cost $300. A bargain, considering her initial quote.

Sincerely,
Lally Katz

To the photo I wish had never been taken

ANNA ACHIA

To whom it may concern,

I would like to nominate the enclosed as the photo I wish had never been taken. I'm certain that the reasons will be perfectly clear once you have clapped eyes on this hideous snapshot of holiday fun, but I shall elaborate nonetheless!

I will dispense with the most obvious reasons first: I am wearing bathers, am rather fat, have no makeup on, and I am stupidly spending my holidays with skinny brown people. However, there is one reason that troubles me the most and which may perhaps surprise you, as it did me. But I'll get to that later.

Until now, I believed there were no photos of me in bathers, not since the frilly-bottomed bloomers I sported as a toddler, or my Brian Rochford striped one-piece that I was so proud of in year seven. Not until this photo surfaced like a floater in the kiddie pool of my past.

I don't know anyone who wants to have their photo taken when they are wearing bathers – not even the people in this picture with me, and they look like an ad for Australis. The only people who are happy having their photo taken in their swimmers are models, surfers and a certain Liberal Party leader. Then there are the rest of us, who find it confronting at best, mortifying at worst.

In my twenties, supposedly my 'prime', I used to wonder why I was single for so long, but this photo has cleared up that perplexing mystery.

My summertime companions are all rock stars now, and you'll note that they are all slim and brown and naturally beautiful. They've always been this way. I'm reminded of the *Sesame Street* song: 'One of these things is not like the other ones/ Which one could it be?' What was I thinking hanging around with these people? They were my best friends, sure. They were my adopted family for my formative years, sure. But maybe, just maybe, I would've done better with the boys if I'd chosen less attractive friends.

There are very few photos of me from my fat-Elvis period. At the time I remember feeling typecast as the 'funny one' – funny Anna! Yes, I was the jolly fat person, the cursed role of miserable fat people the world over. And this was the nineties when there weren't many fat role models on TV, except for Roseanne.

A goodly part of the nineties for me was spent alternately listening to Britpop and listening to a tragic conga line of stricken men telling me how much they loved one or the other of my friends, and could I put in a good word for them? Please? Such compliments as I did receive at this time were predictably slightly insulting: that I had a 'great personality', that I was 'really smart', or, worst of all, that I had 'a nice face' (which only begs the question: 'But what about the rest?')

At a gig, a mutual acquaintance once told my boyfriend Dave that he'd picked the wrong girlfriend, helpfully informing him, 'You should've picked Anna's sister, mate – she's got a heaps hotter body than Anna.' At a party at my 'hot' sister's house, a workmate of my brother-in-law regaled me with a series of what he thought were charming and flattering remarks, which were all actually ridiculous, ill-considered and borderline offensive. So much so that we later nicknamed him 'The Diplomat'. He concluded his insulting litany with this purler: 'You're very attractive ... (he paused here expecting my gratitude) I love overweight women.'

In all seriousness, the only women who actually need to be skinny are models, and possibly actresses. Although why actresses need to be stick-thin to do their acting is a little puzzling – but for models, skinny is their job, and they are really good at it. Onya, models!

For me, weight is largely (pardon the pun) irrelevant. I've been fat and happy before, and I've been skinny and unhappy and I thought I was fat anyway. I really wasted those skinny years thinking I was fat. I could have worn crop tops. Crop tops!

The discovery of this photo was made, coincidentally, just two weeks before I was informed of our topic for this event. My best friend, Talei, who is in this photo, rang one morning and said, 'I have to tell you something. Have you got a minute?' Her 'maybe you should sit down' tone was alarming. My stomach sank, and my mind started processing the frightening scenarios. Has something happened to the baby? Has somebody died? Am I in trouble? I was somewhat relieved it was none of those, but then she said the five ominous words that strike fear into the memory cards of all of us who use the interweb: 'There's a photo on Facebook.'

We can't remember when this was taken, or who took it. But we are guessing, using my fluctuating weight and the carbon dating of boyfriends pictured, that it must be sometime after 1998 but before 2001.

My memories of this time are complex, painful, heartachingly nostalgic and riddled with the contradictory and oh-so-clichéd 'issues' of youth. The anguish and the cheek-reddening shame of remembering what a fucked unit I was, alongside the delight of the joyful and debaucherous party life we led – how happy and free we seemed! The tantalising (and now so distant) feeling of not caring what happened tomorrow, while we simultaneously analysed and dissected every moment. Sickening memories of how we tortured ourselves with self loathing, and a longing for those days when we could just hang out at the beach without a care in the world, blissfully unaware that the photos would one day resurface and make us feel ill. Then, of course, those other times when all the cares in the world could be washed away for a few hours with some excellent Mokbel-era party drugs, or some of those new-fangled antidepressants, which were partly responsible for my doughy appearance in the late nineties.

These days I take great comfort in my constant state of photo-readiness. I never leave the house without my hair and makeup done, although the makeup varies by degrees and is, I hope, always situation-appropriate. For instance, I would never wear going-out makeup to the gym, nor wear meeting makeup to a gig, and I would never wear gig makeup to a party, unless I am going straight to the party from my gig (of course).

As a by-product of my burlesque career and many photo shoots, I now possess a keen instinct for what makes a good picture. If I sense a camera nearby, I am ready in the wink of an appropriately made-up eye, shoulders back, chin out, with a toothy yet glamorous smile, and my body twisted to a 45-degree angle for the most flattering effect. On a recent Italian holiday, my mum tried continuously, and in vain, to capture a casual, un-posed photograph of me; she was denied. My camera instincts are ninja-like – like Mr Miyagi catching a fly with chopsticks, I catch myself and correct before the shutter closes.

I've been looking at this picture a lot, so my stomach no longer turns and my cheeks no longer burn with shame, and I have finally discovered why I hate this picture so much. I've realised I don't hate that I am fat in this photo. I don't even hate that I am in those giant bathers, or that the bottom parts of my legs appear to be missing. What bothers me most of all is that my hair is not done. It is neither teased nor sprayed, and it is as flat as Julia Gillard's vowels.

My obsession with big hair started in primary school, when my sister began a hairdressing apprenticeship and immediately assumed the management of my childish locks. No longer a victim of Mum's demented fringe cutting and lopsided, mismatched plaits, I became the gleeful bearer of my first fashion fringe (the mid-eighties puff-ball) and my first colour rinse in 'plum'. I was hooked on hairstyling. Years later, I rejected the fashion trend for The Rachel, with my sister cutting my hair short just like Elizabeth Taylor's in *Cat on a Hot Tin Roof*. Two years ago, wanting length without compromising height, I got my first perm. Hair straighteners be damned!

I have never been able to control my weight, but I have always had complete mastery over the dominion of my hair.

I have accepted that I will never be skinny, will never have long slender legs, and will always look kind of stocky, and it's actually a relief to accept this. Thirty years of wishing I was something I was not were futile and depressing. I've lost twenty-five kilos since this photo was taken, maybe more (cue Oprah-style audience applause), mostly from doing ridiculous dances like the Monkey and the Mashed Potato. And I am much happier for it, but my figure will never be lean or athletic-looking. However, the bigger the hair, the smaller the hips! If my hair was up, this photo mightn't be so bad. It is a question of balance.

Everyone knows I used to be much fatter, but no one has ever seen me without my hair done. Being seen with my hair un-styled is, for me, the equivalent of being caught naked in the middle of high-school assembly.

I pride myself on my fancy high hair, permed fresh from the salon, teased up massive as if I'm on my way to a Poison concert, or hot-rollered and set just like Marilyn's – but never, ever flat. All it takes is one can of Cedel a week!

This hair is now famous in its own right. A man once stopped me in the street and asked, 'Are you Anna? Yes? I recognised your hair!' Another, peering at me across a bar, exclaimed as he drew closer, 'You're not just a hairdo, are ya?' (I think he noticed that I also have a 'nice face'.)

Strangers comment on my hair up to five times a day, every single day. Which, if you don't count the days I don't leave the house, and you don't include the pointing and whispering, equates to roughly 1600 comments a year.

This particular style inspires many and varied reactions: astonishment, derision, dismay, alarm, joy, merriment, envy and wonder. Not to mention giggles, squeals, whispers and general pointing. People are so delighted or disgusted by my hair that their gaze rarely travels to my thick ankles and thunder thighs.

Young girls who straighten their hair often register horror; they seem to resent the rebelliousness of my heavily sprayed and teased perm, as though it is mocking them. Children are enchanted. And occasionally others, like shopkeepers and public transport users, respond with pure happiness. A woman on the tram thanked me for brightening her day. A butcher cheered. An elderly lady stopped to tell me about a hairstyle she had when she was young. A homeless man gave me two thumbs up: 'Nice one, mate!'

My hair has become an integral part of my identity, and I have almost come to think of it as a separate entity with a personality and powers all its own. Perhaps the distraction created by my bouffant diverts people from their personal problems, gives them something else to talk about, or provides momentary relief from worry or stress. Maybe, as they marvel at my hair, the myriad concerns of their lives are forgotten for just an instant.

My frustrated mum, impatient for me to finish my styling before we went out, once asked me, exasperated, 'Why do you bother?' I snapped in reply, 'Because my hair is a community service!'

We laughed, but in truth, I have come to think of it thus.

Sincerely,
Anna

FIONA O'LOUGHLIN

I actually believe in regrets – they do exist – but they are pointless without acknowledgement. I have an awful photo in my head of my daughter and me, moments after her birth. Thank heavens it was never really taken. Sometimes acknowledgement takes time, and that's okay. I finally wrote this letter to my daughter twenty-two years after she was born.

We were up against it, Biddy. I don't know how I let your birth be run into such a ditch. In hindsight, I was too young, and Henry's caesarean birth had partly sealed our fate eighteen months before.

I don't mean I was too young to have you, but more that I was too young to assert myself properly and get the many obstacles that were in our way out of our moment.

We had a long, long, hard day and it ended in heartbreak and tears, and then you were given to me in my darkest hour, and I think you have been bewildered by it ever since. I don't know how much a newborn can remember but I know that awful birth took its toll on you and robbed you of the safe landing you deserved, and you are the only one who had it so tough on the day you were born.

Maybe, if I be as honest as I can in my recollection of Valentine's Day of 1988, you might be able to make some sense of it all. I think you still carry a question mark in your heart. 'Where's my mummy?'

The night you started knocking on the door of your life, we were at Papa's house, and even though I was only in very early labour and you were coming ten days early, I was in a hurry to get out of John-stone Street and to the hospital. To the care of Doctor O'Conner – a sexist man with more letters after his name than brains in his head. South Australians are fools for doctors. Like peasants in a village, they still look at a doctor like he's a celebrity, and they shine like fuckwits when 'The Doctor' casts his spell. I was no exception back then, and my ignorance put you and me in danger.

Your dad, Chris, wasn't there – he had to work. No one questioned that. I never said a word, but I felt let down and really sad. And I was even sadder when he left two days after you were born. Every mother and baby had a husband and father sitting by the bed, except you and me.

God knows what you were going through, trying to be born, but for a long time we worked together, for about twelve hours. The pain was intense but we managed – every four to five minutes we'd crash through it together. I knew if I didn't panic and stayed up above the pain, we would be fine. I blocked out every soul in the world but you and me. I knew what to do; I understood what was happening.

Dr O'Conner came in and examined me at about two o'clock in the afternoon. We'd been in labour for fifteen hours, and then he started making a mess that you and I are still cleaning up to this day. He told me not to be a hero and that it was going to be a long, hard labour, and that it was time to think about an epidural.

That would have been a good time for him to reassure me that I was doing well. That I could, without question, give birth to you. That I was doing a great job.

I knew that he was wrong, that an epidural slows down labour, that it takes away the pain but at all sorts of other costs. I tried to argue with him. I needed a woman doctor or midwife – I was do-ing women's business in stupid, ignorant, male Adelaide. No wonder you hate Adelaide, Biddy. If only he had the brains or the wisdom to credit a woman with knowing what her birth was telling her. He took away my resolve, like a drug dealer peddling free heroin.

He replaced my 23-year-old gumption with fear, and I let him take the reins. He injected me in the spine to numb me from the waist down and it was like a deadly calm before the storm. I felt nothing for half an hour. We weren't communicating any more, you and I. It's like we were both underwater and we couldn't see or hear each other. Meanwhile, they had also injected me with Syntocinon. Syntocinon is a drug that makes the uterus contract relentlessly, and it's too strong to have without an epidural. So my body wasn't in charge of anything any more.

The pain hit me within an hour. Something had gone wrong and the epidural wasn't attached to my spine anymore, so I had nothing to defend against the Syntocinon with. For the first time I screamed and I wasn't up above the pain any more. I was inside it. You must have been as frightened as me. Every contraction crashed your little head up against a birth canal that hadn't been readied and there was nothing for either of us to hold on to.

And there was no turning back. The Syntocinon was already tearing through me, but there was no exit for you or relief for me. We couldn't regroup and we couldn't land – we needed to land on a beach but it was like we were crashing into the rocks instead. All around me now were doctors and nurses getting ready for a caesarean section. The anaesthetist was being called and we were wheeled upstairs to where the operating theatre was. You and I lay on a trolley, being bashed against the rocks. Chris arrived in the middle of this. There was nothing he could do but say hello and goodbye. You and I were completely on our own, but we had lost contact, both holding on, I guess, but not to each other any more. And then you found me while people were flying past and in and around the corridor. We were back together again.

It was unbelievable. You finally started to be born, the way you were meant to be born. The pain changed like a sharp transition, and that's exactly what it's called in the birthing books. We were going through transition! You and me! After everything that had happened, nature took over again, and Fiona and Biddy were doing what had been planned.

Transition is when the baby finally leaves the uterus. It's still painful but it's a different pain because it finally has a purpose. I knew it without ever having felt it before, because I'm no different to a horse in a stable or a sheep in a paddock, which do and know the same thing. You were being born at last and I tried to tell someone but no one would listen.

Then I realised it didn't matter and I set about bearing down and pushing you out right there on the trolley. I was so relieved that you weren't going to be cut out of me, and not because I was scared of a caesarean at all, but because, in my heart, I knew it wouldn't be right. Birthing is so primal that wrong and right are instinctive forces. I knew better than anyone that my baby was being born.

But humans can be the dumbest of animals. They wheeled us into that theatre and put me to sleep and the last thought I had was, The baby is right here, it's so nearly born, there's no way they can do a caesarean.

I woke up to a pain that I couldn't locate. Where was the pain? I reached down and knew I had been cut. They had done a caesarean. I was absolutely devastated. I cried and I cried and I cried. They gave you to me but we couldn't find each other again. You weren't supposed to be given to a wounded mother, you were supposed to be given to a mother who was whole and awake and strong for you. But I had been drugged unconscious and intubated and cut and stitched up, and I just knew that you felt rejected. 'Where's my mummy?'

I was the only person in the world to you, and I wasn't waiting on the other side to meet you.

We found each other about twenty-four hours later, but it

shouldn't have been like that for you. I've always wondered about its impact on you and my throat constricts every single time I see a birth on telly. Your birth never leaves me, Biddy, and I have cried for us both a thousand times. I know that's why you would never go to anyone else for nine months afterward. You didn't trust the world with you and your mother, and you weren't going anywhere without me again.

Fiona O'Loughlin

SALLY FORD

Dear photo I wish had never been taken,

It's been a long time since I saw you (or even thought of you, to be honest), but when I was invited to be part of Women of Letters, you popped straight into my mind.

I searched through my sister Helen's photo albums and finally found you in the 'Winter, 1986' folder. You haven't changed at all from what I remember. You show me standing on the verandah of Helen's shack up at Meredith, in my pyjamas. I look like a sad koala, and my eyes are puffy from crying, though I must say my hair has a body and a fullness that has deserted me in more recent years.

Had I cried myself to sleep again? Or was I getting to the end of the tears by that stage? Actually, I think I let it all drag on until well into 1987.

God, what a waste of time and energy. Well, not totally – I did write a whole bunch of pretty good songs inspired by this guy.

I first met the cause of these sessions of self-inflicted morbid despair in the very late '70s. He was a singer, not exactly handsome, and starting to lose the little hair he had. He even had poor hygiene, if I am totally honest, and let's face it, these days I have absolutely nothing to lose by being honest. But I was intrigued by him. He had a slight lithp, which I found incredibly sexy. He was very smart and really funny. A fabulous singer. He was way out of my musical league. (Oh, and did I mention he was married?)

I'd been playing tenor saxophone in an all-girl band called Flying Tackle. I could hardly play – I did my first gig with the band three weeks after producing my first toneless note. It was 1977 and the height of the punk movement, so no one else could play their instruments very well either. But that wasn't the point. We were feminists in overalls and we wanted a piece of the action! My next gig was as part of the Substitutes, the four-piece horn section of Paul Kelly's first Melbourne band, the High Rise Bombers.

Meanwhile, the guitarist from Flying Tackle had joined a new band with the reason I looked like shit in you, photo I wish had never been taken, and another guy from a very cool band, the Millionaires. I would later get involved with the bass player, who, if truth be told, was really my shortcut to the main player in the ghastly drama that was about to unfold.

The bass player had asked me to come along to a rehearsal as they were looking for another instrumentalist for the new band, and each member was going to bring someone to try out. Could they really want a sax player who wasn't all that good? But I went along and got the gig. Actually, I think I was the only one who turned up.

It's a pretty seductive thing, playing in a band. Creating music. Writing songs. Recording them. Making film clips. Touring. The 'sex' part of sex, drugs and rock 'n' roll is not all about groupies. Just look at Fleetwood Mac. The creative process is an intimate one and being onstage when things are going well is a unique communion and communication between musicians.

It's hard to say, dear photo I wish had never been taken, what impels someone to persist in a relationship with a married man. Is it masochism? Delusion? Vain hope that he will leave her? For God's sake, they had two kids. From where I am now, in a happy, 22-year-old relationship that has seen its own ups and downs, I realise that he had absolutely no intention of leaving his wife. I just fantasised that he would.

Apart from gigs, rehearsals and touring, we spent so little time together – it was a joke! In five years, we spent one full night together. The relationship mostly took place in my head, during the day or very late at night after a gig.

And it all took place in the days before mobile phones. I tried not to leave the house for long in case he called. He always told me he'd call but he rarely did, and if he did call, he never left a message, afraid of being caught out. Sometimes he would call me from the phone at the end of the street to make sure I was alone before he dropped in. I wonder how people conduct clandestine affairs these days. It's all so traceable.

I now realise he was paralysed into inaction by guilt. His guilt was enormous but I had no sympathy for it. I was *so* self-absorbed. It was all about *me*, and why he would say he'd call and then not do it. I raged. But the rage was internal, never directed at him. My sisters and my friends were getting sick of my tears.

One weekend a friend who had had a brief fling with this same guy (but sensibly had moved on) offered to come over to help me make a veggie garden. I lay on my bed wrapped in self-pity while she busily dug and created the beds out in the sunshine. I was stoned. I was *pathetic*. And I needed a swift kick in the pants.

In 1986, I didn't know yet that I had hep C. I still drank Scotch, ate Smith's crisps and smoked dope. A lot. I was liverish, quick to anger, depressed, miserable.

I was hanging around people with successful recording careers, but I had no discipline, hardly ever practised, had an ordinary tone, didn't know any theory, hadn't done the work. Coming from the punk thing, I had a sense of entitlement, but I was lazy with no awareness of my limitations. Helen pointed out I was punching above my weight and that it would only end in tears.

When I look at you, dear photo, I remember that time as a period of great indulgence, self-pity, anger, frustration, despair, loneliness, emptiness. I once overheard two of my sisters talking about me and saying I had no inner life – they were right but I hated them for saying so. I hated a lot in those days. I hated myself. Hated my father. Hated that I wasn't more successful. Hated how hard it was to get a gig. Hated anyone who had a gig.

I saw a therapist during this period and told her I was involved with a married man. She asked who was stronger, my mother or father? Then she asked who was stronger, his mother or father? The answers were my father and his mother. The therapist said that we were each waiting for the other to end the relationship. I walked out of the session and I never went back.

In early 1987, I mustered some energy and got together a really cool funk band called Washington Wives. We were four men and four women. We had 500 people at our first gig and for six months we rocked. Then the singer left, saying she wanted to be a millionaire before she was thirty and that our band wasn't going to do that for her. We auditioned sixty women trying to replace her. The last singer to audition was Linda Bull, who was perfect. She said she wanted to sing with her sister, so we said, Fine, we'll have her too. A week later they joined the Black Sorrows.

I got a job in a friend's family donut van. I was also asked to write a story about Melbourne in winter for *The Age*. The story ran on the cover of the EG section. My father saw it and called to tell me it was the funniest thing he'd ever read, that it was better than anything Helen had ever written, and why didn't I give up the sax and become a writer, and was the woman in the donut van's real name Doris? It was the only time he ever praised me.

Around that time I steeled myself for a final conversation with the married man.

Me: I can't see you anymore.

Him: Why? Have you found someone new?

In the past twenty-two years, I have seen him only twice. But it wasn't until I had more therapy that I was able to get him out of my head. The therapist said, Sally, he was a big part of your life, can't you leave a small space for him in your heart? So I have. A tiny place.

My life changed for the better in late 1988, when I decided to take singing lessons and generally get a grip, and when my darling Patrick came into my life – and yes, we met playing in a band! We clicked immediately, although I refused to get involved until he left his girlfriend of the time. We went on to make three fabulous and fun bands, in the roots and Latin genres: Gringo Stars, Texicali Rose and the Pachuco Playboys. And I learnt an amazing thing: you can work and live with the person you love.

Dear photo, this has not been an easy letter to write. Not because I don't want to face how I looked in 1986 (Patrick doesn't think I look too bad in you!), but because going over in my mind what happened in my thirties no longer serves any purpose.

I am learning to be mindful and to live in the present. I am learning detachment, I am learning to meditate, I am studying to be a yoga teacher. I have walked away from the business called show, or at least from the treadmill of gigland, and I have never been happier.

Much love,
Sally

Sally Ford

LOU SANZ

A traditional school photograph, me with my two black eyes, alongside my brother and his sexually ambiguous haircut (I can say that because we're related). This photo once represented my scamp-like nature. When people looked at it they would often remark, 'Oh my, how did you get those two black eyes?' And I would laugh and say, 'Oh, that's just a result of my scamp-like behaviour, of course.' And then we'd all laugh, and their general delight in me would flow on further throughout the night and well into the morning.

It was a photo that sparked conversation. It was a photo that ignited a thirst to know more in all who came across it, in all who wanted answers to questions. It was a photo that made people laugh. It was a photo that made people cry, especially when they found out that my parents had managed to retain custody of me after the incident in question. I was just another child who had fallen through the cracks, who the authorities hadn't managed to save. The guilt they would feel from just glancing at this photo, which I sent them every Christmas for the next twenty-five years, would fill them with so much despair, they would eventually give up on life, have their wills rewritten to make me their sole heir, and have 'do not resuscitate' bracelets made up, followed by a full page ad in the *Saturday Age* that just read, 'Sorry, Lou.'

Of course, I was unaware of all of this guilt the authorities were feeling until *Today Tonight* landed on my doorstep, asking me to comment. I feigned disbelief and yet also offered the appropriate amount of gratitude, and they asked to see the photo and I at first said no but then they just insisted, and I still said no, and they asked again in adamant voices, and I told them, 'No, this photo isn't for you, it's already done enough damage,' but then they saw the twinkle in my eye, and I opened the door and said, 'Go on, in you come, and don't forget to wipe your feet,' and they scurried in, the reporter remarking as he pushed past me, 'You're such a little scamp,' and I said, 'You don't know the half of it, and feel free to help yourself to a Scotch Finger biscuit.'

But all of that feels like a lifetime ago. Because now, every time I look at this photo, I only see betrayal and lies, and I wish, now, that it had never been taken. It is a photo that hides an unimaginable depth of betrayal, secrets kept from me for over twenty-five years by those closest to me.

Betrayal doesn't just happen; betrayal is the result of long-maintained untruths that have somehow become facts over time. And so I will present to you the that events I believed that photograph captured, and then the truth of the events and the truth of the betrayal.

In 1987, my best friend was Tamara Minogue, the prettiest and most popular girl at Blah Blah School. We shared mutual interests, insofar as she hated me and I hated myself. We would often play four square at lunchtime – 'we' being the gang I was an associate member of, having not achieved full membership as a result of no one wanting me to achieve it.

Even Georgia White, who was born on a leap year, was a full member, and she wasn't even two years old yet (because she was eight and born on a leap year – Google it if you're struggling). For whatever reasons, I constantly found myself falling short of their requirements for full membership. Not even a well-timed hand job would work, partially due to the fact none of the gang members had penises, but mostly because I didn't know what one was.

On this day, as we played, I found myself dominating the field. I won't lie to you – it felt good. Real good. My palm was like an iron fist, only flatter. The ball smashed down on each victory. Dunce: *SMASH!* Jack: *SMASH!* Queen: *SMASH!* King: *SMASH!* I was a fucking champion, and I wasn't afraid to shout it from the rooftops!

'I'm pretty good at this, Tamara. In fact, I'm better than you today. Wanna feel the touch of a champion? High five!' Needless to say, Tamara left me hanging, and I was told in no uncertain terms that my company was no longer required, and that perhaps I would find more suitable friends at the other end of the playground. Of course, as we were only eight, the conversation went more along the lines of:

'No one likes you, Louise.'

'Yeah, go away.'

'You smell like wog.'

'Fuck off, you cunt.'

Or something like that. It was so long ago. You can hardly ask me to recall specifics.

Abandoned, rejected and isolated, with nowhere to call home, I ventured to the other end of the playground. It was a wasteland, filled with boys who picked their noses and ate their snot; a place for little girls with itchy vaginas who got their periods on slides, vegetarians, a guy we suspected was Asian, chronic farters and boys fascinated with their penises. As I scratched my vagina, I thought, Perhaps these are my people. Maybe they'll truly accept me. But to be accepted here I would have to convince the overlords – Fat and Skinny. You'll never guess how they got their nicknames.

Fat and Skinny ruled from a fort that overlooked the playground with their army of My Child dolls. I'd never owned a My Child doll, only a Cabbage Patch doll. Lucy was her name, but she was rarely spoken of. She was short and fat, and had freckles and red hair – I took one look at her and knew I could never love her. But I was forced to adopt her. Forced into motherhood. I tried to make it work, gave it the best shot I could, but do you know how hard it is to bring a kid home to play after school when you've got a kid of your own? God forbid it's someone you really like, and then one day you walk in on him and the doll, and you're all like, 'I don't understand!' and he's all like, 'She gets me,' and I'm all like, 'But she's a doll,' and he's all like, 'Exactly, Lou, exactly.' No one knows what happened to Lucy after that, but, as a mother, I can theorise that maybe the little skank found herself getting into a heated argument where she was knocked down onto the hardwood floor in the kitchen and her body was stuffed into someone's limited edition *Blossom*-branded sleeping bag under their bed while the assailant waited for their parents to go to bed, at which time they took the body and tied it to the back of their bike and rode it down to the park, whereupon they stuffed her body along with the sleeping bag into a barbecue and doused it all with petrol, then setting Lucy on fire, while they finally felt human again. At best I can only theorise, but I do know that's the day my heart turned to stone and it's why I've never really been able to get close to another human being. (And breathe, Lou, breathe.)

Anyway. As I climbed the 6-foot jungle gym/fort to Fat and Skinny's lair, a black crow landed in front of me – looking back now, this was possibly an omen, an omen screaming, 'Stay away, little Lou, stay away!' But all I remember thinking at the time was, 'Oh, a black bird! How pretty! I love black birds, and black birds clearly love me!'

Reaching the top of the fort, I came face to face with Fat, a chubby blonde girl who always appeared clammy or lightly moistened. She stared at me through eyes that revealed a future of hepatitis, diabetes and glaucoma. 'Welcome, Lou. Would you like a biscuit?' said Fat, handing me a Salada. I was too polite to point out that a Salada wasn't a real biscuit, so I just took it.

A second voice crept up behind me: 'We've been watching you.' It was Skinny, a mouse-like girl who liked to gnaw on things – and people, if the scarring on Fat's arm was anything to go by.

'You're the small girl whose friends don't like her. We know all about you.'

'I'm in the same class as you guys.'

'Class means nothing here on top of the fort,' declared Skinny, clearly the more dominant in their girl-on-girl struggle to be on top.

'So, Louise,' said Skinny, 'have you ever done a backflip off a fort before?'

'Um, yeah, totally, like, all the time. If there's a fort, I'm flipping off it.'

I was clearly lying, but my need for gang acceptance was too strong, or my self-esteem too low.

'We thought so. From the first moment we saw you, we both knew, and I think I speak for Fat on this as well, that you were a girl with a daredevil spirit.'

'Some people describe me as a bit of a scamp,' I interjected.

'Yes, that's exactly what we thought. You're a bit of a scamp. And you know what we said we were missing in this gang?'

'A bit of a scamp?' I asked

'Exactly. Our gang needs a bit of a scamp, and you, Lou, might be just that bit of a scamp we're looking for – that is, if you can prove your worth.'

I stepped to the edge of the fort. I'm not sure what it was – maybe it was the fact that I'd finally found some friends who had unbridled faith in me, maybe it was the crowd that had gathered at the bottom of the fort, the faces of the disenfranchised looking up at me: David with his penis in hand, the Asian kid who years later we'd discover was really just a New Zealander, the fourteen-year-old girl who was still in grade three due to foetal alcohol poisoning. Suddenly I realised that yes, I could flip, I could do it. I grabbed the metal bar with both my hands and felt a tap of support on my back from Fat or Skinny, and I flipped/plunged to my death.

But something strange happened as I hurtled through the air

that day, all 32 kilos of me. My best friend Tamara, dressed as Bette Midler, appeared beside me and spoke words of such wisdom, chanting the lyrics of 'Wind Beneath My Wings'.

And then everything went black.

They're not sure how long I lay unconscious on the tanbark after my 6-foot fall (or 'moment of freedom'), but it couldn't have been more than ten minutes. Then, somehow, I managed to drag my battered and broken body to the teachers' lounge. Doctors say that after some head traumas, the human body can appear to function as normal before the haemorrhaging kicks in.

Not two weeks after the best failed backflip in the history of our school, photos were taken, and this is how this photo came to be – a memory from my day of empowerment, a day when maybe I didn't make it into Fat and Skinny's gang, but at least I tried and that's all that matters. This photo reflected the scamp in all of us. That is, until a few months ago.

Mum and I were talking about photos, the way that mothers and daughters often do. I was reflecting on this particular school photo in a moment of nostalgia and started to recount the story of my quest for greatness in the school playground one afternoon, when suddenly my mother sobered up and interjected.

'You didn't fall,' she stated. 'You were pushed. They tried to kill you.'

I said nothing for a moment, trying to take it all in.

'It was always suspected,' she continued, 'but no one could ever prove it. They found a Salada not far from where your body landed.'

'That doesn't mean anything,' I spat back, angry and confused.

'The teacher's report said they lured you onto the fort with biscuits – they'd been trying to get a kid up there for days to push off. You must've just blocked it out.'

I wanted answers! 'Why didn't anyone tell me?'

'There never seemed like a good time. We thought maybe when

you graduated from primary school, but then you got cystic acne. And then we thought maybe in high school, but there was still the acne, and you got your period and breasts on the same day. That, coupled with your unwanted hair problem, your distinct lack of interest in cock, which led us to believe you might be a lesbian, and your penchant for wearing Jack Daniels promotional t-shirts, Blundstone boots and elasticised Kmart trousers – well, there never seemed to be a good time to bring it up, you know, without the possibility you might kill yourself. And Lou, this was in the days before funeral insurance.'

So look at this photo, everyone. Look at it carefully, because it's no longer a photo of a scamp-like girl and her effeminate younger brother – it's the photo of an attempted murder victim and her effeminate younger brother.

It is a photo of betrayal, for, in the words of Arthur Miller, better known as the man who married Marilyn Monroe, 'Betrayal is the only truth that sticks.' Sticks like my face, covered with my blood and mucus, did that day in 1987 to tanbark below the fort.

Lou

To the person
I misjudged

EMILY MAGUIRE

To the girls in my kindergarten class,

I misjudged you. I saw the ironed ribbons in your hair and the way your bone-coloured socks were folded in neat, straight lines over your delicate ankles; I saw the kittens and fairies on your lunch boxes. And I scowled, and took my un-ribboned bowl cut and chunky ankles and brown paper bag, and defected to the boys' side of the playground.

They didn't want me over there, though, because they thought of me what I thought of all of you. I tried to convince them they were wrong, that I may have had a girl's name and been forced to wear a girl's uniform but I was actually more like a boy. I liked to get dirty and play rough. I was bad at being quiet and sitting nicely. Sometimes all I wanted to do was kick a brick wall for a while. But they, sexist little twerps, could not see that just because I was – technically – a girl, I was not at all like, you know, ugh, a girl.

Oh, lovely girls in my kindergarten class: I misjudged you, I realise now, because I believed too completely in the world as presented to me in the books I loved, where girls stood in towers watching their hair grow, or spent their days cleaning up after dwarves or stepsisters, or carrying baskets of food to sick old ladies. Girls were mothers calling the boys in for dinner, and sisters whining about getting their dresses dirty, and great useless beauties who provoked brave men to risk their lives. Girls were Wendy, and I – I was Peter Pan.

Book-obsessed kid that I was, it took me a long time to get the real-life social-interaction thing happening. It wasn't until the first year of high school that I managed to notice that, unlike adventure-story girls, real-life girls were often cool and smart and funny. Unfortunately, this happened around the same time that boys – and their attention – became even more important to me.

———

To the cool, funny, smart girls who formed a tight, cuddly knot around me in years seven and eight,

I misjudged you. It didn't matter that nine out of ten conversations we had were about the books and movies we loved or hated, about the places we would travel to and the careers we would have and the languages we would speak. No, because one in ten conversations were about clothes or hair, and because you each sometimes referred to us as a group as 'girlfriends', and because you were giggly and childish when you talked about boys. And because one of you got into an argument with a guy I worshipped, for reasons I can't remember or even guess at now, and when the rest of us backed you up he sneered and said we were obviously all on the rag. And another girl, not in our group, leant into that boy and told him that because we hung out together all the time our periods were probably in sync, and the disgusted snorts of laughter from that boy were like a kick in the womb.

Instead of talking to you all about the shame and discomfort I felt, I quit the group. I didn't even tell you; I just stopped waiting at our meeting spot outside the tractor shed in the mornings, stopped replying to notes or returning calls. I got in with a group of cool guys by making them laugh. I made them laugh by telling stories about how you all spent Saturday nights making up dance steps to Bananarama songs and talking about movie stars you had crushes on.

And when two of you cried about my behaviour, I responded by saying , loud enough for my new dude friends to hear, Oh, how *typical*, so emotional, crying over every little thing. And when the smallest, sweetest, shyest of you did not cry, but fronted up to me and said in a sharp, icy voice, Emily, you are not as special as you think you are – well, I went and told my new friends that, hey, you've got to watch out for the little sweet ones, do one thing they don't like and they turn on you, wild like hornets, vicious like rabid dogs. The boys nodded: girls, you know, they get so worked up about stuff, take everything so seriously.

Not like you, though, the boys said, and I felt the hot, bright light of acceptance shining down on me. You, they told me, are just like a bloke. It was the most wonderful compliment I had ever received and the wonderfulness of it was reinforced every single day when I heard the things people said about girls: the disgust with which comedians we all liked described female bodies; the ridicule the writers on our favourite music magazine heaped on bands with mostly female fan bases; the simple, contemptuous way that almost everybody – kids, teachers, even members of my own family – used that word, *girl*, as the ultimate insult.

Anyway, my disgracefully dumped girlfriends, you know my defection didn't turn out well. Things got messy for me and I had to leave the school, but I never stopped keeping track of what was going on in your lives. I watched from afar as you dealt with personal tragedies and illnesses and crushing academic workloads. I am not at all surprised that you have each fulfilled your dreams, becoming, in turn, a teacher, a biologist, a lawyer, a GP, a surgeon. You incredible, talented, resilient, interesting women – I misjudged and mistreated you, and the loss, we must all agree, has been mine.

At my new school I found a girl-tribe quickly and held them close. I had, at least, learnt from my experience. Kind of.

To my fellow members of what became known variously as the Deev Club, the Year Nine Pissheads and the Monday-Morning Shame Gang,

I loved you girls so hard. I love you still and I know you know it and for that I am grateful. But I have to say I misjudged you. We misjudged each other, didn't we?

Remember in English class the discussion about that passage in *To Kill a Mockingbird,* that thing Scout says: 'Ladies seemed to live in faint horror of men, seemed unwilling to approve wholeheartedly of them. But I liked them. There was something about them, no matter how much they cussed and drank and gambled and chewed; no matter how undelectable they were, there was something about them that I instinctively liked.'

God, we were in love with that. We thought Scout was so right, so much smarter than all those 'ladies' who apparently disapproved of men, men who were awesome. Our teacher banged on about the restrictive gender expectations of the society in which Scout lived, but we zoned out. What would she know? Typical sad old maid, with her floral smocks and tightly permed grey hair, probably spent all her spare time knitting booties for the babies she would never have because she would be a virgin for life.

Oh, God, Ms Williamson, thinking of it now – I'm fairly positive I misjudged you as well. In fact, now I think about it, I sound an awful lot like you these days.

Anyway, my Scout-loving sisters, we misjudged each other because we didn't understand then that enjoyment of drinking and cussing and all the rest were not exclusively or naturally male behaviours. After all, we enjoyed such things while some male persons – our dads, for example – did not. We were smart girls; we really should have picked up on that. But we didn't, and so we continued to tell each other to 'man up', to stop being pussies, kept encouraging each other to drink and smoke and fuck like men.

I'm glad we're still friends, darling Deevs, and that we have the opportunity to set things right and raise those kids, who I can hardly believe you all have, to understand that girls can fuck up their livers, lungs and reputations just as enjoyably and casually as boys can.

———

To the first girl I hated, my older sister, who I many times declared shallow and petty and an all-round natural bitch,

Have I ever misjudged anyone as badly? You are a goddamn inspirational powerhouse disguised as a meek and stylish librarian. You make me want to write a children's book just so I can make you the protagonist and have a generation of kids grow up with you as their favourite superhero.

———

To all the girls I hated or looked down on without knowing the first damn thing about you except that you were female,

I misjudged you. Even those of you who actually are total arseholes, I never gave you the credit I would have given similarly nasty boys. The least I can do now, you horrible human beings I misjudged as typical girls, is to admit I had you all wrong. You're arseholes because you've worked at it, damn it. You're as good at it as any arsehole man is, and don't let anyone tell you otherwise.

———

To the girls in kindergarten, to my first girl gang who I rejected and the second who I didn't, to Ms Williamson, to my big sister, to all the girls I loved and to the ones I hated,

I misjudged every one of you.

I was, as Caroline Bingley says of Elizabeth Bennett, 'one of those young ladies who seek to recommend themselves to the other sex by undervaluing their own'. And although Caroline Bingley is a woman who we are all quite justified in disliking, in this matter she was completely right. It *is* a paltry device and a very mean art, no matter how successful it proves to be with some boys and men.

But valuing the opinion of the kind of men who appreciate self-hating women is an epic misjudgement in itself, and one I'm happy to say I have thoroughly corrected.

Emily Maguire

ROBYN BUTLER

Dear Pearl,

'Have you had your bowels open today?'

I thought starting this letter with that question might remind you of who I am.

It's me, Robyn. Pam's daughter.

I'm standing in front of you.

Or rather you're sitting, towering, in front of me. You're enormous, Pearl, you really are. You have coarse, short white hair and one front tooth. Actually, just one tooth. You're wearing a housecoat. It's white, with big orange and green bunches of flowers. You're a giantess in a floral housecoat.

I ask you, 'Have you had your bowels open?'

You don't answer. Even though I'm clutching a clipboard, I feel a certain lack of authority, given that you're pretty old and I am only five.

I stand on my tippy-toes. 'Have you had your bowels open?'

Still nothing. I don't think you can see me.

I look to see if my mother is coming. I really need her.

My mother, Pam. You remember Pam? She ran the nursing home. We lived next door. That's why I was always there. Helping, and doing jobs with my mother. Like asking everyone if they'd had their bowels open. We weren't allowed to say poo; my mother said it wasn't respectful.

I stand very still and listen. Over your wheezy, grunty breathing, I can hear my mother talking to Sharpie in the corridor. Sharpie's the nice nurse who smells like cigarettes and always gives me biscuits. Sharpie likes to chat. There are two other women at the end of the room, but for my task-oriented little self, it's just you and me.

Alone.

Honestly, Pearl, I'm a little frightened. I know, I'm five; that's maybe understandable. But here's the thing: the other women in the nursing home don't frighten me. And they probably should.

Millie, from the front room, who, when she's not stripping off her clothes and strolling around naked, is escaping into the backyard and climbing up the big tree. Once the fire brigade came to get her down.

Ida, from across the corridor, who takes the other ladies' full commode pots to the nurses and professes that the contents belong to a wounded soldier and that they need to be examined.

Mrs Grace, from upstairs, who asks me every day to take the big suitcase off the end of her bed and every day I remove the big suitcase and she thanks me, relieved that it's gone – even though there is no suitcase.

Stella and Ida and Mrs Grace don't frighten me because I understand climbing trees and wanting to take your clothes off and make-believe: I'm five.

You, I don't understand.

Suddenly you lurch forward in your chair. You're itchy. You yank the floral housecoat right up to your belly and scratch your massive, naked thighs. And you're moaning.

I wish my mother would hurry up and finish talking to Sharpie.

The other thing about Stella and Ida and Mrs Grace is that they look like little old ladies. Like in books. They're crinkly and shrunken, but they still look like ladies.

Standing in front of you, Pearl, I'm not sure you are a lady. I'm not saying you're a man. But if I had to draw a picture of a lady, I would not draw a picture of you.

At last my mother springs through the door, keys and scissors and fascinating mini torches banging against her uniform.

She looks at me, surprised. 'Are you still with Pearl?'

'She won't notice me.'

My mother leans down close to you.

'Pearl?'

You slowly zone in on my mother. I see a light go on in your face and you grin that one-tooth smile for all it's worth. My mother makes you look softer. She hugs you.

'Oh, you're beautiful, aren't you?'

I look quickly to see if my mother is joking. I'm sure she must be; I don't think the little beard that sprouts from your chin can be called beautiful. But my mother's eyes are crinkled by her 'kind' smile; she isn't joking.

'Robyn wants to know if you've had your bowels open today.'

Your head sways around a little until, finally, you see me. Your gappy smile beams all over me. With a rush of understanding, you bellow, passionately:

'Yes!'

You startle me but I dutifully tick the column under 'Yes' next to your name. I ponder that it must have been quite a poo you've pooped to elicit such a triumphant response. I trace over the 'Yes' a couple of times, anxious to communicate your success.

When I look up, you're still beaming at me, but now you're holding your arms out wide to me. I spin around to my mother but she's already gliding over to one of the women at the end of the room. You hold your arms out wider. I don't move. You tilt your head, beckoning me forward. I glance down at your naked thighs. I think about being squished between them. You lean towards me. I take a step back. You open your mouth. Your one tooth has a ropey trail of saliva clinging to it.

'Give me a hug.'

I can't. I run to the other side of the room and clutch my mother's hand.

———

It's forty years later, Pearl, and, just recently, I was talking about you to my mother. 'Oh, Pearl loved you!' my mother told me.

'She terrified me,' I said.

'Really?'

Just like I have here to you, I tried to explain to her how scary I found you, how different you seemed from the others.

This my mother understood. 'She was a lot younger.'

No wonder you didn't look like a little old lady. I was shocked when my mother told me that you were only about forty. Wasn't this a geriatric nursing home?

'Darling, Pearl was mentally retarded.'

'She was?'

'She came with the others from Gladesville.'

At this point, I needed my mother to start from the beginning.

So she told me that when the ancient and overcrowded Gladesville Mental Hospital was forced to release its residents into the community, my mother had a good reputation for working with mentally ill patients, so lots of you were assigned to her. Millie, Ida and Mrs Grace were among those who came with you.

This is starting to make sense, right?

My mother told me that Ida, obsessed with the stolen stool samples of her wounded soldier, had been a nurse in World War One.

Millie, the tree climber, who loved whipping her clothes off, had been one of Australia's first female pharmacists. And, before that, a prostitute. Poor Millie – being a prostitute exposed her to tertiary syphilis, which accounted for her mad desire for nakedness and the tops of trees.

I don't know what your story was, Pearl. My mother thinks you'd been in that mental hospital forever. I'm glad that they sent you to her, because when Mum looked at you, unlike me, she didn't see a moaning giantess in a floral housecoat. She saw a woman trapped in an unforgiving mind and body.

Five-year-old me clings to my mother's hand and risks a glance back at you. You look sad.

I've been so lucky, Pearl. I have a mind and body that have rarely let me down. But I wanted you to know that I'm kind of growing my own beard now. My chin sprouts black hairs and my hair sprouts white splotches and my skin sags and wrinkles and my bosoms hang like used piping bags, and I see that one day I too will become a woman trapped in an unforgiving body.

I'm so sorry I wasn't brave enough to give you a hug.

Robyn But

SOPHIE BLACK

I started writing this letter to you the night you died.

It was a good plan: I would send the letter off the next day, it would only take a day to reach you. I'd type it up properly at work, just after the editorial meeting and just before deadline.

But in the morning I woke to an email telling us all that you had passed away.

Procrastination is never the best option in these circumstances, but for someone who considers themselves a writer of sorts, I never seem to have a pen on me.

One way or another, though, this letter had to get written. So here it is: a letter to the person I misjudged.

On reflection, however, my very first impression of you was absolutely correct.

You were interviewing me for a job. And you were very amused.

I stunk of starch and the desire to please. Inexplicably, you'd chosen to interview me in the middle of the open-plan office. Directly in front of the equally amused receptionist.

You didn't say much at all, just lobbed the occasional grenade of a question.

I prattled. Perhaps partly out of relief that you were not, as the mysterious name Private Media and the newspapers covering the windows suggested, a publisher of pornographic magazines.

You had a twinkle in your eye while I opined about the importance of journalism.

The only people to actually boast twinkles in their eyes are Father Christmas, the grandma on the front of those packets of instant cake mix and maybe Moonface from the Faraway Tree – but I'm sorry, you did too, you had a twinkly face. A constant wry look, like you were the only one in on the joke.

It was only after meeting you that I looked up who you were.

I was horrified.

It seems back in the day you had nurtured a then little-known talent by the name of Tim Winton. Oh, and someone called Helen Garner. Again: horrifying, terrifying.

You'd created a publishing company in the '70s that had become a phenomenon, mostly because of your eye for talent, but also because you happened to be one half of a female team, which means you were truly a trailblazer.

You were a *thing*.

For the first time, I'd accidentally applied for a job that I really, really wanted. So much so that it made me want to vomit.

You finally rang me to tell me I had the job. The receptionist didn't ring me, or the HR rep, nor a deputy, but you – the person who was a thing. You told me that I was your kind of people.

I dined off that in my own head for days and yet that marked the start of me not misjudging you so much but, to employ an excellent George W. Bushism, misunderestimating you.

You and your business partner, an ex-newspaper child prodigy turned media mogul, had started a tiny weekly magazine called *The Reader*, with no advertising and no distributors, that you stuffed (or, more accurately, we stuffed) into envelopes every Wednesday to send to a readership that never hovered above 3000.

Every Thursday your other business partner, an equally eminent designer and artist, would set up his laptop at the little table where we juniors sat – what we called the kids' room – to lay out the magazine.

My job was to collect newspaper clippings of interesting things and file them into manila folders. I was creatively entitled 'monitoring manager'.

Never for a moment did I think, What are you, Diana Gribble, publishing legend who just made a mint selling your latest company to Fairfax, what are you doing setting up a tiny magazine with a team of children in a building that's falling down around your ears? What are you doing, woman?

You very often scared the bejesus out of me. Everyone speaks of your grace and your quiet wisdom, but you were also a loud talker. In a 'put your fists up and mount an argument' kind of way, in your no-bullshit dinner-party smack-down style, tearing strips off me for taking a predictable greenie line on genetically modified foods, or arguing a line on Indigenous politics, or throwing your hands up at a lazy excuse for a take on the latest government.

Misunderestimating how lucky I was to be yelled at by you was one of my mistakes. And, of course, I should've yelled back. After all, that's what you wanted.

Years later, after you'd taken a punt on me and made me editor of *Crikey*, I watched you tear strips off my deputy after he'd expressed his disappointment that Hillary Clinton was coming to Australia instead of Barack Obama by labelling the Secretary of State in a tweet as 'sloppy seconds'.

You slammed him for being misogynist and when he protested that he hadn't known what the expression really meant (he really didn't, he thought it meant leftover mashed potato), you told him that ignorance was no excuse and explained the origins of the expression including a rather detailed description of gang rape. He died a thousand deaths of shame. It was very fun to watch.

But back at the beginning, in the falling-down building on the banks of the river, I was too wrapped up in my own gripes, my own ambitions, my own desire to outdo everyone in the building and to prove myself as a writer and an editor.

In my typically self-absorbed twenty-something way, I didn't think about you enough at all.

I didn't think about how unusual it was to see an accomplished businesswoman sitting under the giant window of our crappy former yoga studio with no air conditioning, on a 40-degree day, cheerfully tapping away at a computer with an umbrella perched on her shoulder to keep the sun off.

I didn't think about what a delightful privilege it was to see your boss in the backyard sucking on a fag, nursing a scotch and pruning the lavender while talking on the phone.

I didn't think about how revoltingly ungrateful we were when we rolled our eyes at the idea of a spontaneous party. You sent out invitations with 'Chatham House Rule' emblazoned down the bottom (and then explained to us what 'Chatham House Rule' meant) to people who were former prime ministers, writers, activists, posh types and hippies, and who also happened to be your friends. We were so achingly too cool, our first instinct was to find the whole thing awkward. I hate us when I think of that.

I didn't think to bum a cigarette off you in the back garden as a way to steal some conversation; I didn't think to ask you about your farm; I didn't think to ask you much at all.

I didn't think about how tiny we all were, and how you never ever made us feel that way.

You allowed us our big egos and bravado, and just hovered above it, no doubt sharing knowing looks with your business partners.

By the time you'd made me editor, I didn't get the opportunity any more to bum a cigarette.

After you'd given me one of the best pieces of advice just before I took the gig, – 'Don't try to sound like anyone else,' you said, 'stamp this thing with your own personality' – you'd disappeared from your desk on a daily basis to look after your sick husband.

I was at least wise enough then to lament the fact that I couldn't slump in the chair in your office and seek your advice on the latest lawsuit or to argue over an editorial line.

And yet I still continued to misunderestimate you after you were diagnosed.

When I told your business partner that I wanted to ask your advice about getting a book published but I didn't want to bother you under the circumstances, he wrote back in seconds, in italics: *bother her.*

I misunderestimated how much you missed talking shop. How by all accounts you didn't want to talk about the illness at all, just to gossip.

And then you sent an email. When we were all in the middle of forgetting about your own looming deadline, you sent an email right on my deadline, ping in the inbox.

To me and to the CEO and to the general manager: all women, all women you'd shown faith in.

It read:

Just because you can't see me, doesn't mean I'm not watching all the wonderful things you are doing.
Love you all,
Di

The last time I saw you, I was lucky enough to be in your house – your light-filled, art-filled, book-filled house full of footy conversations. We had made up some feeble excuse of picking up some boxes of stuff, just to get inside the door, just to steal some of your time.

You showed us your husband's workshop, the workshop full of his sculptures that you'd spent months clearing and cleaning, after he, ridiculously, incomprehensively, had died, three months before you were diagnosed. You hugged me before we left. And you held me at arms length and said, 'You're doing a great job.'

Then you died, and I found out everything about you.

For someone who hated being talked about, and hated talking about herself, you seem to have befriended a great number of literary types whose first instinct was to immortalise you in print.

They all evoked your fortitude and grace, your influence, your soft power – immense and deep – they all remembered how direct and clear-sighted you were in both your praise and criticism.

But I already knew all that.

There was one thing, above all else, I'd misunderestimated about you. It wasn't until after you'd gone that it became so very clear how large you loomed to your family and to your business partners, who were friends, some of your best friends, before they were anything else more complicated than that.

At your light-filled, art-filled, book-filled house, there lay a pile of envelopes, addressed to you. Your friend and business partner had painted a card for you for every day since your diagnosis.

He had crafted a letter, a piece of gossip, one line, a poem, a joke, every day for over three months, then stamped them and popped them in the post box to you. Every single day.

Unlike me, he clearly always had a pen on him. That's the letter that counts: the one that's sent before you're gone. The letter you actually get to read is the letter that matters.

To inspire those letters in people is what you did, Di, to inspire them to write them, and, more importantly, to send them. I'm sorry this one is so late.

Love,
Sophie

357

HELEN GARNER

C Helen Garner
Flemington
Victoria
Australia
The Southern Hemisphere
This World

27 November 2011

Dear Mrs Dunkley,

In 1952, when I was nine and my name was Helen Ford, I came from Ocean Grove State School, where the teachers were kindly country people, to a private girls' school in Geelong. I was put into your grade five class.

You were very thin, with short black hair and hands that trembled. You wore heels, a black calf-length skirt and a black jacket with a nipped-in waist.

We had Arthur Mee's *Children's Encyclopedia* at home, and I thought I was pretty good at general knowledge.

'In what year was the Great Plague of London?'

Up flew my hand. '1665.'

You stared at me. 'I beg your pardon?' You mimicked my flat, nasal, state-school accent. You corrected it. You humiliated me.

I became such a blusher that other kids would call out, 'Hey, Fordie! What colour's red?'

I was weak at arithmetic. On such weakness you had no mercy. 'Stand up, you great *moon calf*.' You made us queue at your table to show you our hopelessly scratched out and blotted exercise books. Close up you emitted a faint and terrifying odour: a medicinal sort of perfume. On your lapel twinkled a sinister marcasite brooch.

Every morning, first thing after the bell, you would write in chalk on the blackboard the numerals of the clock face, then take the long wooden pointer and touch the figures, one by one, in random order, in a slow, inexorable rhythm. We had to add them silently in our heads, and have the answer ready when you stopped. The name of this daily practice was 'the digit ring'.

You made us keep our hands on the desks so we couldn't count on our fingers, but I learnt to make my movements too small to be visible: to this day I can add up on my fingers like lightning. But the psychic cost of the digit ring was high. My mother had to wake me from nightmares. 'You were calling out in your sleep,' she'd say. 'You were screaming out "The digit ring! The digit ring!" What on earth,' she asked innocently, '*is* a digit ring?'

Dear Mrs Dunkley. You taught us not only arithmetic. One day, making us all sick with shame that our mothers had neglected their duties, you taught the whole of grade five to darn a sock. You taught us to spell, and how to write a proper letter: the address, the date, the courteous salutation, the correct layout of the page, the formal signing off. But most crucially, you taught us grammar and syntax. On the blackboard you drew up meticulous columns, and introduced us to parts of speech, parsing, analysis. You showed us how to take a sentence apart, identify its components, and fit them back together with a fresh understanding of the way they worked.

One day you listed the functions of the adverb. You said, 'An adverb can modify an adjective.' Until that moment I had known only that adverbs modified verbs: *they laughed loudly; sadly she hung her head.* I knew I was supposed to be scratching away with my dip pen, copying the list into my exercise book, but I was so excited by this new idea that I put up my hand and said, 'Mrs Dunkley. How can an adverb modify an adjective?'

You paused, up there in front of the board with the pointer in your hand. My cheeks were just about to start burning when I saw on your face a mysterious thing. It was a tiny, crooked smile. You looked at me for a long moment – a slow, careful, serious look. You looked at me, and for the first time, I knew that you had seen me.

'Here's an example,' you said, in an almost intimate tone. '*The wind was terribly cold.*'

I got it, and you saw me get it. Then your face snapped shut.

I never lost my terror of you, nor you your savage contempt. But if arithmetic lessons continued to be a hell of failure and derision, your English classes were a paradise of branching and blossoming knowledge.

Many years later, dear Mrs Dunkley, when I had turned you into an entertaining ogre from my childhood whose antics made people laugh and shudder, when I had published four books and felt at last that I could call myself a writer, I had a dream about you. In this dream I walked along the sandstone verandah of the school where you had taught me, and looked in through the French doors of the staffroom. Instead of the long tables at which the teachers of my childhood used to sit, marking exercise books and inventing horrible tests and exams, I saw a bizarre and miraculous scene.

I saw you, Mrs Dunkley, moving in slow motion across the staff-room – but instead of your grim black 1940s wool suit, you were dressed in a jacket made of some wonderfully tender and flexible material, like suede or buckskin, but in soft, unstable colours that streamed off you into the air in wavy bands and ribbons and garlands, so that as you walked you drew along behind you a thick, smudged rainbow trail.

In 1996 I described this dream in the introduction to a collection of my essays. A few months after the book came out, I received a letter from a stranger. She had enjoyed my book, she said, particularly the introduction. She enclosed a photo that she thought I might like to see.

The photo shows a woman and a teenage girl standing in front of a leafy tree, in a suburban backyard. It's an amateurish black and white snap of a mother and daughter: it cuts off both subjects at the ankle. The girl is dressed in a gingham school uniform. Her hairdo places the picture in about 1960. She is slightly taller than the woman, and is looking at the camera with the corners of her mouth drawn back into her cheeks, but her eyes are not smiling; they are wary and guarded.

The woman in the photo is in her late forties. She has short, dark, wavy hair combed back off her forehead. Her brows are dark and level, her nose thin, her lips firmly closed in an expression of bitter constraint. Deep, hard lines bracket her mouth. She's wearing a straight black skirt, and a black cardigan undone to show a neat white blouse buttoned to the neck. Her hands are hanging by her sides.

I showed the photo to my husband. 'What enormous hands!' he said.

I knew your hands, Mrs Dunkley. Not that they ever touched me, but I recall them as thin and sinewy and fierce-looking, with purplish skin that seemed fragile. They quivered, in 1952, with what I thought was rage, as you skimmed your scornful pencil point down my wonky long divisions and multiplications.

'My mother,' wrote the stranger in her letter, 'was an alcoholic.'

I thought I knew you, Mrs Dunkley. I thought that by writing about you I had tamed you and made you a part of me. But when

I looked at that photo, I felt as if I'd walked into a strange room at night, and something imperfectly familiar had turned to me in the dark. The real Mrs Dunkley shifted out from under the grid of my creation, and I saw you at last, my teacher: an intense, damaged, dreadfully unhappy woman, only just holding on, fronting up to the school each morning, buttoned into your black clothes, savagely impatient, craving, suffering: a lost soul.

Dear Mrs Dunkley, you're long gone, and I'm nearly seventy. But oh, I wish you weren't dead. I've got some things here that I wouldn't be ashamed to show you. And I've got something I want to say. I would like to thank you. It's probably what you would have called *hyperbole*, but, Mrs Dunkley, you taught me everything I know. Other teachers, later, consolidated it. But you were the one who laid the groundwork. You showed me the glory and the power of an English sentence, and the skills I would need to build one. You put into my hands the tools for the job.

Dear Mrs Dunkley. I know that your first name was Grace; I hope you found some, in the end.

Please accept, in whatever afterlife you earned or were vouchsafed, the enduring love, the sincere respect, and the eternal gratitude, Of your Great Mooncalf, Helen

Helen Garner

To the woman who changed my life

BENJAMIN LAW

Dear Mother,

Well, this is embarrassing. First of all, it's sort of weird that I'm writing you a letter at all, because I distinctly remember teaching you how to use email. The last time I turned on your computer, though, there were over a thousand unread messages in your inbox. And even though most of it was probably junk mail from your Myer One subscription, it still makes me feel as though I've somehow failed you as a son.

I'm also vaguely embarrassed that, with this letter, I've decided that the one woman who has changed my life most is . . . well, you. (Didn't I write a book about this?) Is that gross? You've always said you don't like mummy's boys, and yet here I am, declaring you've touched me more profoundly than any other woman in the world – which I really hope people take in a non-incest kind of way. This whole dedication – it seems kind of, well, *gay*. But as you'll probably say to me after this, 'Ben, you *are* gay.' And then you'll laugh, you bitch. And later, when we're talking to perfect strangers, you'll – as always – introduce me to them as 'my gay son, Benjamin. He's really gay, you know.'

Thanks, Mum. I really appreciate that.

But, to be fair, you *have* changed my life. As most of our arguments over the years have gone, you've changed my life because you *gave* me life – and therefore I apparently *owe* you my life, even though

I never asked to be born. And then you'll finish off by saying, 'Ben, you don't get me at all, because you'll never understand what it's like to be a mother!' But how can I, Jenny? How can I when it's illegal for me to adopt – or steal – a child in this state, and, more importantly, I don't have a uterus, much less one that's as fertile and prolific as yours? You can't close every disagreement we have by saying, 'You'll never know what it's like to be a mother,' even though I have to admit it's a pretty good trump card, you diabolical genius, you.

You're right, though: I'll never understand what it's like to be a mother. But from what you've told me over the years, I now understand that motherhood is something that's at once both sublime and horrifying, like skydiving or Madonna's face.

When you were twenty-two years old, you had your first child. And, as you would tell us many years later, you peered down at your newborn daughter's face and thought to yourself, 'Wow, babies really smell like pussy.' But there were other thoughts too, including the palpable sense that everything that happened to this person – the baby daughter who'd grow up to be my big sister – depended entirely on you. You started with one kid, then had two, then bam: suddenly you had five kids – which I think is technically a litter – fully aware that everything you said and did from now on would affect the lives of these miniature humans, for better or worse.

I can't imagine that pressure. I'm twenty-nine now. At my age, you already had three kids. At my age, I cannot keep basic herbs alive. At restaurants, I walk into clear glass doors. I've dropped furniture on my toenails, causing them to go black. I once crashed my car trying to park it at a shopping centre. As much as this statement will set gay rights back, there is a reason why clumsy gay men can't – or shouldn't – reproduce easily: we would accidentally kill our children.

When you're a mother, you change your kids' lives automatically, just by having them. Even if you bundle them up and abandon them in the woods to be raised by wild wolves, rats or other Chinese people, you will have changed your children's lives permanently. In fact, you change your kids' lives before they're even born.

Say you had stayed in Hong Kong where you spent your teens and early twenties, a place where people, on average, have 100 square feet of living space to themselves – the size of a small ensuite here. If we'd been born there, we would have lived like my cousins, whose bedrooms are so compact and compressed, they're like a Jenga puzzle of desks and wardrobes and beds, arranged just so, until there's only enough space for them to slot themselves into bed at night.

You took a leap of faith in moving to Australia with my dad, to a completely foreign country to which you'd never been before. It was because of that brave move that your children have grown up to become independent, to have space to roam, and can travel around the world with a barely restricted passport and earn incomes that don't confine us to houses the size of a Guantanamo cell. Because you moved to Australia, we became lucky. And we became bogans. Bogans who use words like 'eh' and 'uni' and 'moot'.

When I was finally born, you left your mark on me immediately. One of the first and most important responsibilities in parenthood is naming your child, and some parents fail miserably in that department. Really, who looks down at the face of a newborn babe with flushed cheeks and blinking eyes like a calf, and says to themselves, 'You, my sweet bundle of joy, I will name *Agatha*'?

I have encountered two actual people in my life named Michael Hunt – think about it – which I feel is insanely cruel. Celebrities are notoriously awful: Sylvester Stallone named two of his children Seargeoh and Sage Moonblood (who both, no doubt, have lucrative careers in professional menstruation), and there is a Canadian in Saskatchewan whose given name is Dick Assman, who insists his German name is pronounced 'ooze-man', though I'm not convinced 'Dick-Ooze Man' is much of an improvement.

But, Mum, you did relatively well in the naming department,

I must say. For my eldest sister, you chose Candy – a sweet name, though I feel it's sad she eventually became a primary school teacher, considering she has the perfect name for a prostitute. Then came regal-sounding Andrew, then me. For my English name, I'm glad you went with Benjamin, because I feel it suits me. (It's Hebrew, and we're such Jews.)

And I'm also glad that you chose a suitable Chinese name for me as well. *Yook-Nung*. It means 'ability' and 'the rising sun', which makes me feel both Chinese and Native American. But on my birth certificate you spelt the name 'Yook' with the letters Y U K. Nurses in Nambour Hospital would have laughed, knowing you looked down at your newborn baby and thought, Yuk. Thank you, Mum. Thank you for the gift of life, and for reminding me every time I look at my passport that I'm disgusting.

But perhaps 'Yuk' is fitting after all, because in my adult years, I've somehow found myself with this reputation for being the grossest person my friends know. I'm regularly sent emails with pictures or videos of conjoined twins, faecal accidents, explosive cysts, men who have sexual relationships with inanimate objects, men who have sexual relationships with explosive cysts – all with the message, 'Saw this and thought of you, Ben.' Mother, how did you know I'd turn out like this? Was it my face? Did you already know then that later in childhood all my cousins and relatives would know me as Doctor Sex? That I'd teach my primary school friends what lesbians were and what sodomy meant – and how it was done – in between classes? Was nature or nurture responsible for me becoming this person – Yuk?

When I think back to all those times we watched Sophie Lee's *Sex* together, or the other times you screamed at us, 'Kids, kids! There is sex on the television. *Come look!*', I suspect you played your own special role. We always watched far more SBS than ABC, shunning shows about English gardens and instead opting for Spanish movies filled with naked women and men doing interesting things with each other and processed meats, and replays of the erotic breastfeeding film *The Tit and the Moon*.

But you've changed my life in so many ways, Mum. You taught me to read before I started school. You taught me about self-respect and the importance of moisturising. Because of you, I have deep – and I think legitimate – suspicions, which border on revulsion, towards people who don't rinse the suds off their dishes. When I came out at seventeen, you told me there was nothing wrong with being gay – that it simply meant something had gone wrong in the womb – and it's only now that I realise how lucky I was, to have such an utter fag hag for a mother.

But it was after your divorce, as your kids began to move out, that you started to change your own life. Rather than being responsible for the task of naming any more children, you renamed yourself, reclaiming your maiden name. You had all the documentation laminated and framed, and put it in places where other women would hang their marriage photos.

So thank you, Mum. And sorry, too. Sorry for the times I've said, 'I love you', when really, I just wanted to hang up. Sorry for all the times I made you think I'd died as a kid, and for that time I lifted up your shirt and accidentally showed Andrew your boobs. And I'm being a brat about the emails, of course. I know you read all our emails, and that you're just completely getting spam-fucked by Myer One. And I'm sorry about being embarrassed about this letter. Because God knows, you've had reason to be embarrassed by us.

Lots of love, from the really gay son, the one you looked down upon and thought to name,
Yuk

Benjamin Law

KEIR NUTTALL

Dear St Columba of Rieti,

I'm writing to you in the hope you may be able to help me out of a bind.

I read on Wikipedia that you are the patron saint to turn to in matters of sorcery and witchcraft, and frankly, I hope that you will be the second woman to change my life. I will tell you about the first later.

I know it's a bit rich asking for your help, given I am not Catholic or even baptised.

In my defence, though, I did grow up surrounded by Catholics. The country primary school I attended, Clintonvale State, had nineteen students and one teacher who was my dad. My family were one of three in the entire district who weren't Catholic, so I absorbed a lot of Catholicism by osmosis. For example, I still love to get drunk and feel guilty about it afterwards.

I'm sure you would have approved of the pious atmosphere at Clintonvale Primary. One day my classmate Danny Ramsey brought a Gene Simmons mask to school. The other students said that Kiss were devil worshippers, and that their name stood for Knights In Satan's Service. They confiscated the mask and buried it under the library.

When Danny Ramsey protested that it was a birthday gift from his mum, we hurled large pieces of cactus at him.

Around this time (grade three), my best friend Lawrence Ryan told me that a lady who was a devil worshipper had been jogging in the park in Warwick and one of her boobs had fallen off. When the ambulance came, they found it on the ground, full of maggots. This definitely happened, and if you don't believe me, just ask Lawrence's aunty, who doesn't have a phone.

Of course, St Columba, you have seen way weirder stuff than that, having raised the dead and toured the Holy Land without your body, so I'm sure you totally get it. My point is, I was not without spiritual guidance. And I can't say I wasn't warned about the devil.

My parents, one atheist and one agnostic, were unaware that in Clintonvale I had started praying. I mainly prayed for Donna Cootes to love me, but I also prayed for selfless things like having a space-ship land in the school grounds to take us all for a ride. I see that just recently the Vatican has announced it's okay to believe in aliens, so I think you'd have to agree I was way ahead of you guys on that one.

When I was in grade six, we moved to Toowoomba. I could tell it was a big city because it had a McDonald's.

For high school, my parents sent me to Toowoomba Grammar. You'll be pleased to know that my grade eight science teacher, Mr Randolph, was a very devout man. During one lesson on physics he told us that there was no such thing as perpetual motion – it was impossible. Despite this, he said, two of his friends once drove all the way across the Nullarbor with no petrol in their tank, just by using the power of prayer. Mr Randolph said if we were interested in hearing more of this sort of thing, or even if we weren't but liked free pancakes, we should come to the Inter-School Christian Fellowship meetings held every Tuesday at lunch.

While ISCF was nowhere near as cool an acronym as KISS, the pancakes were a real drawcard.

At one of the meetings, Mr Randolph told us the story of one of the members of his youth group. She had been smoking lots of mari-juana and didn't know why. 'Why are you doing that?' they asked her. 'I just don't know,' she would say. 'I don't know why I'm doing it.'

Nobody at the youth group could work it out. Then one day they realised she had been listening to 'Another One Bites the Dust' by Queen on her walkman. Hidden under the music was a backwards message that said, 'It's fun to smoke marijuana.'

Then Mr Randolph played us a video that seemed to feature my entire music collection.

It turned out Iron Maiden, Twisted Sister and even XTC were in league with the devil. And they confirmed that Kiss was indeed an acronym for Knights In Satan's Service, and AC/DC stood for Anti-Christ/Devil's Child, and WASP for We Are Satan's People.

Overnight my albums had become dark and fascinating. I could feel them luring me towards evil.

At another ISCF meeting, a mysterious guest from outside the school came. He stood at the front of the room and looked at us all. After a moment, he announced he had the power to see demons, and that he could see them right now. They were hanging off our backs and sitting on our shoulders, whispering in our ears, telling us to sin. Demons of pride and hatred and lust.

Lust! No wonder I was so horny! It all made perfect sense. I ate my free pancake.

Columba, I know you can relate when I say there was a battle going on inside me between good and evil. Throughout this time I had become obsessed with the guitar, and, in particular, trying to play the guitar as fast as humanly possible, with no regard for timing, dynamics or taste. The pivotal moment came when I saw the movie *Crossroads*. Not that travesty starring Britney Spears – this *Crossroads* was all class. It was *The Karate Kid* with guitars.

In the movie, Steve Vai plays a guitarist who has signed his soul over to the devil in exchange for the ability to shred heinously on his axe. That means 'play guitar well'. I saw him and I wanted to be him.

And here is where I got myself into a pickle, St Columba, so please forgive me in advance.

I prepared a contract between myself and the devil. In exchange for my eternal soul, I would become the best guitarist in the world in a famous rock band. I cut my finger open and signed my name in blood, then burned the contract and scattered the ashes. I had learned the finer details on how to do this from my ISCF friends.

Within months, my guitar chops were blazing. Sure, I practised a lot, but it was obvious to me it was mostly the devil making good on his end of the bargain. I stopped attending the ISCF meetings and started sinning in earnest.

St Columba, I confess that I smoked a lot of cigarettes, got drunk for the first time and had sex with a Postpak. I won't go into details here.

I bought remaindered *Penthouse* and *Playboy* magazines off my friend whose parents owned a newsagency and sold them at an outrageous profit to the boarders at school. Now I could eat all the pancakes I wanted.

I must have been listening to a lot of Queen, too, because pretty soon I was smoking heaps of marijuana and I didn't know why. One day the Gideons visited our school and handed out pocket-sized Bibles. My friend Dave and I discovered that their pages were the perfect size for rolling joints.

That summer I worked my way through nearly the entire Book of Revelations.

The ISCF had made it very clear to us that sex before marriage was a big no-no, but I knew those rules no longer applied to me.

Still, no matter how hard I tried, I couldn't stop being a virgin.

Then I met Tammy LeStrange.

I saw her after school at McDonald's hanging out with Harry Delbrige and his girlfriend. I called him up and asked him who that girl in the pink miniskirt was and could I have her number. He said he'd ask. Two hours later, my phone rang. It was Tammy herself.

'So, Harry says you think I'm hot?' she said.

'Um, yeah.'

'Well,' she said. 'Do you want to have a root then?'

'Oh . . . Yes, please.'

I don't know why I told you that, Columba. I guess I thought you might be curious, seeing as how you went to your grave a virgin and all. No offence. Please watch over Tammy.

I didn't worry too much about school, safe in the knowledge that my contract with you-know-who would soon pay off and I'd be set for life. I know what you're thinking, St Columba, and you're right. They call him the devil for a reason!

But I've always been pretty slow on the uptake. For example, I never saw my own face in profile until I was nineteen. It was a real shock. Similarly, I didn't realise that the devil wasn't living up to his end of the bargain until I was thirty.

I was already three years older than Hendrix, Joplin and Kurt Cobain had been when they'd died. The bands I had played in over the years – Uncle Stinky, More, Funk Me Dead, Cradle, Seethe, Eat Biscuits, GACK, Dogmachine, Earthfish and Complicated Game – had all either broken up, failed or no longer required my services.

Now I was in a band called Transport. We were all ageing and saw it as our last shot at the big time. To show our dedication, we got band tattoos. Transport had got further than any other band I'd been in: we had a song on high rotation on triple j and a real manager. She got me a meeting with music publisher and ex-member of Icehouse Keith Welsh. I was pretty excited, thinking it might lead to a big break for us. Keith shook my hand, looked me in the eye and said, 'You're past your use-by date.'

I didn't know it at the time but I had already fallen in love with the woman who would completely change my life. Katie was also a struggling musician. After much debate about mixing business and pleasure, I started playing guitar for Katie and writing some songs with her. When she needed a whole new backing band, Transport stepped in. Over the next couple of years, her success grew and grew.

Often Transport would play an early show backing Kate in front of a sold-out crowd and then go to another venue and play our own show to five bored punters. Kate got a record deal while Transport maxed out our drummer's credit card touring the country playing to nobody. The day Kate was presented with her first gold record, I watched all my dreams come true, but not for me.

Look, I'm not complaining in any way. I'm extremely grateful. If it wasn't going to happen for me, having it happen for the person I love most in the world is the next best thing. And I still get to play guitar and write songs for a living, which, let's face it, is like having won the lotto.

But as I get older, my own certain death has become less of an abstract concept, and more of a feeling in my spinal column.

St Columba, I'm not sure if I believe that lady's boob fell off in Warwick, or that prayer can run a car as well as petrol or that there are demons hanging off all of us, making us sin. I don't know if there really is someone called the devil, and I'm not sure you can even read this letter. But, for some reason, it's not hard for me to believe I might have a soul. Please – can you help me get it back?

I've reviewed the small print in my contract with the devil, and I think I have a good case. It read, and I quote, 'I will become the best guitarist in the world', unquote, and, quote, 'in a famous rock band', unquote. My wife, Katie, has attained a B-grade level of fame at best and plays pop music, not rock. And Steve Vai is still the best guitarist in the world. I think you'll agree, the devil didn't honour his contract.

But I'm sorry, no, I don't have a copy. I burned it.

Yours faithfully,
Keir Nuttall

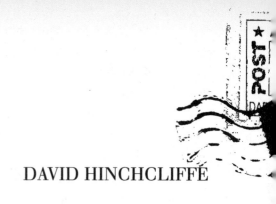

DAVID HINCHCLIFFE

There's something about your senior years that makes you want to escape the present and lurch back down the tunnel of time — to go right back, as it were, to the beginning of it all . . . To return to that most female of inner sanctums, the very womb itself.

So I write this to the ovum that, against the odds, gave me life, from the perspective of a grateful little spermatozoon and the man to be created.

Dear Mother Ovum,

There I was, happily swimming around without a care in the world.

One of the gang, really.

None of us actually stood out. All 2 536 942 of us were pretty much cookie-cutter copies of each other, all going with the flow, you might say. Remarkable, really, so many of us, so singularly lacking in singularity. Uncanny.

We hadn't really formed much in the way of personality or features. Just little squiggles of 'hope'. I suppose the more unkind would have described us as sort of androgynous, amorphous amoebas.

Anyway, there we were — pathetic little tadpoles thrashing around in this gushing torrent like we were contestants in one of those topless jelly-wrestling matches you see on a Friday night at the Port Office Hotel.

Then, all of a sudden, the green light went on, the whistle blew, the floodgates broke and – *whoosh*.

We found ourselves rushing helter-skelter down this long, dark passage into a deep, mysterious unknown.

Frankly, I was spooked.

Nothing had prepared us for this. But somehow something kicked in.

Something primal and predetermined clicked in each of us and suddenly it was every spermatozoon for him or herself. I flicked my flagella like my life depended on it – which of course it did. I took one long deep breath and just went for it. I elbowed others out of the way, and kicked and clawed to the front of the pack.

Without knowing it at the time, I was living the great Darwinian dream – survival of the fittest.

But I have to admit that at the time it was all a bit of a blur, really. My head was spinning. I was on autopilot.

(Honestly, if I hadn't gone through those rebirthing classes at the Natural Medicine Clinic several years ago, I doubt I'd remember a thing.)

But I can say now that I do clearly recall the moment I first saw you. The object of my primitive, carnal desire. You were this enormous warm, inviting, fecund presence.

I melted. I was immediately captivated. I didn't need any 'egging' on. I made a beeline from the very get-go. I attached myself and nuzzled deep into that luxurious interior and I did not let go.

My twenty-three chromosomes found your twenty-three chromosomes absolutely irresistible, as though it were a match made in heaven.

We connected, physically and metaphysically. It was more spectacular than a Riverfire Fireworks display! It was more blinding than an F-111 dump-and-burn!

I remember that extraordinary and instantaneous transformation from my aimless spermatozoon and your egg cell to that wonderful new hybrid organism we created – what the gynaecologists call the 'totipotent zygote', or, as I prefer to call it, *me*.

I became the sum of our parts. I was bigger than a hyperactive speck of sperm or a warm, seductive ovum.

It was a turning point. It changed my life. Well, in fact, it gave me life. I was the ugly worm transmogrified into the beautiful butterfly.

If it hadn't been for that one cataclysmic, climactic moment, I would have worn myself out just swimming around in ever-decreasing circles.

I would have shrivelled up and died and been replaced by an army of new recruits. And that would have been the end of my potential.

Who knows how our little history would have been changed? I wouldn't have grown up to marry Meg and gone on to beget Tom and then Joe, who in turn will no doubt go on to do their own begetting, and so on, and so on. Generations would never have been born if a certain frisky little spermatozoon hadn't encountered you at the end of that long, dark tunnel.

Each of us represents a single sperm in an absolute ocean finding its way to a single egg. How the course of human history would change if those incalculable odds changed. I boggle at the sheer mathematical improbability of it all.

In chaos theory, they call it the 'butterfly effect'.

According to this theory, a small change at one place can result in large differences somewhere else. The effect derives its name from the theoretical example of a hurricane's formation being contingent on whether or not a distant butterfly had flapped its wings several weeks before. If a buttefly flaps its wings in the Amazon, a hurricane can be produced down the track as far away as in the South China Sea.

So this little butterfly owes you – my dear mother ovum – absolutely everything.

I know it's taken me a while to get around to putting this in writing. In fact, it's about fifty-seven years and four months since that fateful day.

I just want to declare – openly and unqualifiedly – that everything I am today I owe to you.

To say you changed me is a gross understatement. Against odds of 2 536 942 to 1, our chance encounter converted me from a shapeless, brainless, thoughtless, hopeless amoeba that wriggled into your warm embrace fifty-seven years and four months ago, to the world-weary, well-worn, shopsoiled, befuddled but eternally grateful specimen that stands before you today.

I toast the mother ovum that – against all the odds – gave each of us Life.

[signature]

TIM McGUIRE

Dear Buffy the Vampire Slayer,

Today my mother swears she didn't let me watch you when I was six, but she did. I don't know why I loved you from such a young age. I don't know why you didn't frighten me, when the Bunyip song on the Blinky Bill tape had the power to send me screaming into my parents' bedroom every night. You were a sassy sixteen-year-old girl who fought vampires; I was an asthmatic six-year-old boy who swam with the aid of an orange flotation device called a 'booby ring'. There was no common ground between us, no reason in the world why I should have decided, at six, that I wanted to be you.

It was difficult to get this ambition off the ground. Nobody at school wanted to play Buffy during lunch, especially since I cast myself in the title role every time. So instead, when we played tiggy, I would run like you did in episode 46, all shoulders and frantic glances, screaming in a whiney, prepubescent voice that sounded eerily similar to your whiney American one: 'Somebody, please help me! Stop, please, I need help!' This did little to improve my popularity, which had already taken hits from the advanced vocabulary you'd taught me, getting me to repeat words like 'kleptomaniac', 'orgasm' and 'orgy', while in class we learned 'Olympics' and 'mountain' and what an adjective did to a noun.

I think I can say with some confidence, then, that you were also the catalyst for my premature sexual awakening. 'I had sex,' I told my father when I was eight. He asked some questions very quickly and was relieved when he could tell me that, just because I'd lain on top of a girl and kissed her with my mouth open, it didn't mean I'd had sex with her. I didn't understand this logic and concluded that for it to be sex, one of us probably needed to be a vampire. If this is true about sex, then my dad will be relieved to know I'm still a virgin.

It didn't matter that I was too young to understand all of the plot lines. You were a constant in my life at a time when so much else was uncertain. I could change schools and addresses and know that you would always be there with a wooden stake and a clever pun to make me feel better. You see, Buffy, I owed who I was to you. You'd taught me how to dance, how to fight and how to make my legs look damn good in a Little Red Riding Hood Halloween costume. What I didn't know was that this was just the beginning of our relationship, that you had instilled lessons and values in me that I would come to depend on later in life. Because I got my wish, Buffy – I did become you. Whether by wishful thinking or grand design, we took the same journey, just a few years apart, and when I was finally on it, I appreciated for the first time how hard it had been for you, and how much I didn't want it after all.

Buffy, this was our concurrent journey:

We start a new school and have trouble fitting in with any-body except the library staff. Rumours about us circulate almost immediately and we worry about what will happen if our secret is discovered. It's not something we chose or asked for; it's just a part of who we are. The fact that we discover and then have to deal with it when we are teenagers is cruel and unfair. We stay up nights, preoccupied with it, worried that this thing will define us more than everything else we are and want to be. We are close with our mother, but we don't tell her our secret until our second-last year of high school. Having seen what happened when you told her yours, I am ready to be kicked out of home when I tell her mine.

But even though we are the same, our mothers must be different, because mine doesn't let me walk out of the house. Instead, she continues loving me, as yours does when you give her the chance, and both of them show us again and again, in sweetly oblivious ways, how proud they are of us. Your mother tries to go with you on vampire patrols; mine writes 'courage and honesty always' in permanent marker on my cast when I fracture my wrist, which makes for awkward cover stories at my all-male high school. But we love our mothers very much.

Somehow, we make it through high school. Then, when we are nineteen, we meet a boy at university. We date and it is wonderful. He is wonderful. He's everything we want a boyfriend to be: dependable, charming, honest. And he loves us. He tells us this himself, but we already know: by the way he saves you from the Polgara demon in your case, and in mine by the way he brings me back a bookmark he made out of reeds on his camping trip. He is so genuine and good that we take him for granted. He wants to see us more, love us more, but there is something wrong with us and we can't seem to let him. We suspect it's our secret again. Even though he knows it – even though he has one too. We believed for too long that we weren't supposed to be happy and in doing so we fucked up our first real chance at it. When we realise it isn't going to work out, we cry, because we know that he is perfect, and that when we lose him we're going to be alone again. It takes seeing him a year later with someone else to make us understand we could never have made him happy. We are so glad that someone else could, but we wish it could have been us.

When we are twenty, we decide to better ourselves. We want to learn about who we are and where we're going. We want to be great. We aren't, though, because at twenty I graduate with a degree in fine arts, and you kill yourself.

I am twenty now and this might be a safe time to stop following in your footsteps before I end up dead too, or, worse, blonde.

It amazes me that, after fifteen years of watching you, my age still hasn't caught up to yours. When the show ended you were twenty-two, which means I still have two years left where I can turn on the television and compare my life to yours. One of the many skills you taught me, though, is courage, and so I'm stopping today, with this letter, even though I really wanted to make it to the musical episode, and the one where you have sex with Spike.

But even when I have outgrown you, I know that you will still come back to me in strange and unpredictable ways. Like how in the final episode you say to the source of all evil, 'I want you to get out of my face!' Today I repeat this line whenever I need to excavate a pimple or a blackhead from my T-zone. I throw a leg up onto the bathroom sink, lean right up close to the mirror, squeeze the offending blemish between my fingers, and say the line at the moment of eruption: 'I want you to get out of my face!' In my passion, I usually forget to hold a tissue to the area and warm pus spatters against the glass.

So thank you for everything, Buffy. Like you, I have been blessed with many wonderful women in my life. Family, friends, girlfriends, teachers, women whose uteruses I will ask to borrow in ten years time. They know who they are. They might be thinking that I should have written this letter to them, because they have saved me, from myself and from others, many times over. But you saved the world, Buffy, and they ain't got nothing on you.

Your number one fan,
Tim

ROBERT MANNE

Dear Pauline,

This letter will not please you. But write it I must. First, a word or two of personal explanation.

When I was quite young, I learned that people's political views are either left-wing or right-wing. As I was interested in politics, I wondered which side had truth or justice on its side and to which side of politics I should belong.

One way of deciding whether I wished to belong to the left or right wing of politics was to listen to my parents. My father was a far more politically aware person than my mother. As a small business-man, he was tempted to vote for Mr Menzies, but my mother refused to let him do so. She had grown up in Weimar Germany, and one of her favourite stories was about how, as a schoolgirl in 1925, she had torn down a poster of the right-wing presidential candidate, General von Hindenburg. Although neither of my parents talked about it much, around this time I learned that the extreme right in Germany had produced Adolf Hitler, and that he had decided to wipe my people from the face of the earth. So the answer to the question of whether I should belong to the left or the right of politics was now answered.

Or was it? If the overwhelming political question was whether or not one preferred a world of racial or social hierarchy and privi-lege, or a world of rough equality, the answer for me was obvious.

I preferred equality. This placed me on the left. Things then, however, turned out to be more complicated than I'd first thought. I soon discovered that an even larger number of people had been murdered by a regime of the extreme left, Josef Stalin's Soviet Union, than had been murdered under the Third Reich of Adolf Hitler. And people on the left had still not abandoned their illusions about the movement to which Stalin belonged – communism. This placed me on the right.

For a quarter century, as a consequence of all this, I was a political hybrid – an anti-communist social democrat. For eight years I even edited the conservative anti-communist cultural magazine *Quadrant*, leading it slowly, amid much grumbling and gnashing of teeth, to the left.

This leads me to you, Pauline, the woman who changed my life.

In 1996, you were preselected as the Liberal Party candidate for the unwinnable outer-Brisbane seat of Oxley. When you wrote a letter to the editor complaining about the privileges afforded to Aboriginals – radical for 1996, innocuous by the racial standards of 2011 – you lost your preselection. Then, standing as an independent, you won the seat of Oxley handsomely, recording the highest anti-Labor swing in the country. No one thought much about you until six months later, when you gave your maiden speech to an empty House. Your main complaint was about the way the coercive ideology of 'political correctness' had been used by Prime Minister Keating and his supporters among the left-wing 'elites' to impose, on ordinary, average Australians, an alien set of values favouring Aboriginals and Asians and, later, Muslims and asylum seekers.

You will not demur, I am sure, when I call this the most consequential maiden speech in Australian political history. Not in spite of but because of your lack of cosmopolitan sophistication, you became immensely popular. You were and still are defined by your two-word response to a question about xenophobia: 'please explain'. What you stood for – no, please, let me finish – was an old world where racial prejudice and Anglo-Irish superiority was merest common sense. Your essence, if I might put it so, was captured by the fact that in your many public appearances, you often appeared to be on the edge of breaking into tears. Unlike your American equivalent, Sarah Palin, who is disgustingly cheerful, you were then decidedly lachrymose. You intuited that your world was under threat. You will remember, Pauline, the time when you prepared a video in readiness for the assassination you believed to be imminent. As the last representative of a dying world, you seemed to expect that you would be shot.

Even before the great Australian indifference machine transformed you from a political leader into a television personality on *Dancing with the Stars* and *Celebrity Apprentice,* I did not fear you, I promise, Pauline. You might be surprised to hear that I did, however, fear the reaction to you of the new Australian Prime Minister, John Howard, who eventually stole almost all your political clothes. Shortly after your maiden speech, you may recall, Howard used the occasion of a Queensland Liberal Party conference to speak about the way his government had lifted the yoke of political correctness from the necks of the Australian people. Concerning you, Pauline, Howard held his tongue, for very many months. Was it because he didn't want to give you any political oxygen? Or was it because he secretly sympathised with what you had to say? I'd be interested in your view.

Now let me explain, Pauline, why I have felt compelled to write this stern and strange letter.

For a quarter century, Australian political leaders struggled to transcend the racism that had scarred their country's history. The most noble accomplishment of the Australian political class, from Whitlam to Keating via Fraser, was to turn its back on the White Australia Policy and to open its eyes to the vast injustices committed against Indigenous peoples following the arrival of British settlers in Australia.

John Howard was the first political leader since Billy McMahon uninterested in this path.

For years I had been blind to the new forces emerging on the conservative side of politics, to which you and I, in very different ways, belonged. Unlike many, I had not understood the implications of the fact Howard would not allow the word multiculturalism to pass his lips. I had not understood what it foretold when he expressed doubts about the pace of Asian immigration. I had not seen the meaning of the misgivings he had expressed about Mabo or the idea of Aboriginal self-determination. I had not even heard the dog whistle in the slogan the Liberal Party used in 1996 – 'For All of Us'.

It took Howard's sphinx-like silence over you, Pauline, to open my eyes. Quite suddenly, I saw Tampa on the horizon. That is to say, I saw that Howard intended to reconstruct the Liberal Party, from its small-l liberal origins into a party of populist conservatism. Quite suddenly, I saw the significance of the idea that neo-conservatives had begun to deploy against the supposed political correctness of the supposed cosmopolitan elites, to which I had not so long ago been embarrassingly sympathetic. I've read the manifesto of the anti-Muslim, anti-multicultural fanatic Anders Breivik who recently murdered scores of young Norwegian Social Democrats. It begins with a dissection of the evils of political correctness. To be brutally honest, the manifesto is reminiscent of the book your followers released on your behalf, which was called *Pauline Hanson: The Truth*. Am I right to believe, as I always have, that you never actually read it?

Almost everything I have written for the past fifteen years has been against this way of looking at the world. Every major battle I have fought since then has been against the representatives of this world – Rupert Murdoch, John Howard, Keith Windschuttle, Andrew Bolt. By 1996, my political journey had taken me back to where my true feelings lie – to the egalitarian and anti-racist traditions of the left.

So the woman who truly changed my life was you, Pauline. Because I am far too arthritic to appear on *Dancing with the Stars*, and far too old and cerebral to be chosen as a *Celebrity Apprentice*, I have chosen to write this letter to offer to you my heartfelt gratitude.

R. Manne

DANIEL EVANS

Dear Mrs Potterzinski,

It's me, Daniel. Evans. Daniel Evans. I'm not sure if you remember me, but I certainly remember you. If it helps, I'd like to take you back to where it all started, back to 1992.

A leap year. Apartheid is being dismantled. Charles and Diana are still together. Paul Keating is in office. In Summer Bay, Bobby Simpson is alive and well, her nautical demise off the back of Adam's boat still a season away. And in a time before *So You Think You Can Dance*, if you have aspirations of child stardom, you're learning to bust it at Mrs Potterzinski's Dance School.

That summer I had proven to my parents that I had what it takes. I'd staged two successful neighbourhood productions of *Jesus Christ Superstar* and *Grease*. The former involved my six-year-old sister dressed as prostitute Mary Magdalene, and the latter lots of scantily clad children gyrating about the bonnet of my dad's Ford Falcon, mouthing words to songs that, on reflection, possibly weren't age-appropriate.

Your studio used to be located in the middle of an industrial estate between a whitegoods factory and an army disposal store. Kind of fitting given you had the energy and enigma of a Navy seal and ran the establishment like a prepubescent Guantanamo Bay.

Children huddled in hushed awe as you passed through the foyer, your face set in steel. There were whispers that you had danced at the

389

Moulin Rouge. This, combined with the high-cut, hyper-colour g-string leotards you wore over tights, fed the pornography rumours. One boy, Shaun, told me you were, in fact, a high-class prostitute. Another girl called Chelsea said you were married to *Family Feud* host Rob Bruff. We were enthralled.

Having been a choreographer for *Man O Man* and a cheer coach for *Gladiators*, it may have been B-grade glamour you peddled, but suburban escapees like me ate it up. Like a finely tuned interrogator, you would let silence speak volumes. And in those silences your eyes slid around like a serpent and you'd look us up and down with your head cocked to one side. 'This is about focus and discipline,' you said repeatedly. 'NOW GRAB A MAT AND WARM UP.'

With no air conditioning and sometimes in 35-degree Bikram heat, we'd sweat as our bodies contorted into Linda Blair-style configurations – all limbs and bones and impossible angles. And as you walked around correcting us, we all observed the most important rule: no matter how painful, no matter how difficult, furrow your brow and never complain.

We obeyed because we had to, and we had to because of the results. You may have been merciless but you won – lots. Your routines scooped the eisteddfod circuit.

The dance to Annie Lennox's 'Why' was my favourite. That was the one where, before letting us go on stage, you would make the entire ensemble look at *National Geographic* photo essays on Ethiopian famine. You told us we were doing this dance for kids far less fortunate than ourselves. Two girls cried and you told them wisely to 'use it'. And they did.

Your students were transfixing to watch, executing choreo that made the parents nervous, and in costumes that working-class families could barely afford.

One day Brodie Farraday's mum tried to suggest that the 'Blame It on the Boogie' routine did not need diamanté-laced gloves. Shortly after this conversation, Brodie was moved from her centre position to the back row – a space reserved for the disabled, those of a larger build, ethnic girls with moustaches and what you called 'developing bodies'. The back row – my home ground.

The fastest ticket to fame, we'd all figured out, was a position somewhere in the front row. Front-row kids were of prime performance pedigree – I realise now you placed them there for their excellent bone structure, flawless complexion, killer show smiles and extra-enthusiastic dispositions. Front row-ers got the solos, were always first to start the canons, and, like some kind of extraterrestrial cyborgs, could always pick up the most complicated move after only one demonstration. The front row was a front line and you wielded those kids like weapons against the stiff lips and keen eyes of the adjudicators. Then, like an Aztec high priestess, you'd sacrifice them for the greater good, expediting the very best to Hollywood . . . on the Gold Coast.

We watched as Potterzinski's favourites were cast in a local television series filmed at Movie World, a national miniseries filmed off the coast of Cairns, an internationally touring musical bound for New Zealand. You were a celestial gatekeeper, sending children into outer orbit. And I so desperately wanted you to one day pick me – if not for a bit part on *Ocean Girl*, then, at the very least, for the front row.

After Brodie Farraday's mum withdrew her from classes, it became immediately obvious that there would an opening in the front row for 'Blame It on the Boogie', and I thought that maybe it might be me promoted to front and centre. I had been practising so hard. The song was on repeat morning, noon and night, I knew all the moves off by heart, and in class, I didn't just dance, I flew. I dared you not to look at me – I dared you to take your eyes away from me. I wasn't just good, I was excellent, and you knew it. For an entire run one Saturday, you just stared at me, and I could've sworn your mouth opened a touch in sheer adoration . . .

I waited – with baited breath, fingers crossed, smiling to the point of collapse – for you to announce Brodie's replacement. The successful candidate would get an entire 45-second solo at the beginning of the dance before being joined by the rest of the troupe in staggered stages. The replacement had to be brilliant. The entire dance rested squarely on their shoulders. And I was ready. I was so ready. And I willed, with every fibre of being, you to pull me from back-row obscurity into the hallowed front row.

'You'll never get that spot,' Shaun said to me by the vending machine. 'You're not good enough.'

The words stung, Mrs Potterzinski. They pricked somewhere deep in my heart, because secretly I had suspected that maybe I wasn't centre-spotlight material, that I wasn't good enough to transcend this suburb, launch up and away, because I didn't have 'it'. And no matter how sparkly my spirit fingers, how aerodynamic my leaps, I'd never possess those two letters, 'I' and 'T', which were my passport to a life on the stage.

'She says you aren't easy to watch,' he continued, slurping back a Pasito. 'That's what Courtney says. She says it's because of your left eye.'

I'm still not sure if that's true – if my lazy left eye had somehow factored into your decision-making process. I'd tried to make up for my defect by always pitching my moves at a further 45 degrees. Still, there was no denying I did have serious hand–eye coordination issues. The following week, I held both eyes open like some sort of stunned animal. You didn't cast one look my way.

'Front and centre,' you announced, 'will be danced by . . .'

For the briefest of moments your eyes slipped effortlessly to mine, and a small smile broke at the corner of your mouth, and for the tiniest of seconds my entire body exploded into fireworks. And then –

'Shaun.'

There you were – God of dance-floor war. Shaun – the hero. Me – collateral damage. The tears came more quickly than I'd anticipated, falling out of the corners of my eye – my lazy left eye – as we resumed our beginning positions, and I danced on in the back row, obstructed and hidden.

I'm not sure if this has rung any bells, or if, in your mental Rolodex, you're still looking for an image of me. I spent another three years performing for you, alternating between back row right and back row centre. Occasionally I'd be trotted out to do the 'funny bit'. Like playing a sumo wrestler in the 'Kung Fu Fighting' routine, or the dog for New Kids on the Block's lesser-known hit 'Dirty Dawg'. After the acne ruptured across my face and the braces were installed, I finally gave up and packed it in.

On cue, Shaun went on to star in an ABC children's program, before featuring alongside Heath Ledger in the short-lived series *Roar*. Next was the musical. Then a couple of commercials. After that I stopped following his career. I think he still works on and off.

You changed my life by not changing my life. You set me on a different course, Mrs Potterzinski, one without *TV Week* covers and bit parts in *Blue Heelers*. Maybe you deliberately saved me. Was that it? Did you see more? Or maybe you were just a middle-aged heartless cunt who took sadistic pleasure in breaking the dreams of young children?

Something I want to tell you is that the back row is not for losers. You may have tried to hide us, the liabilities, the ones who smudged your perfect canvas. But in keeping us captive at the back, you made us survivors. You made us tougher, and more determined to shine. And when the rows in front of us would part, we'd be there, time after time, working our fucking guts out.

So thank you for making me – for making me tougher, more determined to shine. What I lacked in physical perfection, in hand-eye coordination, I've made up for in hot-blooded resilience.

I've learnt to forgive. The forgetting is harder. Every time I take to the dance floor, every time I hear an infectious disco beat and a young Michael Jackson beginning to croon, I'm dragged back to that industrial estate. I just have to grin and bear it. Throw down the gin with the tonic, and sometimes without the tonic. And lay blame for my shortcomings, my disappointment somewhere more ethereal. I lay my blame on the boogie.

And so, Mrs Potterzinski, wherever you are – this one goes out to you.

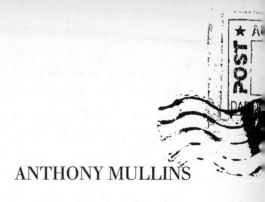

ANTHONY MULLINS

Dear Krissy,

It's day three in Paris and we're spending a rainy afternoon in the apartment, eating brie and mortadella baguettes and sleeping off the last of the jetlag. My feet hurt like crazy. In the past few days we've wandered the streets of Le Marais without much of a plan, discovering the neighbourhood that will be our home for the next three weeks. And our sources were right. It is beautiful. A perfect place to celebrate twenty years together.

Later I'm planning on playing some music on a ukulele you encouraged me to buy for the trip. I was able to stash it in the cabin luggage, and I take the fact that you wanted me to play some music while we were away as a sign that everything is good in our relationship. Especially because 1) it's a ukulele, which, along with the accordion and bagpipes, I'm pretty sure makes up the house band at the gates of hell, and 2) I don't really know how it works yet. I'm not even sure what key it's in. But I'm okay with this. I kind of prefer the mystery. It's something I've come to trust in myself across twenty years of lazy, rainy afternoons like this one with you.

They usually involve you writing on the couch while I sketch out ideas on one of the numerous guitars I own – imaginary soundtracks to non-existent movies that play exclusively in our flat for an afternoon, then fade out into some obscure DVD release in the sky.

You're always very tolerant as my fingers explore the fretboard, looking for an intriguing passage to travel down without any idea of where I might arrive. I imagine it sounds more like someone repairing an instrument than playing one but you seem to like it. It's not how I normally do things. I usually have to be quite dogged and systematic about how I do my work. Filmmaking is hideously expensive, involving dozens, sometimes hundreds of collaborators. There is always a plan, even when you want it to look like there isn't one. And it rarely offers the opportunity to stumble around in the dark like this and discover a strange and utterly pointless gem. But here, on these afternoons, there is no plan. There's only the chance to stumble across an unusual melody, a new voicing, a curious phrase. And to follow it.

Paris seems to be a place that will constantly reward a complete lack of planning. The city has been kind to us so far, despite us only having a jumbled list of recommendations gleaned from well-travelled friends, and a few phrases of apology and request. The avenues, alleys and doorways of Paris seem to invite just the right amount of discovery and chaos. A shop opens its door into a tiny laneway, apparently hoping to catch customers who are either lost or chancing a shortcut somewhere else. A delivery truck creates a traffic jam in a narrow alley and no one protests the unscheduled hold-up. You and I agreed a long time ago we liked this about France. Australia seemed too organised, too neat, everything so meticulously arranged that we become upset at the slightest disruption – it's not good for us. It brings out a mean streak in us all.

I've started recording a few tracks now, having figured out how the chords work – they're similar to a guitar but the D string is a different gauge so playing a routine chord throws up an unfamiliar voice. I don't read music well enough to transpose it in my head so I still have no idea what key I'm playing in, but it's nice. I'm discovering that ukuleles don't have to sound like you're selling a used car – they can be soft, intimate, even moody.

When I met you I was at a point in my life when it was time to get a plan. I'd already dropped out of a fine arts degree, worked for a while, gone back to uni to become a history teacher, and then ended up studying film and television. Having just graduated, with few prospects for work, I was fast running out of things to do next while I worked out what to do next and I seriously contemplated going back to the one-hour photo lab job I'd had between degrees. Maybe I could become the manager. I think I actually said those words to you, and either you didn't hear me or it was early enough in our relationship that you were willing to give me another chance. But it wasn't the end of it.

Not long after that, an old school friend visited our flat under the guise of discussing a 'business opportunity' because he 'respected my opinion', and I was too naive, unassertive, polite or all of the above to decline. And I continued to be far too polite as he and his abnormally bright-eyed mentor sat across from us on the milk crates that formed the sum total of the furniture we owned and drew with whiteboard precision a shape to fit my seemingly fragile future into. It was a once-off, ground floor, first look, first cab off the rank, first ship to sail, first man on the moon, exclusive offer to me, his friend, that must end today. To drive home his case, he pointed out, 'respectfully', the aimless direction my life had taken since school and how this was an opportunity to do something practical, sensible, reliable.

I nodded thoughtfully while my stomach ate itself. I'd recently started using words like practical, sensible, reliable, far more than I thought any arts graduate had a right to. For the first time in my life, I wasn't sure what came next, and here was my friend, my generous friend, offering me a plan to follow, a direction, a new way, an Amway. He underlined the word enthusiastically with his marker. Amway. The presentation was over. That was it. That was the future. He put down the pen, smiled at me and rubbed his hands as if he was about to hoe into a bowl of his favourite curry.

You saw the mix of speechless confusion and dread on my face and understood the situation with the clarity that I have come to love and rely upon. 'This is fucked,' you said. And it was.

A few days shy of twenty years later and we are in Paris. There was never much of a plan to get where we both are in our lives. We're just here. Together. And happy. You are on the couch writing what I think will be your next novel and I have just finished another gloriously pointless melody to nowhere. I set it to play to the only audience it will probably ever have as I make a cup of tea. It is sweet and melancholy in a way that seems in tune with the rainy streets outside. You look up from your writing and listen, smiling and nodding your approval. You like it. I knew you would. I hand you a cup of tea and we sit and discuss where we should go for our twentieth anniversary in a few days. We throw some ideas around but we don't get very far – 'We'll see.'

TODD MacDONALD

Dear Mary MacKillop,

Saint Mary? Your holiness? I'm not sure how to address you . . .

First up, let me just say I am not a religious person at all, I confess, and I don't mean that in a disrespectful way. But you hold a certain position in my life, which I cannot deny. And I suppose in a way I am covering my bases with you here, in case I have it wrong and you really are up there taking notes.

I wanted to write to you, I suppose, to apologise or explain myself, to ask forgiveness, perhaps – I'm not sure.

I get confused – is this a letter, or a prayer, or what? Perhaps you may recall a prayer we sent to you some years ago now, when our daughter was very ill.

Hold on, I'll back track a little . . . It started with Rebecca. We met in Edinburgh and fell in love in the Highlands of Scotland – heady festival days of too many cigarettes and pints, and then weeks later we nursed each other through the coughing up of black God-only-knows-what into the sink of Jenny Higgie's London flat. Then on the drug-hazed dance floor of a London nightclub there was a wild, cocaine-fuelled mutual promise that if we ever were to get married, we would have to do it at the Big Pineapple because we were from Queensland. And we did.

Soon after, two more women arrived to change my life – two little women. Twins. Not that we knew until twenty weeks into the

399

pregnancy. It was a surreal moment at the ultrasound as I came in late to see Bec, belly lubricated, on the technician's bench, and she looked at me and simultaneously cried and laughed – 'There're two in there!'

Then: waters breaking on the morning of the baby shower, high-risk pregnancy, emergency caesarean. Umbilical cords around necks, gaping hollows of an empty pregnant belly that I wasn't supposed to look back and see, but I did. A week in hospital learning to feed a bub, wash a bub, change a bub, and how to hold two at once. And, oh God, I forgot to buy a car for us to get home from the hospital in – it wasn't the best state of mind to be in when trying to make a major purchase.

Ruby barely fit in my hand, and Lola was so serene, as we put them in the blue capsules that friends lent us, with lamb's wool lining, before clicking seatbelts over tiny chests and then driving back down Punt Road from the Mercy to our Northcote rental. That hospital is gone now, turned into apartments – it's strange to think that someone now lives in the room where our children were born.

We survived the following months, somehow, with so much breastmilk and so little sleep. And then there was that Christmas in Queensland – that mad week after a year of twins. Our physiologist had said to us, 'That was the hardest year of your life and you survived.'

Not quite, hey, Mary? We held each other through that dark, blurred day of doctors entering our hospital room to tell us, 'Unfortunately your daughter has tuberous sclerosis, an incurable genetic disorder with a broad array of possible mental and physical effects.' They spoke of seizures and epilepsy.

I am not the praying type, but I did it anyway. It was a difficult time, and it's still hard, and certainly I am not through this at all – it's so very difficult not to fall into the darkness and be led by it, to be taken by the negative and the hopelessness at times when it truly seems insurmountable, when you are lost and searching and thinking so much about everything, good, bad, ugly.

The horrid and beautiful mess of life follows no script and has few fairytale endings to have faith in. Sometimes choice is stolen from you and all you can do is react and survive.

I still feel occasionally like my emotions live on the surface of my skin, fragile and dangerous, after so long of feeling betrayed by my own thoughts. But what else can I do, Mary? What else could anyone do, feeling so overwhelmed by what has happened and what is happening? And people tell you that they could never do what you do, and I think, Of course you could. You just . . . Do. What. You. Have. To. Do. For God's sake (sorry).

The things I thought, through the grief – that she might never smile, never say 'Dad'.

She might never be off medication, never say, 'Bravo!' or get hopping mad or play table tennis, write an assignment, go to school, have a boyfriend, or run.

She might never get married, or have children, or procrastinate at uni, or break up, make up, pash, or meditate, or play a team sport, or want a pony, or share a daiquiri with me, or cry in a movie, or make me a playlist.

I might never teach her to waltz or to play the guitar badly or to drive, or write a poem with her, or tell her my fears, give her advice, or hold her and tell her everything will work out in the end.

She would be bullied, teased, picked on, tricked and taken advantage of, used, forgotten about, ignored, and unseen.

She would be the special kid, the nuff nuff, the dumb kid to push around, the slow girl, retard, spaz, Dumbo, dopey, Frankenstein, scar face, spotty, bleach-marked, loser, freak . . .

But I, that am not shaped for sportive tricks,
Nor made to court an amorous looking-glass;

I, that am rudely stamp'd, and want love's majesty
To strut before a wanton ambling nymph;
I, that am curtail'd of this fair proportion,
Cheated of feature by dissembling nature,
Deformed, unfinish'd, sent before my time
Into this breathing world, scarce half made up,
And that so lamely and unfashionable
That dogs bark at me as I halt by them;
Why, I, in this weak piping time of peace,
Have no delight to pass away the time,
Unless to spy my shadow in the sun
And descant on mine own deformity:
And therefore, since I cannot prove a lover,
To entertain these fair well-spoken days,
I am determined to prove a villain
And hate the idle pleasures of these days.
Plots have I laid, inductions dangerous,
By drunken prophecies, libels and dreams.

And I hated those fucking support groups. All the backwards fucking suburban drop-kick, smoking, fat, bitter and hateful parents – of those sick, sick children – who probably smoked when they were pregnant and deserved every bit of misery they got.

The doctors frogmarched into the hospital room, four of them. We were huddled around the stainless-steel cot and they lined up and talked, as if they had a large, pale-blue pill and they were telling us, 'Well, I'm really sorry, but now you are going to have to swallow this.' And you think, No, thanks, can't you give it to someone else? Can't you break it in half and — 'No, no, just open up.'

Sorry, Mary – there are things you can never say but you still feel them sometimes. It's not right, it's not fair, it's not easy . . .

But you know all this, I suppose.

And I digress – back to the prayer we sent to you, for help.

It would probably be clearer if you read the letter I wrote to our friends in response to that prayer. I'm not sure if you received that group email? I'll include it here as a reminder, and as a way of thanking you.

Dear friends,

We would like to thank you all so much for being part of our healing prayer circle for Lola. Thank you also to all the other people who received the prayer and participated in the novena who may not know or have met Lola or us – thank you!

The response has been overwhelming, with up to a thousand people praying or sending positive thoughts and energy.

We have felt so supported by your words, emails and commitment.

Leading up to the novena, Lola had started having seizures for the first time since Christmas, up to four times a day. Her last EEG (the procedure that monitors the electrical activity in the brain) had been increasingly active and was getting out of control. We were preparing to take the next step in medical intervention, which was steroids.

On day three of the novena, Wednesday, 2 August (my birthday), Lola was scheduled for another EEG. To everyone's surprise, the reading had completely normalised. The doctors' words were: 'This is an EEG of a child without epilepsy. I would have expected this result only after trying steroids and two other drugs.' Our next appointment is now in December. The results could not have been better, and I can think of no better birthday present – a miracle indeed.

Since then, Lola has continued to improve. She's like a different girl, like a light has been switched on, and is so much more connected, happy and interactive. It is an inexplicable and amazing thing. Not a complete cure but an incredible, wonderful help. We realise Lola's condition is very unpredictable and will be with her for life, so please keep her in your prayers. She is so young and we won't really be able to know how well she is doing for a little while yet.

Quite a few people have suggested that we continue with some sort of organised prayer. So we were thinking that on the first three days of the month, we could come together again to send positive light and love for Lola.

This has been healing not only for Lola but also for us, as it has helped mend our broken hearts.

We are feeling so inspired by the power of what we can achieve together when we join and focus with love and clear intentions.

Thank you for your prayers and thoughts.

Lots of love,
Todd, Bec, Lola and Ruby

Mary, please accept my apology for not continuing with this prayer circle. And thank you.

I'm still not religious, but the sheer force and positivity of thousands of people thinking about us and our struggle was palpable and did effect change – of that I am sure.

And I have to tell you also that, since those dark days, with the guidance of an incredible neurologist and surgical team, Lola has now been seizure- and medication-free for three years, and is about to go into grade one at West End Primary. I have to pick her up from ballet after I finish writing this! She is a beautiful singer and a wonderful dancer, and sports a mighty scar from the craniotomy that changed her and all of our lives.

Mary, that moment with you, that flash of faith, sustained us, I think, and lay a crash mat under us that allowed us to fall as we had to, as we always would have. But the faith in the fall allowed us to survive.

So thank you, Mary, for the faith. This road in front of us now is the open road of choice, and we'll be able to make a clear and love-filled choice together.

Yours in faith,
Todd MacDonald

CONTRIBUTORS

ANNA ACHIA is the founder of Australia's premier go-go dancing school, Anna's Go-Go Academy. Anna has spent the last six years amassing a go-go army and teaching them silly dances, but her other credits include burlesque performer (Hi Ball Burlesque), MC, producer and entertainer. She has appeared on the telly and the radio, in lots of papers and magazines, and is now seeking a hairspray sponsor, since she uses so much of it.

WALEED ALY is a lecturer in politics at Monash University. He is also the host of the *Drive* program on Radio National and *Big Ideas* on ABC TV.

PINKY BEECROFT is a songwriter, singer, speaker, irregular TV host and frontperson of The White Russians.

SOPHIE BLACK is an editor, journalist and writer. Fresh from a stint as the editor of the independent online news service *Crikey*, she currently lectures in media and journalism at the University of Melbourne. She's now giving new motherhood a shake, and correspondence from her desk mainly involves writing witty thank-you cards. Her newsier thoughts can be found on twitter @sophblack.

From the successful creative and radio show partnership Hamish and Andy, HAMISH BLAKE is a nationally popular and versatile talent. His career is very much in tandem with his performing partner Andy Lee.

After stepping out from university life and the demands of commerce degrees, they teamed up with their mates to create comedy/variety program *Radio Karate* for Channel 31. Rave reviews followed. Hamish and Andy's story reads as one accomplishment after another. From hosting student radio, the duo was swept up by Fox FM for *The Almost Midday Show*, where their popularity soon promoted them to the drive slot on Fox in 2006 hosting their own show, *Hamish and Andy*. As a solo performer, Hamish made an appearance in ABC comedy series *TwentySomething*. He will also be co-starring in his first feature film with Bret McKenzie (*Flight of the Concords*) in *Two Little Boys*, shot in New Zealand. Hamish has appeared on various Australian television series, including *Spicks and Specks*, *Thank God You're Here*, *Australia's Brainiest Comedian*, *The Librarians*, *The Panel*, *Rove*, *Talkin' 'bout your Generation* and *The Footy Show*. He has also featured in the British version of *Thank God You're Here*. In 2008 he was a speaker for the negative team in the Melbourne International Comedy Festival's annual televised Great Debate.

JULIAN BURNSIDE is a barrister and author. He is married to artist Kate Durham.

ROBYN BUTLER is a writer, producer and actor who mostly remembers to feed her two children and her dog.

ITA BUTTROSE AO, OBE has enjoyed an extensive career in print, radio and television. She has edited leading magazines and newspapers, including Sydney's *Daily* and *Sunday Telegraph*s, *The Australian Women's Weekly*, *Cleo* and *ITA*. She is a regular social commentator on Channel 9's *Today* show and in popular demand on the professional speakers' circuit. She is National President of Alzheimer's Australia, Vice-President Emeritus of Arthritis Australia, and National Patron of the Macular Degeneration Foundation.

LESLIE CANNOLD is the author of the historical novel *The Book of Rachael* (Text, 2011), which inspired this letter. She has also written two non-fiction books about women's reproductive freedom. She is an award-winning columnist who has twice been named as one of Australia's top public thinkers and in 2011 she was named Australian Humanist of the Year. She tweets like a bandit at @LeslieCannold. Glutton for punishment? Find out more at Cannold.com.

LOENE CARMEN is best known as a singer/songwriter of four critically acclaimed albums, as well as for her occasional acting roles in films such as *Red Dog* and *The Year My Voice Broke*. Loene's written contributions have also appeared in *Women of Letters* as well as in the anthologies *Meanjin: On Rock 'n' Roll* and *Your Mother Would Be Proud*.

Actress, singer and, more recently, marriage celebrant, JANE CLIFTON is often asked if there is anything she can't do, to which she simply replies, 'Ballet and making money.' An arts graduate from Monash University's halcyon days of sex and demos and rock 'n' roll, Jane has carved out a four-decades-long show-business career. Her memoir *The Address Book* is her third book.

COCO is an author and actress who most recently appeared in the ABC TV series *The Straits*. Her memoir, *Coco: Autobiography of My Dog* (2012), is published by Five Mile Press. She lives in Sydney with a writer who answers to the name MANDY SAYER.

DEBORAH CONWAY's career encompasses recording, performing, composing, producing and acting. Her trademark entrepreneurial spirit has forged numbers of innovative collaborations, most particularly the one with her husband that has resulted in eight studio albums and three daughters. Conway is a dog owner.

CATHERINE DEVENY is a writer, comedian, and social commentator well known for her work as a columnist with *The Age* newspaper and as an ABC regular. Her seventh book and first novel, *The Happiness Show*, was published by Black Inc Books in November 2012.

MONICA DUX's next book *Things I Didn't Expect* will be published by MUP in early 2013.

ADAM ELLIOT is an Academy Award-winning animation writer, director and producer whose bittersweet films are based on the biographies of his family and friends. His five films have been viewed by millions of people and have won over 100 awards including an Oscar for *Harvie Krumpet* in 2004.

DANIEL EVANS is a writer, journalist and playwright from Brisbane. He is a regular contributor to *frankie* magazine. If you invite him to a party he will – at some stage – insist you play 'The Horses' by Daryl Braithwaite, then corral your guests onto a makeshift dancefloor in your hallway. Then he'll break something. Probably your cat.

CLEMENTINE FORD is a Melbourne-based writer who inherited a love of musical theatre and endless cups of tea. She wishes her mother were still alive so she could enjoy the thrill that is *Game of Thrones*.

SALLY FORD has been a professional musician (sax, flute, voice) for thirty-five years in bands too numerous to mention. She currently plays sax with Nicky Bomba's Melbourne Ska Orchestra, sings in the alto section of Melbourne Mass Gospel Choir and teaches hatha yoga.

HELEN GARNER was born in Geelong in 1942, and has been writing and publishing since her first book, *Monkey Grip*, came out in 1977.

Nadine Garner has worked across film, television and theatre for the past twenty-six years. Beginning her career in 1984 in Crawford Productions' *The Henderson Kids,* she continued to foray out into an industry that has afforded her opportunities to work with many of the country's theatre companies in both contemporary and classical productions, and given her television and film experience that has taken her all across Australia and to the U.K. Mostly recently she starred in *City Homicide* for Channel Seven for almost five years and she is currently shooting *The Mysteries of Dr Blake* for the ABC. Nadine directed her first short film in 2010 and hopes to explore more writing and directing in the future.

Virginia Gay graduated from WAAPA in 2005, then pretended to be a nurse for four years on Channel Seven's *All Saints.* Following that, she pretended to be Julia Gillard in the STC Wharf Revue *Pennies From Kevin,* and has just finished shooting the second season of *Winners and Losers,* where she pretends to know a lot about high finance. This last one, particularly, is a stretch. Her one-woman cabaret, *Dirty Pretty Songs,* is about to headline at the Edinburgh Fringe in The Famous Spiegeltent, and had a sellout season at the 2012 Adelaide Cabaret Festival. She makes regular appearances on the *First Tuesday Book Club,* The Chaser's new show *The Unbelievable Truth* and *Good News Week,* and occasionally hosts and writes Erotic Fan Fiction for the Sydney Writers' Festival.

Libbi Gorr is a writer, performer and, currently, a broadcaster with ABC 774 in Melbourne. Her award-winning McFeast slate created for ABC TV sold worldwide in the 90s, but, in a reinvention worthy of that other icon of the 80s and 90s, Madonna, Libbi has refashioned her work profile from insouciant wild child to the new-millennium figure of Oprah on crack. Libbi's two books, *The A-Z of Mummy Manners: An Etiquette Guide for Dealing with Other Children's*

Mothers and *The Bedtime Poem for Edible Children*, reflect Libbi's efforts to balance her inner creativity with her outer – that is, remaining in a secure family unit with her long-term love Stewart Burchmore and their two young children. Visit Libbi at libbigorr.com.au or tweet @MissGorr.

In the daylight hours, ANGIE HART teaches yoga, guiding people towards being more mindful and self-aware. When the sun goes down, she writes and performs music, where she is led by her muse and, occasionally, is led to ruin. She aims to practise more of what she preaches.

JUSTIN HEAZLEWOOD is a writer, musician and humourist once described as 'the Gen-Y commentator it's okay to like'. As The Bedroom Philosopher, he has released three albums, including the multi-award-winning *Songs From The 86 Tram,* which his nan described as 'fine'. He recently published his first book, *The Bedroom Philosopher Diaries*, through Affirm Press and is working on a second about being an artist in Australia. He has written for *frankie, The Big Issue, jmag* and *Mess+Noise*.

As well as being a professional artist with more than forty exhibitions under his belt, DAVID HINCHLIFFE has served for twenty-four years as a Labor councillor for the city centre in Brisbane, rising to the position of Deputy Mayor. His father, grandfather and brother are all journalists and he trained as a journalist. 'Ink runs in our veins,' says David.

COURTENEY HOCKING is a Melbourne writer, comedian, broadcaster and actress. She has written for *Good News Week, The Age* and *Crikey*; created Melbourne's only political comedy room, Political Asylum; and was recently selected as a finalist in the Qantas Spirit of Young Australia Awards.

PATIENCE HODGSON is one half of indie rock band The Grates. She lived in Brooklyn, New York, for two years, with guitarist John Patterson, while they wrote their third album *Secret Rituals*. These days they live together in Brisbane with a one-eyed cat, run a tea room and make music at night. Patience also makes two podcasts with comedian Melinda Buttle.

KATE HOLDEN is the author of the memoirs *In My Skin* and *The Romantic*, a long-time *Age* column and sundry other bits of published writing which can be found at kate-holden.com.

CHRISTA HUGHES shot to fame as 'KK Juggy' – the outrageously confronting front chick with platinum selling rock band Machine Gun Fellatio. A world renowned cabaret performer in her own right, Christa's toured the world as ring mistress for Circus Oz, is the subject of an AFI-winning documentary, has recorded an ARIA-nominated album with her dad, Dick Hughes, and has starred in a couple of avant-garde operas and films. Christa's latest project is her band, Christa Hughes and the Honky Tonk Shonks.

TRACEE HUTCHISON is a Melbourne-based broadcast journalist and author with twenty-five years of experience in radio, television and print. A former triple j and RRR announcer, she currently presents rolling news/current affairs coverage on ABC News Radio and Radio Australia across Australia, Asia and the Pacific.

KAMAHL is the name that, for over four decades, has identified the music and the unforgettable voice of a man who is one of the most sensational recording stars in Australian history. The story of his life, which took him from a child in the cow paddocks of Kuala Lumpur, Malaysia, to performing for presidents and royalty, and to counting among his friends some of the great and mighty, is one of the most extraordinary adventures in show business. From being bombed in Malaysia to a sometimes turbulent but enduring marriage in Australia, to making and losing a fortune, and making it again. His philanthropy along the way is legendary, and for it he was made a Member of the Order of Australia and given the Centenary Medal. Following Prime Minister John Howard, Kamahl was made Father of the Year in 1998 and included in Variety's Entertainers of the Century. Above all, Kamahl is still entertaining – and still packing them in.

LALLY KATZ is a multi-award-winning playwright. Her work has been performed many times on all the main stages of Melbourne and Sydney and in independent theatres across Australia and overseas.

MORAG KOBEZ-HALVORSON is a food writer, regular contributor to 612 ABC Radio, restaurant reviewer for the *Queensland Good Food Guide* and author of the blog missmoragsmorsels.com.

JAE LAFFER is recognised as one of Australia's finest songwriters; with his band The Panics he has crafted several albums of classic songs that embrace both stark intimacy and unapologetic grandeur. Music critics often say listening to The Panics' songs is like immersing yourself in the soundtrack to your own life. In their albums and EPs, people discover the cinematic score to their own lost Australian summers.

SAMANTHA LANE is a Melbourne-based journalist who writes for *The Age* and appears on Channel Ten's AFL show *Before the Game*. She cried while reading at Women of Letters, but the experience triggered a life-affirming conversation with her significant ex.

BENJAMIN LAW is the author of the black comedy memoir *The Family Law* and *Gaysia*. He writes regularly for *frankie*, *QWeekend* and

The Monthly, and was once described by Andrew Bolt as 'a gay with startling comprehension issues'.

PIP LINCOLNE is a frock-loving, clog-wearing, reality TV-loving lady. She lives with her family in Melbourne and has written three craft books. She is penning a fourth book as we speak and writes the blog meetmeatmikes.com most days, too.

JOHNNY MACKAY is a maker of noise, scribbler of word and general layabout who does his best to avoid winter and being left out in the cold in any way. He occasionally takes to the stage with Children Collide and Electric Smile Band among other featherbrained pursuits.

EMILY MAGUIRE is the author of four novels and two non-fiction books. Her articles and essays on sex, religion, culture and literature have been published widely.

ROBERT MANNE is Professor of Politics at La Trobe University. He is the author or editor of twenty books and a regular contributor to *The Monthly*.

HELEN MARCOU is the co-founder of live music lobby group SLAM. Through her work with SLAM, Helen continues to advocate for reforms in the contemporary music sector. National SLAM day, an annual day of awareness and celebration of live music, was initiated in 2012 with participation and widespread media coverage all around the country. Helen is a member of key live music advisory committees including the Victorian State Government's roundtable, the Melbourne Lord Mayor's roundtable and the City of Yarra's music working group. Helen and her partner Quincy McLean are the owners of Bakehouse Studios in Melbourne. Since 1991, Bakehouse has contributed to and nurtured the careers of hundreds of local and international musicians. In 2010, Helen was listed as one of *The Age Melbourne Magazine*'s top 100 most influential and creative Melburnians. *The Age EG*'s inaugural outstanding achievement award went to Helen and Quincy in 2010, and Helen has been nominated for 'Female of the Year' in *Rolling Stone* magazine. She describes herself as 'a big fan of live music who became the inadvertent spokesperson for a community, never expecting to be in this role'. She also likes cooking and crochet.

Born in the coastal New South Wales town of Byron Bay in 1987, HAYLEY MARY has come a long way since she made her singing debut as a child, busking on the streets of her home town with her father. Now based in London, for the past five years she's been the voice of Australian quartet The Jezabels, who since forming in Sydney in 2007 have become one of Australia's most promising and popular acts. To date the quartet have released three EPs – two of which have been certified Gold in their homeland – and their 2011 debut album, *Prisoner*. Debuting at number two on the Australian charts, *Prisoner* has also been certified Gold, with the band performing sold-out headline shows across Australia in support, as well as in countries such as America, Canada, Germany, England, Singapore and more. Having recently completed a series of UK shows supporting Garbage and a recent spot on the 2012 Lollapalooza bill in Chicago, Mary will spend the remainder of the year touring in support of *Prisoner*, before focusing on the writing and recording of album number two.

TODD MACDONALD is an actor and theatre director, producer and programmer. He is currently Artistic Associate at Queensland Theatre Company where he programs the GreenHouse season. Todd is the co-founder and past Artistic Director of The Store Room theatre in Melbourne. He is the proud father of twins Ruby and Lola and married to artist Rebecca McIntosh.

LINDSAY MCDOUGALL is the semi-annoying guy you hear at 3 p.m. every weekday afternoon and put up with until 5.30 p.m. on triple j. He has also been in a vaguely successful pop band, Frenzal Rhomb, for the last fifteen years, in which time he has been to a lot of places around the world and seen the inside of the bars and hotels in most of them.

TIM MCGUIRE is a freelance writer from Brisbane. His work has been published in *The Big Issue* and *The Lifted Brow* and is featured regularly by the Brisbane-based literary collective Stilts, for which he is the events coordinator.

LAURA JEAN MCKAY is a writer and performer published in *Best Australian Stories* and *The Big Issue*. She writes fiction about Cambodia and non-fiction about her adventures by cargo ship. Find out more at laurajeanmckay.com.

SHAUN MICALLEF is a televisual artiste specialising in anything that is offered him. His credits include: *The Micallef Program*, *SeaChange*, *Micallef Tonight*, *Newstopia* and *Talkin' 'bout your Generation*. His debits include: *Welcher & Welcher*.

KATE MILLER-HEIDKE is a multi-platinum selling singer-songwriter from Brisbane. In April 2012 she will release her third album, *Night-flight*. Kate has performed to large audiences all over the world. She has been nominated for several Arias, but hasn't won any.

KEVIN MITCHELL, aka Bob Evans, aka frontman of Jebediah and member of Basement Birds, has wormed his way into the hearts of many around the world with his wide repertoire and charisma. His albums and live shows have received high praise and numerous accolades.

DI MORRISSEY is one of the most successful authors Australia, having produced twenty bestsellers in twenty years. Each book is inspired by a particular landscape. She lives and researches in the location of every novel. Her latest book is *The Golden Land*, set in Burma.

RHYS MULDOON is a contributor to *The Drum*, as well as an actor, director and radio presenter. In 2010 he co-authored a children's book, *Jasper & Abby*, with Kevin Rudd.

ANTHONY MULLINS is an award-winning filmmaker. The projects Anthony has written and directed have won numerous international awards including a Primetime Emmy, an International Digital Emmy, two BAFTAs, three Australian Writer's Guild Awards and Official Selection in the 2000 Cannes Film Festival. He is currently the creative director of Hoodlum, a Brisbane-based production company.

GEORGE NEGUS has written, directed and presented Australian television current affairs since 1975 – with a special passion for international affairs and Australia's place in the world. He worked independently via Negus Media International for more than twenty years as well as having roles as presenter/interviewer and reporter for ABC's *Foreign Correspondent*, *Australia Talks* and *George Negus Tonight*; Channel Nine's *60 Minutes* and *Today Show*; Channel Seven's coverage of both Gulf Wars; SBS's flagship international affairs program *Dateline*; and Channel Ten's 2011 news analysis program. He continues in 2012 as occasional international/national affairs commentator on Australian TV/radio. His books include *The World from Italy*, *The World from Islam* and *The World from Down Under*, produced with Negus Media and published by HarperCollins.

KEIR NUTTALL is a songwriter, guitarist and producer who mainly works with his wife, Kate Miller-Heidke, and country artist Franky Walnut.

When Alice Springs mother of five FIONA O'LOUGHLIN started doing stand-up later in life than most comics, her hilarious stories of housewifery and motherhood were an immediate hit. Fiona has taken her story-based stand-up around the world, headlining LA's world-renowned Improv Comedy Club, playing repeat seasons in Hong Kong and performing at Edinburgh Fringe, as well as Montreal's invitation-only Just For Laughs and the Leicester Comedy Festival. Fiona's also been a hit on the telly with guest appearances on *Sunrise*, *Good News Week*, *Spicks and Specks*, *The World Stands Up* and a heap of Melbourne International Comedy Festival Galas.

KRISTINA OLSSON is the author of the novels *In One Skin* and *The China Garden*, which won the 2010 Barbara Jefferis Award, and the biography *Kilroy Was Here*. Her latest work is a memoir, *Vigilance*, which will be published by UQP in 2013.

In 1999 JACQUI PAYNE was appointed as a magistrate and was the first Aborigine to be appointed to judicial office in Queensland. Jacqui's mob is Batjalla. Her grandmother was born on Fraser Island. Jacqui was born in North Queensland and grew up in Gladstone and came to Brisbane in the late '70s to study law. After getting her law degree, Jacqui's first job as a solicitor was at the Aboriginal and Torres Strait Islander Legal Service where she practiced exclusively in the area of criminal law. Eventually Jacqui opened her own criminal defence law firm where she worked for a number of years. It was while operating her own firm that the then Attorney-General of Queensland, Matt Foley, offered her an appointment to the magistracy which she accepted. Jacqui works as a magistrate for fun but her real job is the mother of six and, at this time, the grandmother of three.

ANDREA POWELL is an actor, author and comedian renowned for her characterisations. She can be heard regularly on radio and has appeared on *The Panel*, *Kath & Kim*, *The Librarians*, *Whatever Happened To That Guy?*, *City Homicide*, *Neighbours* and *Judith Lucy's Spiritual Journey*. Penguin published Andrea's book *Strain Your Gherkins by Ethel Chop* in 2007.

ALICE PUNG'S first book, *Unpolished Gem*, won the ABIA Award in 2007 for Newcomer of the Year, and was shortlisted for numerous other state and national awards. Her second book, *Growing Up Asian in Australia*, is a collection of edited stories which is studied as a VCE text. Her latest book, *Her Father's Daughter*, was published in 2011. Alice is the current writer in residence at Janet Clarke Hall, and has been writer in residence at Ormond College, Peking University and the International Writing Program at the University of Iowa.

Award-winning musician, writer, composer and comedian GERALDINE QUINN (*Rockwiz*, *Spicks and Specks*, The Comedy Channel) has toured her unique style of musical comedy internationally since 2005. She resides in Melbourne and wants a dog for her birthday.

HANNIE RAYSON is a playwright. She has written thirteen plays, which have been performed throughout Australia and overseas. She is currently working on a commission for The Manhattan Theatre Club.

MICHAEL ROBOTHAM is a hopeless romantic with a very sick mind. A former journalist and ghostwriter, he is one of Australia's most widely read crime writers.

LOU SANZ is a comedy writer, blogger, 'sometimes comedian' and enabler currently residing in Melbourne.

TOBY SCHMITZ is an actor, writer and director working across theatre, television and film. And occasional corporate work, where his soul really lies.

RONNIE SCOTT is a contributor to *The Believer*, *The Big Issue*, *Meanjin*, the *Australian Book Review* and ABC Radio National. In 2007, he founded *The Lifted Brow*, a freeform arts and culture magazine. Visit him at ronalddavidscott.com.

EDDIE SHARP is an artist, writer, performer and theatremaker. He is a co-creator of The Imperial Panda Festival, Erotic Fan Fiction Readings, The Mad Max Remix, Some Film Museums I Have Known and countless other things you have never heard of. He is also severely claustrophobic and was once politely asked to leave a private party at Yahoo Serious's house.

SOFIJA STEFANOVIC is a writer and filmmaker. She co-wrote the TV shows *John Safran's Race Relations* and *Myf Warhurst's Nice*. She developed the AFI-nominated documentary *Beyond Our Ken* by joining a cult for six months. For her documentary and writing work, Sofija has competed in the Miss ex-Yugoslavia beauty pageant, met with Japanese pro-whaling officials and participated in exorcisms.

KAV TEMPERLEY, Eskimo Joe frontman and member of Basement Birds, is a multi-award-winning, multi-platinum-selling singer, musician and songwriter.

HENRY WAGONS is one of Australia's great live performers. Wagons' take on country music is based on the early classics, drenched in humour and delivered with his distinctive baritone. Like the mischievous child of Cash, Orbison and Presley, Henry Wagons defies expectations when holding a guitar on stage. In 2009, Henry was named in the Top 100 Most Influential Melbournians by *The Age Melbourne Magazine* and has recently released a fifth album, *Rumble Shake and Tumble*, which took out an AIR Award for Best Country Album and two *Age EG* Awards for Best Album and Best Group.

MAX WALKER – philanthropist, noted media personality, former architect and legendary sportsman (Australian Test cricketer and VFL/AFL footballer) – has headed his own highly successful company for nearly thirty years. He is always willing to share his wisdom, lateral thinking, enthusiasm for life and love of learning. Max's varied background and business acumen, when combined with a warm, vibrant personality and a genuine interest in people, has made him a sought-after professional guest speaker, MC and cor-porate host. Max is also a prolific reader and writer of books and articles for various magazines, journals etc. To date he has written and published fourteen books, seven of which have been number-one bestsellers. On a personal level, Max is a dedicated family man who enjoys leisure pursuits in the arts, photography, architecture, fine wines, collecting fountain pens and adventurous travel. Max Walker, AM, has become a brand that is synonymous with integrity, credibility and success.

FELICITY WARD. Comedian. Actor. Writer. Grown from the salty air of the Central Coast of NSW, was bound to move away from her dish-pig upbringing. Resides mostly in Melbourne. Well, she collects mail there. Mostly seen on stage doing stand up. Sometimes seen on the telly (*Randling*, *Spicks and Specks*, *Thank God You're Here*, and a number of axed shows). Once seen in the movies (*Any Questions For Ben?*). Often seen at the supermarkets in her pyjamas. Dress-ups are for night-time.

PARIS WELLS started as a Fairfax employee, playing underground shows with DJ friends around Melbourne. It wasn't long before she built a monstrous buzz in Melbourne, signed to Illusive Sounds and shortly afterwards released her debut EP. The release, *Mum Hasn't Slept Yet*, was a catalyst for her supporting slot in Justin Timberlake's FutureSex/LoveShow tour in Australia and New Zealand. Since then she has performed at Australia's best music festivals and along-side other artists such as Bliss N Eso. Her latest release, *Various Small Fires*, has sent her on an east-coast tour of Australia and won her a Melbourne Design Award for her video clip, 'Let's Get It Started'. Paris is currently writing for a new release in 2012.

DAVID WILLIAMSON is Australia's best known and most widely performed playwright. His first full-length play *The Coming of Stork* was presented at La Mama Theatre in 1970 and was followed by *The Removalists* and *Don's Party* in 1971. His prodigious output since then includes *The Club, Brilliant Lies, Dead White Males* and *Let the Sunshine*. His plays have been translated into many languages and performed internationally, including major productions in London, Los Angeles, New York and Washington. As a screenwriter, David has brought to the screen his own plays including *The Removalists, Don's Party, The Club, Travelling North* and *Emerald City*, along with his original screenplays for feature films including *Libido, Petersen, Gallipoli, Phar Lap, The Year of Living Dangerously* and *Balibo*. His many awards include twelve Australian Writers' Guild AWGIE Awards, five Australian Film Institute Awards for Best Screenplay and, in 1996 The United Nations Association of Australia Media Peace Award. In 2005 he was awarded the Richard Lane Award for services to the Australian Writers' Guild. David has been named one of Australia's Living National Treasures.

ACKNOWLEDGEMENTS

We are indebted to our friends and families for giving up their Sunday afternoons for us. Galia and Alan Hardy, Lisa McGuire, Tim McGuire, James McGuire, Liam Pieper, David McCarthy, Bob Ellis (canine), Lorelei Vashti, Nikki Lusk, Ben Law, Kitty Robertson, Cousin Sondra Davoren, Krissy Kneen, Ronnie Scott, Lee Sandwith, Elaine Reyes, Pete Garrow, Patrick Kelly, Tammy Law, Elize Strydom, Talia Cain, Julz Hay, Jason McGann, Lauren Egan, Sahra Stolz, Fay Burstin, Joc Curran, Alan Brough, Clare Bowditch, Noni Hazlehurst, Tim Rogers, Denise Scott, Gabi Barton, Laura Jean McKay and all of our incredible DJs.

Special thanks is owed to Tara Nielsen, the most gorgeous pixel pusher around, whose impeccable design we love almost as much as her.

Thank you Cate Blake, Ben Ball and everyone at Penguin for turning our little shows into big books.

To all at The Thornbury Theatre.

Our homes away from home: The Red Rattler, The Basement, Melbourne Fringe Club, Splendour in the Grass, The Zoo and Avid Reader.

Thanks to everyone who takes a chance on us, buys a ticket, and has a part in making our shows so special.

And, of course, Edgar's Mission – this is all for you.

Lyrics from 'Hand In My Pocket' writers Glen Ballard & Alanis Nadine Morissette © Copyright Aerostation Corporation / Vanhurst Place Music Universal MCA Music Publishing Pty. Ltd. All rights reserved. International copyright secured. Reprinted with permission.

Extract from *This is Water* by David Foster Wallace copyright © 2009 by David Foster Wallace Literary Trust. By permission of Little, Brown and Company. All rights reserved.